DEPARTMENT OF
PUBLIC INFORMATION

BASIC FACTS
ABOUT THE
UNITED NATIONS

UNITED NATIONS
NEW YORK, 1995

Published by the United Nations
Department of Public Information
New York, NY 10017

Note: Data current as of 31 March 1995

ISBN: 92-1-100570-1
United Nations Publication
Sales No. E.95.1.31

CONTENTS

3   ECONOMIC AND SOCIAL DEVELOPMENT

4   HUMAN RIGHTS

7   INTERNATIONAL LAW

8   INTERGOVERNMENTAL AGENCIES RELATED TO THE UNITED NATIONS

International Finance Corporation (283); Multilateral
Investment Guarantee Agency (283)

APPENDICES

INDEX

LIST OF ACRONYMS

ECA	Economic Commission for Africa
ECE	Economic Commission for Europe
ECLAC	Economic Commission for Latin America and the Caribbean
ECOSOC	Economic and Social Council
ESCAP	Economic and Social Commission for Asia and the Pacific
ESCWA	Economic and Social Commission for Western Asia
FAO	Food and Agriculture Organization of the United Nations
IAEA	International Atomic Energy Agency
IBRD	International Bank for Reconstruction and Development (World Bank)
ICAO	International Civil Aviation Organization
ICRC	International Committee of the Red Cross
IDA	International Development Association
IFAD	International Fund for Agricultural Development
IFC	International Finance Corporation
ILO	International Labour Organization
IMF	International Monetary Fund
IMO	International Maritime Organization
INSTRAW	International Research and Training Institute for the Advancement of Women
ITU	International Telecommunication Union
MIGA	Multilateral Investment Guarantee Agency
MINUGUA	Mission for the Verification of Human Rights in Guatemala
MINURSO	United Nations Mission for the Referendum in Western Sahara
ONUMOZ	United Nations Operation in Mozambique
ONUSAL	United Nations Observer Mission in El Salvador
ONUVEH	United Nations Observer Group for the Verification of the Elections in Haiti
ONUVEN	United Nations Observer Mission for the Verification of the Elections in Nicaragua
UNAMIR	United Nations Assistance Mission for Rwanda
UNAVEM	United Nations Angola Verification Mission
UNCRO	United Nations Confidence Restoration Operation in Croatia
UNCHS	United Nations Centre for Human Settlements (Habitat)
UNCTAD	United Nations Conference on Trade and Development
UNDOF	United Nations Disengagement Observer Force
UNDP	United Nations Development Programme
UNEF	United Nations Emergency Force
UNEP	United Nations Environment Programme
UNESCO	United Nations Educational, Scientific and Cultural Organization
UNFICYP	United Nations Peace-keeping Force in Cyprus
UNFPA	United Nations Population Fund
UNGOMAP	United Nations Good Offices Mission in Afghanistan and Pakistan

UNHCR	Office of the United Nations High Commissioner for Refugees
UNICEF	United Nations Children's Fund
UNICRI	United Nations Interregional Crime and Justice Research Institute
UNIDIR	United Nations Institute for Disarmament Research
UNIDO	United Nations Industrial Development Organization
UNIFEM	United Nations Development Fund for Women
UNIFIL	United Nations Interim Force in Lebanon
UNIIMOG	United Nations Iran-Iraq Military Observer Group
UNIKOM	United Nations Iraq-Kuwait Observation Mission
UNIPOM	United Nations India-Pakistan Observation Mission
UNITAR	United Nations Institute for Training and Research
UNMIH	United Nations Mission in Haiti
UNMOGIP	United Nations Military Observer Group in India and Pakistan
UNMOT	United Nations Mission of Observers in Tajikistan
UNOMIG	United Nations Observer Mission in Georgia
UNOMIL	United Nations Observer Mission in Liberia
UNOMSA	United Nations Observer Mission in South Africa
UNOMUR	United Nations Observer Mission Uganda-Rwanda
UNOSOM	United Nations Operation in Somalia
UNOVER	United Nations Observer Mission to Verify the Referendum in Eritrea
UNPREDEP	United Nations Preventive Deployment Force
UNPROFOR	United Nations Protection Force
UNRISD	United Nations Research Institute for Social Development
UNRWA	United Nations Relief and Works Agency for Palestine Refugees in the Near East
UNSCOM	United Nations Special Commission
UNSO	United Nations Sudano-Sahelian Office
UNTAC	United Nations Transitional Authority in Cambodia
UNTAG	United Nations Transition Assistance Group
UNTSO	United Nations Truce Supervision Organization
UNU	United Nations University
UNV	United Nations Volunteers
UPU	Universal Postal Union
WFC	World Food Council
WFP	World Food Programme
WHO	World Health Organization
WIPO	World Intellectual Property Organization
WMO	World Meteorological Organization
WTO	World Trade Organization

FOREWORD

This updated and revised edition of *Basic Facts about the United Nations* appears during the Fiftieth Anniversary celebrations of the world Organization. This is a time when the world is focusing with renewed intensity upon the role and accomplishments of the United Nations, as well as its potential for the future.

Over the past five decades, international cooperation has brought great advances in every area of the United Nations Charter. The United Nations has invented the concept of peace-keeping. It has fostered a global understanding of human rights, and has helped to erect international legal structures. For many of the most disadvantaged societies in the world, it has provided essential help in economic and social development.

Today, the end of the cold war has brought new challenges to international security and prosperity. Fierce ethnic rivalries menace societies from within, and have led to terrible civilian suffering. Environmental degradation, the growing disparity between rich and poor, and the rise of global economic pressures create challenges to human welfare that defy control by individual States.

Building upon its half-century of experience, the United Nations is seeking ways to respond to this new situation. Peace-keeping operations now operate under greatly expanded mandates, often requiring the reconstruction of entire societies and their institutions. The international community has taken on an unprecedented degree of responsibility for human rights. New legal instruments are taking shape to protect the most vulnerable members of society caught in the midst of intra-State conflicts. The United Nations has organized a continuum of global conferences to address the most pressing new issues of development in a comprehensive and interlinked manner.

The United Nations is also responding to new demands for assistance in creating democratic societies. Democratization can offer vital support for the goals of the Charter in the twenty-first century. It strengthens the foundations of civil society in every dimension.

This edition of *Basic Facts about the United Nations* offers an overview of the broad range of responsibilities, operations and objectives of the United Nations as it strives to engage the problems and opportunities of our time. I hope it will help the world's citizens to better understand their world Organization, and to support and help shape it to deal successfully with the challenges to come.

Boutros BOUTROS-GHALI
Secretary-General

CHAPTER 1

The United Nations: Origin, Purposes and Principles, Structure

The name "United Nations" was devised by United States President Franklin D. Roosevelt and was first used in the "Declaration by United Nations" of 1 January 1942, during the Second World War, when representatives of 26 nations pledged their Governments to continue fighting together against the Axis Powers.

The United Nations Charter was drawn up by the representatives of 50 countries at the United Nations Conference on International Organization, which met at San Francisco from 25 April to 26 June 1945. Those delegates deliberated on the basis of proposals worked out by the representatives of China, the Soviet Union, the United Kingdom and the United States at Dumbarton Oaks in August-October 1944. The Charter was signed on 26 June 1945 by the representatives of the 50 countries. Poland, which was not represented at the Conference, signed it later and became one of the original 51 Member States.

The United Nations officially came into existence on 24 October 1945, when the Charter had been ratified by China, France, the Soviet Union, the United Kingdom, the United States and by a majority of other signatories. United Nations Day is celebrated on 24 October each year.

UNITED NATIONS CHARTER

The United Nations Charter is the constituting instrument of the Organization, setting out the rights and obligations of Member States, and establishing the United Nations organs and procedures. An international treaty, the Charter codifies at the international level the major principles of international relations—from the sovereign equality of States to the prohibition of the use of force in international relations to the basic human rights to which all women and men are entitled.

The Charter opens with a Preamble, and includes sections on United Nations Purposes and Principles, Membership, Organs, Pacific Settlement of Disputes, Action with Respect to Threats to the Peace, Breaches of the Peace and Acts of

Aggression, International Economic Cooperation, and Non-Self-Governing Territories. (For Amendments to the Charter, see Chapter 7).

PREAMBLE TO THE CHARTER

The Preamble to the Charter expresses the ideals and common aims of all the peoples whose Governments joined together to form the United Nations:

"WE THE PEOPLES OF THE UNITED NATIONS DETERMINED to save succeeding generations from the scourge of war, which twice in our lifetime has brought untold sorrow to mankind, and to reaffirm faith in fundamental human rights, in the dignity and worth of the human person, in the equal rights of men and women and of nations large and small, and to establish conditions under which justice and respect for the obligations arising from treaties and other sources of international law can be maintained, and to promote social progress and better standards of life in larger freedom,

"AND FOR THESE ENDS to practice tolerance and live together in peace with one another as good neighbours, and to unite our strength to maintain international peace and security, and to ensure, by the acceptance of principles and the institution of methods, that armed force shall not be used, save in the common interest, and to employ international machinery for the promotion of the economic and social advancement of all peoples,

"HAVE RESOLVED TO COMBINE OUR EFFORTS TO ACCOMPLISH THESE AIMS. Accordingly, our respective Governments, through representatives assembled in the city of San Francisco, who have exhibited their full powers found to be in good and due form, have agreed to the present Charter of the United Nations and do hereby establish an international organization to be known as the United Nations."

PURPOSES AND PRINCIPLES

The purposes of the United Nations, as set forth in the Charter, are:

♦   to maintain international peace and security;

♦ to develop friendly relations among nations based on respect for the principle of equal right and self-determination of peoples;

♦ to cooperate in solving international economic, social, cultural and humanitarian problems and in promoting respect for human rights and fundamental freedoms;

♦ to be a centre for harmonizing the actions of nations in attaining these common ends.

The United Nations acts in accordance with the following principles:

♦ it is based on the sovereign equality of all its Members;

♦ all Members are to fulfil in good faith their Charter obligations;

♦ they are to settle their international disputes by peaceful means and without endangering international peace and security, and justice;

♦ they are to refrain from the threat or use of force against any other State;

♦ they are to give the United Nations every assistance in any action it takes in accordance with the Charter, and shall not assist States against which the United Nations is taking preventive or enforcement action;

♦ the United Nations shall ensure that States which are not Members act in accordance with these principles in so far as it is necessary for the maintenance of international peace and security;

♦ nothing in the Charter is to authorize the United Nations to intervene in matters which are essentially within the domestic jurisdiction of any State.

MEMBERSHIP

Membership of the United Nations is open to all peace-loving nations which accept the obligations of the Charter and, in the judgement of the Organization, are willing and able to carry out these obligations. (For list of Member States, see the Appendices.)

New Member States are admitted by the General Assembly on the recommendation of the Security Council. The Charter provides for the suspension or expulsion of a Member for violation of the principles of the Charter, but no such action has ever been taken.

OFFICIAL LANGUAGES

Under the Charter, the official languages of the United Nations are Chinese, English, French, Russian and Spanish. Arabic has been added as an official language of the General Assembly, the Security Council and the Economic and Social Council.

STRUCTURE OF THE ORGANIZATION

The Charter established six principal organs of the United Nations:

GENERAL ASSEMBLY

The General Assembly is the main deliberative organ. It is composed of representatives of all Member States, each of which has one vote. Decisions on important questions, such as those on peace and security, admission of new Members and budgetary matters, require a two-thirds majority. Decisions on other questions are reached by a simple majority.

Functions and powers

Under the Charter, the functions and powers of the General Assembly include:
♦   to consider and make recommendations on the principles of cooperation in the maintenance of international peace and security, including the principles governing disarmament and the regulation of armaments;
♦   to discuss any question relating to international peace and security and, except where a dispute or situation is being discussed by the Security Council, to make recommendations on it;
♦   to discuss and, with the same exception, make recommendations on any question within the scope of the Charter or affecting the powers and functions of any organ of the United Nations;
♦   to initiate studies and make recommendations to promote international political cooperation, the development and codification of international law, the realization of human rights and

fundamental freedoms for all, and international collaboration in economic, social, cultural, educational and health fields;
 ♦   to make recommendations for the peaceful settlement of any situation, regardless of origin, which might impair friendly relations among nations;
 ♦   to receive and consider reports from the Security Council and other United Nations organs;
 ♦   to consider and approve the United Nations budget and to apportion the contributions among Members;
 ♦   to elect the non-permanent members of the Security Council, the members of the Economic and Social Council and those members of the Trusteeship Council that are elected; to elect jointly with the Security Council the Judges of the International Court of Justice; and, on the recommendation of the Security Council, to appoint the Secretary-General.

Under the "Uniting for peace" resolution adopted by the General Assembly in November 1950, the Assembly may take action if the Security Council, because of a lack of unanimity of its permanent members, fails to act in a case where there appears to be a threat to international peace, breach of the peace or act of aggression. The Assembly is empowered to consider the matter immediately with a view to making recommendations to Members for collective measures, including, in the case of a breach of the peace or act of aggression, the use of armed force when necessary to maintain or restore international peace and security.

Sessions

The General Assembly's regular session begins each year on the third Tuesday in September and continues usually until mid-December. At the start of each regular session, the Assembly elects a new President, 21 Vice-Presidents and the Chairmen of the Assembly's seven Main Committees. To ensure equitable geographical representation, the presidency of the Assembly rotates each year among five groups of States: African, Asian, Eastern European, Latin American, and Western European and other States.

In addition to its regular sessions, the Assembly may meet in special sessions at the request of the Security Council, of a majority of Members of the United Nations or of one Member if the majority of Members concurs. Emergency special sessions may be called within 24 hours of a request by the Security Council on the vote of any nine members of the Council, or by a majority of the United Nations Members, or by one Member if the majority of Members concurs.

At the beginning of each regular session, the Assembly holds a general debate, often addressed by heads of State and Government, in which Member States express their views on a wide range of matters of international concern. Because of the great number of questions which the Assembly is called upon to consider (162 separate agenda items at the 1994 session of the Assembly, for example), the Assembly allocates most questions to its six Main Committees:

- Disarmament and International Security Committee (First Committee);
- Economic and Financial Committee (Second Committee);
- Social, Humanitarian and Cultural Committee (Third Committee);
- Special Political and Decolonization Committee (Fourth Committee);
- Administrative and Budgetary Committee (Fifth Committee);
- Legal Committee (Sixth Committee).

There is also a General Committee, composed of the President and 21 Vice-Presidents of the Assembly and the chairmen of the seven Main Committees and a Credentials Committee, which consists of nine members appointed by the Assembly on the proposal of the President at each session who reports to the Assembly on the credentials of representatives.

Some questions are considered only in plenary meetings, rather than in one of the Main Committees. All questions are voted on in plenary meetings, usually towards the end of the regular session, after the committees have completed their consideration of them and submitted draft resolutions to the plenary Assembly.

Voting in committees is by a simple majority. In plenary meetings, resolutions may be adopted by acclamation, without objection or without a vote, or the vote may be recorded or taken by roll-call.

While the decisions of the Assembly have no legally binding force for Governments, they carry the weight of world opinion on major international issues, as well as the moral authority of the world community.

The work of the United Nations year-round derives largely from the decisions of the General Assembly—that is to say, the will of the majority of the Members as expressed in resolutions adopted by the Assembly. That work is carried out:
*   by committees and other bodies established by the Assembly to study and report on specific issues, such as disarmament, outer space, peace-keeping, decolonization and human rights;
*   in international conferences called for by the Assembly; and
*   by the Secretariat of the United Nations—the Secretary-General and his staff of international civil servants.

SECURITY COUNCIL

The Security Council has primary responsibility, under the Charter, for the maintenance of international peace and security.

The Council has 15 members: five permanent members—China, France, the Russian Federation,* the United Kingdom and the United States—and 10 elected by the General Assembly for two-year terms.

Each Council member has one vote. Decisions on procedural matters are made by an affirmative vote of at least nine of the 15 members. Decisions on substantive matters require nine votes, including the concurring votes of all five permanent members. This is the rule of "great Power unanimity", often referred to as the "veto" power. If a permanent member does not agree with a decision, it can cast a negative vote, and this act has power of veto. All five permanent members have exercised the right of veto at one time or another. If a permanent

---

*The Union of Soviet Socialist Republics was an original Member of the United Nations from 24 October 1945. In a letter dated 24 December 1991, Boris Yeltsin, the President of the Russian Federation, informed the Secretary-General that the membership of the Soviet Union in the Security Council and all other United Nations organs was being continued by the Russian Federation with the support of the 11 member countries of the Commonwealth of Independent States.

member does not support a decision but does not wish to block it through a veto, it may abstain.

Under the Charter, all Members of the United Nations agree to accept and carry out the decisions of the Security Council. While other organs of the United Nations make recommendations to Governments, the Council alone has the power to take decisions which Member States are obligated under the Charter to carry out.

Functions and powers

Under the Charter, the functions and powers of the Security Council are:

♦ to maintain international peace and security in accordance with the principles and purposes of the United Nations;

♦ to investigate any dispute or situation which might lead to international friction;

♦ to recommend methods of adjusting such disputes or the terms of settlement;

♦ to formulate plans for the establishment of a system to regulate armaments;

♦ to determine the existence of a threat to the peace or act of aggression and to recommend what action should be taken; to call on Members to apply economic sanctions and other measures not involving the use of force to prevent or stop aggression;

♦ to take military action against an aggressor;

♦ to recommend the admission of new Members and the terms on which States may become parties to the Statute of the International Court of Justice;

♦ to exercise the trusteeship functions of the United Nations in "strategic areas";

♦ to recommend to the General Assembly the appointment of the Secretary-General and, together with the Assembly, to elect the Judges of the International Court.

The Security Council is so organized as to be able to function continuously, and a representative of each of its members must be present at all times at United Nations Headquarters. On 31 January 1992, the first-ever Summit Meeting of the Council was convened at Headquarters, attended by Heads of State and Government of 13 of its 15 members and by the Ministers for Foreign Affairs of the remaining two. The Council may meet elsewhere than at Headquarters; in 1972, it held a session in Addis Ababa, Ethiopia, and the following year it met in Panama City, Panama.

When a complaint concerning a threat to peace is brought before it, the Council's first action is usually to recommend that the parties try to reach agreement by peaceful means. In some cases, the Council itself undertakes investigation and mediation. It may appoint special representatives or request the Secretary-General to do so or to use his good offices. It may set forth principles for a peaceful settlement.

When a dispute leads to fighting, the Council's first concern is to bring it to an end as soon as possible. On many occasions, the Council has issued cease-fire directives which have been instrumental in preventing wider hostilities. It also sends United Nations peace-keeping forces to help reduce tensions in troubled areas, keep opposing forces apart and create conditions of calm in which peaceful settlements may be sought. Under Chapter VII of the Charter, the Council may decide on enforcement measures, economic sanctions (such as trade embargoes) or collective military action.

A Member State against which preventive or enforcement action has been taken by the Security Council may be suspended from the exercise of the rights and privileges of membership by the General Assembly on the recommendation of the Security Council. A Member State which has persistently violated the principles of the Charter may be expelled from the United Nations by the Assembly on the Council's recommendation.

A State which is a Member of the United Nations but not of the Security Council may participate, without a vote, in its discussions when the Council considers that that country's interests are affected. Both Members of the United Nations and non-members, if they are parties to a dispute being considered by the Council, are invited to take part, without a vote, in the Council's discussions; the Council sets the conditions for participation by a non-member State.

ECONOMIC AND SOCIAL COUNCIL

The Charter established the Economic and Social Council as the principal organ to coordinate the economic and social work of the United Nations and the specialized agencies and institutions—known as the United Nations family of organizations. The Council has 54 members who serve for three-year terms. Voting in the Council is by simple majority; each member has one vote.

Functions and powers

The functions and powers of the Economic and Social Council are:

♦ to serve as the central forum for the discussion of international economic and social issues of a global or inter-disciplinary nature and the formulation of policy recommendations on those issues addressed to Member States and to the United Nations system;

♦ to make or initiate studies and reports and make recommendations on international economic, social, cultural, educational, health and related matters;

♦ to promote respect for, and observance of, human rights and fundamental freedoms;

♦ to call international conferences and prepare draft conventions for submission to the General Assembly on matters falling within its competence;

♦ to negotiate agreements with the specialized agencies defining their relationship with the United Nations;

♦ to coordinate the activities of the specialized agencies by means of consultations with and recommendations to them and by means of recommendations to the General Assembly and the Members of the United Nations;

♦ to perform services, approved by the Assembly, for Members of the United Nations and, on request, for the specialized agencies;

♦ to consult with non-governmental organizations concerned with matters with which the Council deals.

Sessions

The Economic and Social Council generally holds one five-week-long substantive session each year, alternating between New York and Geneva, and at least two organizational sessions in New York. The substantive session includes a high-level special meeting, attended by Ministers and other high officials, to discuss major economic and social issues. The year-round work of the Council is carried out in its subsidiary bodies—commissions and committees—which meet at regular intervals and report back to the Council.

Subsidiary and related bodies

The subsidiary machinery of the Council includes:

♦   nine functional commissions: Statistical Commission, Commission on Population and Development, Commission for Social Development, Commission on Human Rights, Commission on the Status of Women, Commission on Narcotic Drugs, Commission on Crime Prevention and Criminal Justice, Commission on Science and Technology for Development and Commission on Sustainable Development;

♦   five regional commissions: Economic Commission for Africa (Addis Ababa, Ethiopia), Economic and Social Commission for Asia and the Pacific (Bangkok, Thailand), Economic Commission for Europe (Geneva, Switzerland), Economic Commission for Latin America and the Caribbean (Santiago, Chile) and Economic and Social Commission for Western Asia (Amman, Jordan);

♦   four standing committees: Committee for Programme and Coordination, Commission on Human Settlements, Committee on Non-Governmental Organizations and Intergovernmental Working Group of Experts on International Standards of Accounting and Reporting;

♦   a number of expert bodies on subjects such as development planning, natural resources, new and renewable sources of energy and energy for development, and economic, social and cultural rights;

♦   the executive committees and boards of the United Nations Children's Fund, the Office of the United Nations High Commissioner for Refugees, the United Nations Development Programme/United Nations Population Fund, the World Food Programme and the International Research and Training Institute for the Advancement of Women. Also related to the Council are the International Narcotics Control Board and the World Food Council.

Relations with non-governmental organizations

Under the Charter, the Economic and Social Council may consult with non-governmental organizations (NGOs) concerned with matters within the Council's competence. The Council recognizes that these organizations should have the opportunity to express their views, and that they possess special experience or technical knowledge of value to the Council's work.

Over 1,500 NGOs have consultative status with the Council. They are classified into three categories: category I organizations are those concerned with most of the Council's activities; category II organizations have special competence in specific areas; and organizations that can make an occasional contribution to the Council are placed on a roster for ad hoc consultations.

NGOs with consultative status may send observers to public meetings of the Council and its subsidiary bodies and may submit written statements relevant to the Council's work. They may also consult with the United Nations Secretariat on matters of mutual concern.

TRUSTEESHIP COUNCIL

In setting up an International Trusteeship System, the Charter established the Trusteeship Council as one of the main organs of the United Nations and assigned to it the task of supervising the administration of Trust Territories placed under the Trusteeship System. Major goals of the System were to promote the advancement of the inhabitants of the 11 original Trust Territories and their progressive development towards self-government or independence. The Trusteeship Council is made up of the five permanent members of the Security Council—China, France, the Russian Federation, the United Kingdom and the United States.

The aims of the Trusteeship System have been fulfilled to such an extent that all Trust Territories have attained self-government or independence, either as separate States or by joining neighbouring independent countries. In November 1994, the Security Council terminated the United Nations Trusteeship Agreement for the last of the original 11 Trustee Territories on its agenda—the Trust Territory of the Pacific Islands (Palau), administered by the United States. The Trusteeship Council, by amending its rules of procedure, will now meet as and where occasion may require. (See also Chapter 6).

Functions and powers

Under the Charter, the Trusteeship Council is authorized to examine and discuss reports from the Administering Authority on the political, economic, social and educational advancement of the peoples of Trust Territories and, in consultation with the Administering Authority, to examine petitions from and undertake periodic and other special missions to Trust Territories.

INTERNATIONAL COURT OF JUSTICE

The International Court of Justice, whose seat is at The Hague, the Netherlands, is the principal judicial organ of the United Nations. Its Statute is an integral part of the United Nations Charter.

The Court is open to the parties to its Statute, which automatically includes all Members of the United Nations. A State which is not a United Nations Member may become a party to the Statute, on conditions determined in each case by the General Assembly on the recommendation of the Security Council. Switzerland and Nauru are the only non-member States which are parties to the Statute. The Court is not open to private individuals.

All countries which are parties to the Statute of the Court can be parties to cases before it. Other States can refer cases to it under conditions laid down by the Security Council. In addition, the Security Council may recommend that a legal dispute be referred to the Court.

Both the General Assembly and the Security Council can ask the Court for an advisory opinion on any legal question; other organs of the United Nations and the specialized agencies, when authorized by the General Assembly, can ask for advisory opinions on legal questions within the scope of their activities.

Jurisdiction

The jurisdiction of the Court covers all questions which States refer to it, and all matters provided for in the United Nations Charter or in treaties or conventions in force. States may bind themselves in advance to accept the jurisdiction of the Court, either by signing a treaty or convention which provides for referral to the Court or by making a declaration to that effect. Such declarations accepting compulsory jurisdiction may exclude certain classes of cases.

In accordance with Article 38 of its Statute, the Court, in deciding disputes submitted to it, applies:

♦ international conventions establishing rules recognized by the contesting States;

♦ international custom as evidence of a general practice accepted as law;

♦ the general principles of law recognized by nations; and

♦ judicial decisions and the teachings of the most highly qualified publicists of the various nations, as a subsidiary means for determining the rules of law.

If the parties agree, the Court may also decide a case on the basis of equity.

Membership

The Court consists of 15 Judges elected by the General Assembly and the Security Council, voting independently. They are chosen on the basis of their qualifications, not on the basis of nationality, and care is taken to ensure that the principal legal systems of the world are represented in the Court. No two Judges can be nationals of the same State. The Judges serve for a nine-year term and may be re-elected. They cannot engage in any other occupation during their term of office.

The Court normally sits in plenary session, but it may form smaller units called chambers if the parties so request. Judgments given by chambers are considered as rendered by the full Court. The Court has further constituted a Chamber for Environmental Matters, and forms annually a Chamber of Summary Procedures (See also Chapter 7.)

SECRETARIAT

The Secretariat—an international staff working at the United Nations Headquarters in New York and all over the world—carries out the diverse day-to-day work of the Organization. It services the other principal organs of the United Nations and administers the programmes and policies laid down by them. At its head is the Secretary-General, who is appointed by the General Assembly on the recommendation of the Security Council for a five-year, renewable term.

The duties carried out by the Secretariat are as varied as the problems dealt with by the United Nations. These range from administering peace-keeping operations to mediating international disputes. Secretariat staff also survey economic and social trends and problems; prepare studies on subjects such as human rights and sustainable development; organize international conferences on issues of worldwide concern; monitor the extent to which the decisions of United Nations bodies are being carried out; interpret speeches and translate documents into the Organization's official languages; and conduct information programmes to acquaint the world's communications media with the work of the United Nations.

More than 14,000 men and women from some 170 countries make up the Secretariat staff. As international civil servants, they and the Secretary-General answer to the United Nations alone for their activities, and take an oath not to seek or receive instructions from any Government or outside authority. Under Article 100 of the Charter, each Member State undertakes to respect the exclusively international character of the responsibilities of the Secretary-General and the staff and to refrain from seeking to influence them improperly in the discharge of their duties.

Secretary-General

The Secretary-General is described by the Charter as the "chief administrative officer" of the Organization. The Secretary-General is, of course, much more than that. Equal parts diplomat and activist, conciliator and provocateur, the Secretary-General stands before the world community as the very emblem of the United Nations. The task demands great vigour, sensitivity and imagination, to which the Secretary-General must add a tenacious sense of optimism—a belief that the ideals expressed in the Charter can be made a reality. The present Secretary-General of the United Nations, and the sixth occupant of the post, is Boutros Boutros-Ghali, of Egypt, who took office on 1 January 1992.

The work of the Secretary-General involves a certain degree of inherent, creative tension that stems from the Charter's definition of the job. The Charter empowers him to bring to the attention of the Security Council any matter which, in his opinion, threatens international peace and security. It also calls upon him to perform "such other functions" as are entrusted to him by the Security Council, the General Assembly and the other main United Nations organs. Thus the Secretary-General functions as both spokesperson for the international community and servant of the Member States—roles that would seem to guarantee some amount of friction. Far from constricting his work, however, these broad outlines grant the Secretary-General an extraordinary mandate for action.

The Secretary-General is best known to the general public for using his stature and impartiality—his "good offices"—in the interests of "preventive diplomacy". This refers to steps taken by the Secretary-General or his senior staff, publicly and in private, to prevent international disputes from arising, escalating or spreading. Indeed, as events and crises unfold across the globe, the Secretary-General's words and deeds can have profound impact.

But his work also entails routine daily consultations with world leaders and other individuals, attendance at sessions of various United Nations bodies, and worldwide travel as part of the overall effort to improve the state of international affairs. Each year, the Secretary-General issues a report in which he appraises the work of the Organization and advances his view of its future priorities.

Each Secretary-General also defines the job within the context of his particular day and age. In 1992, for example, Mr. Boutros-Ghali, at the request of the Security Council, authored *An Agenda for Peace*, a far-reaching proposal for peace-keeping and peace-building in the post–cold war world. Two years later, he issued *An Agenda for Development*, a blueprint for development into the twenty-first century. At a time when the world community is entering largely uncharted territory, so, too, is the office of Secretary-General being given new dynamism and direction.

Mr. Boutros-Ghali's predecessors as Secretary-General were: Javier Pérez de Cuéllar, of Peru, who served from 1982 to 1991; Kurt Waldheim, of Austria, who held office from 1972 to 1981; U Thant, of Burma (now Myanmar), who served from 1961 to 1971; Dag Hammarskjöld, of Sweden, who served from 1953 until his death in a plane crash in Africa in 1961; and Trygve Lie, of Norway, who held office from 1946 to 1953.

BUDGET OF THE UNITED NATIONS

The regular programme budget of the United Nations is approved by the General Assembly biennially. The budget is initially submitted by the Secretary-General and reviewed by a 16-member expert committee—the Advisory Committee on Administrative and Budgetary Questions. The programmatic aspects are reviewed by the 34-member Committee for Programme and Coordination.

For the 1994-1995 biennium, the budget appropriations, as initially approved in 1993, totalled $2,580,200,200, divided into 12 main categories of expenditures, as follows (in United States dollars):

1.	Overall policy-making, direction and coordination	37,049,800
2.	Political affairs	169,496,800
3.	International justice and law	50,819,400
4.	International cooperation for development	296,711,400
5.	Regional cooperation for development	343,680,000
6.	Human rights and humanitarian affairs	120,941,800
7.	Public information	133,145,300
8.	Common support services	876,856,000

9.	Special expenses	57,973,200
10.	Capital expenditures	77,148,000
11.	Staff assessment*	404,949,400
12.	Office for Inspections and Investigations	11,429,100

The main source of funds for the regular budget is the contributions of Member States, who are assessed on a scale specified by the Assembly on the recommendation of the 18-member Committee on Contributions. The fundamental criterion on which the scale of assessments is based is the real capacity of Member States to pay. The Assembly has fixed a maximum of 25 per cent of the budget for any one contributor and a minimum of 0.01 per cent. (For scale of assessments of Member States, see the Appendices.)

Initial income estimates for the biennium 1994-1995, other than assessments on Member States, totalled $477,401,700.

1.	Income from staff assessment*	411,364,200
2.	General income	59,258,800
3.	Services to the public	6,778,700

The overall financial situation of the United Nations has been precarious for several years because of the continuing failure of many Member States to pay, in full and on time, their assessed contributions to the regular budget or to peace-keeping operations. The United Nations has managed to continue to

---

*To equalize the net pay of all United Nations staff members, whatever their national tax obligations, the Organization deducts from their salaries a sum of money designated a "staff assessment". The rate of withholding is roughly equivalent to the amount paid by United States citizens for federal, state and local taxes calculated at the standard rate. The money collected by the United Nations from the staff assessment is then credited towards the United Nations membership "dues" of the staff member's home country.

Most Governments excuse nationals who are United Nations employees from further taxation. The United States is the main exception; its citizens who work for the Secretariat must pay the same income taxes as all other United States citizens. To enable them to pay their taxes, the United Nations refunds to United States employees that part of their staff assessment which is equal to what the national revenue authorities require for taxes. The citizen then pays that amount to those authorities. In this way, United States nationals are not required to pay taxes twice.

The regular programme budget to which these assessments apply covers expenses relating to substantive programmes, programme support and administrative activities of the Organization both at Headquarters and around the globe.

operate, thanks to voluntary contributions from some countries and its Working Capital Fund (to which Member States advance sums in proportion to their assessed contributions). However, as of 31 December 1994, Member States' unpaid assessed contributions totalled almost $1.8 billion.

Out of this amount, Member States owed more than $352 million to the regular budget for 1994 and more than $127 million for 1993 and previous years. Out of 184 assessed Member States, in December 1994, only 75 had paid their assessments for the regular budget in full. The remaining 109 had failed to meet their statutory financial obligations to the Organization.

Outside the regular budget, Member States are also assessed, in accordance with a modified version of the basic scale, for the costs of the United Nations Peace-keeping Force in Cyprus, the United Nations Disengagement Observer Force in the Middle East, the United Nations Interim Force in Lebanon, the United Nations Iraq-Kuwait Observation Mission, the United Nations Angola Verification Mission, the United Nations Observer Mission in El Salvador, the United Nations Mission for the Referendum in Western Sahara, the United Nations Protection Force, the United Nations Operation in Somalia, the United Nations Operation in Mozambique, the United Nations Observer Mission in Georgia, the United Nations Observer Mission in Liberia, the United Nations Mission in Haiti, the United Nations Assistance Mission for Rwanda and the United Nations Mission of Observers in Tajikistan.

In 1994, assessment for peace-keeping operations amounted to $3.19 billion. In addition, some $1 billion of prior years' assessments remained unpaid at 1 January 1994. As of 31 December 1994, unpaid contributions for the 18 current or recently completed peace-keeping operations with separate assessed budgets amounted to some $1.3 billion. Shortfalls in the receipt of assessed contributions were met by delaying reimbursements to States that contributed troops, thus placing an unfair burden on them.

The work of many operational programmes and funds is financed mainly on a voluntary basis. These programmes and funds include the United Nations Development Programme, the World Food Programme, the Office of the United Nations High Commissioner for Refugees, the United Nations Children's Fund, the United Nations Relief and Works Agency for Palestine Refugees in the Near East, and the United Nations Population Fund. Contributions are provided by Governments, and also by individuals, as in the case of the United Nations Children's Fund.

Budget of the United Nations system

In 1994, the approved regular budget of the United Nations system amounted to $2,912,511,826. This figure includes the United Nations, the specialized agencies (except the World Bank, the International Monetary Fund and the International Fund for Agricultural Development) and the International Atomic Energy Agency.

CHAPTER 2

INTERNATIONAL PEACE
AND SECURITY

In the aftermath of a devastating world war, the United Nations was founded in 1945 to help stabilize international relations and give peace a more secure foundation. Since then, it has been both witness and catalyst to an extraordinary transition in global relations. From the ruins of the Second World War, through years clouded by the rivalry of two major power blocs, the threat of nuclear war and seemingly endless regional conflicts, the United Nations has evolved into an organization in which the collective search for stability founded on peace and development has become an overriding concern.

As the cold war faded, hopes were high for an era in which warfare as an instrument of policy would be rejected. Instead, virtually every continent has seen long-submerged differences flare up in bitter conflicts. The demands on the United Nations have increased sharply, and the Organization has responded by multiplying its peace-keeping operations as well as its peace-making efforts, humanitarian presence and preventive diplomacy.

Today, peace and security are no longer viewed only in terms of absence of military conflict. The common interests of humankind are also seen to be affected by social and economic realities such as poverty, hunger, environmental degradation and human rights violations—problems that are often at the very heart of national and international tensions.

PROMOTING PEACEFUL RELATIONS

The elaboration of principles to promote peace is carried out primarily by the General Assembly under Article 11 of the Charter, which states that the Assembly "may consider the general principles of cooperation in the maintenance of international peace and security...and may make recommendations with regard to such principles to the Members or to the Security Council or to both".

Over the years, the General Assembly has helped promote peaceful relations among nations by adopting several resolutions and declarations on peace, the peaceful settlement of disputes and international cooperation in strengthening peace.

In 1980, the General Assembly approved the establishment in San José, Costa Rica, of the University for Peace, as a specialized international institute for studies, research and dissemination of knowledge aimed at training for peace.

The Assembly has also designated the opening day of its regular annual session—the third Tuesday in September—as International Day of Peace. To concentrate the efforts of the United Nations and its Member States on promoting and achieving the ideals of peace, the year 1986 was proclaimed the International Year of Peace.

PEACEMAKING AND PEACE-KEEPING

Throughout its history, the United Nations has often been called upon to prevent a dangerous situation from escalating into war, to persuade opposing parties to settle their differences at the conference table rather than on the battlefield, and to help restore peace when conflicts occur.

The methods and machinery have taken many forms. In some disputes, the United Nations has dispatched peace-keeping forces, observer or fact-finding missions, good offices missions, mediators and special representatives. In other cases, it has provided the forum for debate and negotiation or an avenue for quiet diplomacy.

Under the Charter, Member States are to settle their disputes by peaceful means in such a manner that international peace, security and justice are not endangered. They are to refrain from the threat or use of force against any State, or in any other manner inconsistent with the purposes of the United Nations.

The Security Council is, under the Charter, the United Nations organ primarily responsible for maintaining peace and security. Under Article 25 of the Charter, Member States agree to accept and carry out the Council's decisions. Recommendations of other United Nations bodies do not have the mandatory force of Security Council decisions, but may influence situations as the expression of world opinion.

The emergence of a collegial spirit among the Council's

permanent members, and the growing readiness of Member States to utilize the United Nations, have enhanced the role of the Secretary-General as a channel of communication between parties. Increasingly, the Secretary-General's good offices have been used to bring parties together to work out equitable agreements. The cases of Afghanistan, the Iran-Iraq war, Namibia, Central America, Cambodia and Mozambique represent various facets of the Secretary-General's peacemaking role.

One of the ways in which the United Nations helps maintain international peace and security is through peace-keeping operations. Such operations are mounted to deal with conflicts that threaten international peace and security, while lasting political solutions are sought.

Peace-keeping involves a United Nations presence in the field (normally including military and civilian personnel) to implement or monitor the implementation of arrangements relating to the control of conflicts (cease-fires, separation of forces etc.) and their resolution (partial or comprehensive settlements), and/or to protect the delivery of humanitarian relief.

These operations are established by the Security Council and directed by the Secretary-General. They must have the consent of the host Governments, and usually of the other parties involved, and must not be used in any way to favour one party against another.

Peace-keeping operations can involve military observer missions, made up of unarmed officers, peace-keeping forces or a combination of both. Peace-keeping forces are made up of troops provided by Member States and financed by the international community. The soldiers of the United Nations peace-keeping forces have weapons, but usually can use them only in self-defence.

With the end of the cold war, the demand for United Nations peace-keeping has increased dramatically. Between 1988 and 1994, 21 new peace-keeping operations were mounted, compared with 13 such operations undertaken during the previous 40 years.

The character of peace-keeping operations has also changed. Most of the 13 operations set up before 1988 were traditional operations. Largely military in composition, they were to monitor cease-fires, control buffer zones and prevent a resumption of hostilities. They sought to maintain calm on the front line, thereby creating an environment more conducive to a negotiated settlement.

Many recent operations have been set up to help implement a settlement already negotiated by the peacemakers. As such, they have involved not only the traditional military activities but also a range of civilian responsibilities. In addition, various peace-keeping operations have sought to protect civilians and to ensure the delivery of humanitarian assistance.

In 1988, the United Nations peace-keeping forces were awarded the Nobel Peace Prize.

ELECTION MONITORING

The United Nations broke new ground in 1989 when, as part of the UNTAG peace-keeping operation, it monitored the entire electoral process in Namibia. Since then, the United Nations has monitored, at Government request, elections in Nicaragua and Haiti (1990), Angola (1992), Cambodia (1993), El Salvador, South Africa and Mozambique (1994), as well as the 1993 referendum in Eritrea. United Nations action has involved all aspects of the electoral process, including voter registration, poll organization, voting, ballot counting and the announcement of results. In each case, the goal was to be able to determine that the electoral process was "free and fair at every stage".

An Electoral Assistance Division was created in 1992 within the United Nations Department of Peace-keeping Operations. Between April 1992 and May 1995, it provided technical assistance in electoral matters to 55 countries.

AN AGENDA FOR PEACE

On 31 January 1992, the Security Council met for the first time at the level of heads of State and Government, marking an unprecedented recommitment by the members of the Council to the purposes and principles of the Charter. At the conclusion of the Summit meeting, the members called on the Secretary-General to recommend ways to improve the United Nations capacity for preventive diplomacy, peacemaking and peace-keeping.

In June 1992, the Secretary-General submitted to the Member States *An Agenda for Peace*,* a report presenting an integrated programme of proposals for more effective United Nations activities aimed at identifying potential conflicts, bringing about their resolution, and building peace among former adversaries in the post-conflict period.

In the area of **preventive diplomacy**, the Secretary-General recommended increased use of confidence-building and fact-finding activities, as well as the establishment of an early-warning system for assessing possible threats to peace. He suggested a new technique—"preventive deployment"—by which United Nations forces would be sent to an area to deter hostilities, rather than waiting until after armed conflict occurred. He proposed that demilitarized zones be considered as a preventive option. He also recommended that the Security Council seek information on economic and social situations, such as massive migration, famine and ethnic unrest, which might threaten international peace and security.

To ensure a more active **peacemaking** role for the United Nations, he called for the full participation of the General Assembly in supporting efforts at mediation, negotiation or arbitration. He urged States to place greater reliance on the International Court of Justice for the peaceful settlement of their differences. He called for increased international assistance, through the United Nations, to improve socio-economic circumstances contributing to a conflict.

He also recommended steps to enable the Security Council to make use of its power, under Chapter VII of the Charter, to use military force to restore international peace and security in the face of a threat to peace or act of aggression. That option, he stressed, was essential to the credibility of the United Nations as a guarantor of international security. In this connection, he proposed the creation of specially trained "peace-enforcement units", which could be deployed in cases where the task of maintaining a cease-fire might exceed the mission of peace-keeping.

---

*An Agenda for Peace. Preventive Diplomacy, Peacemaking and Peace-keeping, DPI/1247, 1992.

With regard to peace-keeping operations, the Secretary-General appealed to States for information on the kind and number of personnel they were prepared to offer the United Nations should the need for new operations arise. He supported financing such missions out of States' defence, rather than foreign affairs, budgets. He recommended that, before deploying United Nations personnel in dangerous situations, the Security Council consider collective measures that would come into effect if there were attacks on the Organization's military and civilian staff.

The Secretary-General recommended a wide range of peace-building activities for the post-conflict period, including joint efforts by the parties to repatriate refugees, remove land-mines, improve transportation and utilize resources such as water and electricity. He stressed the importance of United Nations assistance in monitoring elections, rebuilding or strengthening governmental institutions and protecting human rights.

He also proposed that changes in United Nations mechanisms and techniques for maintaining peace and security should be linked to the increasing role that regional organizations were playing in preventive diplomacy, peacemaking and peace-keeping.

In a position paper issued in January 1995 as a *Supplement*** to *An Agenda for Peace*, the Secretary-General assessed the experience of the United Nations since the publication of the 1992 report. He noted the dramatic changes in both the quantity and nature of United Nations activities for peace and security since the Security Council's 1992 Summit meeting. Most recent conflicts, he observed, had been within States, fought by armies and irregular forces, often in circumstances where State institutions had collapsed and where humanitarian emergencies had developed. In addition to carrying out its humanitarian and military tasks, the United Nations was being called upon to promote national reconciliation and re-establish effective government.

**An Agenda for Peace*. Second edition, with the Supplement and related UN documents, DPI/1623/PKO, E.95.I.15, 1995.

Another kind of operation, the Secretary-General said, had been successful in such places as Namibia, Cambodia and Mozambique, where a negotiated settlement had already been reached. The United Nations was thus called upon to help the parties implement the settlement and undertake an unprecedented variety of functions, from the demobilization of forces to the organization of elections. Such multifunctional operations, he said, highlighted the role the United Nations can play over a number of years, following a settlement, to ensure that the causes of war are eradicated.

In reference to coercive methods for peace-keeping, the Secretary-General pointed out that the increased use of sanctions by the United Nations called for a mechanism to assess, before sanctions are imposed, their impact on the target country and on third countries. The mechanism would also monitor the application of sanctions, measure their effectiveness, ensure the delivery of humanitarian assistance to vulnerable groups within the targeted country, and explore ways of assisting third countries damaged by the sanctions.

The Secretary-General concluded that the necessary financial resources must be provided if United Nations peace-keeping instruments were to be employed effectively. The failure of Member States to pay their assessed contributions for activities that they themselves had voted into being, he said, made it impossible to carry out the activities to the proper standard.

PEACE-KEEPING OPERATIONS, 1948-1995

Current operations (as of May 1995)

United Nations Truce Supervision Organization (UNTSO, established 1948) in the Middle East;
United Nations Military Observer Group in India and Pakistan (UNMOGIP, 1949);
United Nations Peace-keeping Force in Cyprus (UNFICYP, 1964);
United Nations Disengagement Observer Force (UNDOF, 1974) in the Syrian Golan Heights;
United Nations Interim Force in Lebanon (UNIFIL, 1978);
United Nations Iraq-Kuwait Observation Mission (UNIKOM, 1991);
United Nations Mission for the Referendum in Western Sahara (MINURSO, 1991);
United Nations Protection Force (UNPROFOR, 1992) in the former Yugoslavia, replaced in 1995 by three forces: UNPROFOR in Bosnia and Herzegovina, United Nations Confidence Restoration Operation in Croatia (UNCRO), and United Nations Preventive Deployment Force (UNPREDEP) in The former Yugoslav Republic of Macedonia;
United Nations Observer Mission in Georgia (UNOMIG, 1993);
United Nations Observer Mission in Liberia (UNOMIL, 1993);
United Nations Mission in Haiti (UNMIH, 1993);
United Nations Assistance Mission for Rwanda (UNAMIR, 1993);
United Nations Mission of Observers in Tajikistan (UNMOT, 1994);
United Nations Angola Verification Mission III (UNAVEM III, 1995).

Past operations

United Nations Emergency Force (UNEF I, 1956-1967) on the Egypt-Israel border;
United Nations Observation Group in Lebanon (UNOGIL, 1958);
United Nations Operation in the Congo (ONUC, 1960-1964);
United Nations Security Force in West New Guinea (West Irian) (UNSF, 1962-1963);
United Nations Yemen Observation Mission (UNYOM, 1963-1964);
Mission of the Representative of the Secretary-General in the Dominican Republic (DOMREP, 1965-1966);
United Nations India-Pakistan Observation Mission (UNIPOM, 1965-1966);
Second United Nations Emergency Force (UNEF II, 1973-1979) between Egypt and Israel;
United Nations Good Offices Mission in Afghanistan and Pakistan (UNGOMAP, 1988-1990);
United Nations Iran-Iraq Military Observer Group (UNIIMOG, 1988-1991);
United Nations Angola Verification Mission (UNAVEM, 1989-1991), replaced by UNAVEM II (1991-1995);
United Nations Transition Assistance Group (UNTAG, 1989-1990) in Namibia;
United Nations Observer Group in Central America (ONUCA, 1989-1992);

United Nations Observer Mission in El Salvador (ONUSAL, 1991-1995);
United Nations Advance Mission in Cambodia (UNAMIC, 1991-1992), replaced by the United Nations Transitional Authority in Cambodia (UNTAC, 1992-1993);
United Nations Operation in Somalia (UNOSOM, 1992-1993), succeeded by UNOSOM II (1993-1995);
United Nations Operation in Mozambique (ONUMOZ, 1992-1994);
United Nations Observer Mission in Uganda-Rwanda (UNOMUR, 1993-1994);
United Nations Aouzou Strip Observer Group (UNASOG, 1994).

UNITED NATIONS ACTION FOR PEACE

AFRICA
♦ **Angola** ♦ **Congo** ♦ **Eritrea** ♦ **Liberia**
♦ **Mozambique** ♦ **Rwanda** ♦ **Somalia**

ANGOLA

Angola became independent from Portugal on 11 November 1975. But armed opposition to the Government led to many years of civil strife. By the 1980s, the National Union for the Total Independence of Angola (UNITA) controlled large parts of the country with help from the minority regime in South Africa. The Government, for its part, was assisted by Cuban forces.

On 22 December 1988, following U.S.-mediated negotiations, Angola, Cuba and South Africa signed at United Nations Headquarters an agreement aimed at bringing peace to southwestern Africa. The agreement provided for the implementation of a United Nations plan for the independence of Namibia, the withdrawal of Cuban troops from Angola, and measures to achieve peace in the region.

Angola and Cuba also signed an agreement on the withdrawal of Cuban troops from Angola—a condition for South Africa's acceptance of the independence plan for Namibia. Under the agreement, the **United Nations Angola Verification Mission (UNAVEM)** was dispatched to Angola to monitor the Cuban troop withdrawal, which was completed in May 1991.

On 31 May 1991, the Angolan Government and UNITA signed near Lisbon the Peace Accords for Angola. The Government requested the participation of the United Nations in verifying the implementation of the Accords. Under the Accords, the United Nations was to verify the arrangements agreed by the parties for monitoring the cease-fire and the police, and verify—but not be responsible for—the demobilization of troops and the formation of the new unified armed forces. On 30 May, the Security Council entrusted this new mandate to UNAVEM (from then on UNAVEM II), and extended the Mission until general elections, which were scheduled for 1992.

The Peace Accords provided for free and fair elections under international supervision. In December 1991, the Government requested United Nations technical assistance to prepare and hold the elections, as well as the dispatch of observers to follow the entire electoral process.

In February 1992, the Secretary-General appointed a Special Representative for Angola. In March, the Security Council enlarged UNAVEM's mandate to include election observation. The electoral process was conducted by the National Electoral Council (NEC), in which all political parties were represented.

More than 4.8 million eligible voters were registered, representing 92 per cent of an estimated voting population of 5.3 million. The electoral campaign was conducted without major violence, although there were reports of intimidation by some political parties, notably UNITA and the Government party, the Popular Movement for the Liberation of Angola (MPLA).

On election days, 29 and 30 September, UNAVEM II deployed 400 electoral observers throughout the country. They covered all 18 provinces and most of the 164 municipalities, and visited about 4,000 of the 6,000 polling stations. More than 91 per cent of registered voters cast their ballots. On 1 October, the Special Representative stated that the great majority of the electorate had voted in peaceful conditions.

On 3 October and on the following days, UNITA and some other parties complained of massive irregularities and fraud. The Secretary-General urged the UNITA leader, Mr. Jonas Savimbi, not to reject the elections pending investigation of his complaints, and urged him to meet with President José Eduardo dos Santos. The NEC investigated the complaints throughout the country with UNAVEM assistance, but found no conclusive evidence of systematic fraud.

The disbandment of the two former armies had been

formally announced on 27 September, two days before the elections. But UNAVEM continued to carry out its verification functions. By 7 October, about 80 per cent of Government troops had been demobilized, while a much lower proportion of UNITA troops had done so.

A major violation of the Peace Accord occurred on 5 October, when 11 former UNITA generals, including the UNITA army commander, withdrew from the new unified armed forces in protest at what they called fraud and cheating in the elections.

The Security Council sent to Angola an ad hoc Commission, composed of Cape Verde, Morocco, the Russian Federation and the United States, to support implementation of the Peace Accords. But in spite of all diplomatic efforts, the situation continued to worsen.

On 17 October, the NEC President announced the election results. MPLA had obtained 53 per cent of the vote and UNITA 34 per cent in the legislative elections. In the presidential contest, President dos Santos had received 49 per cent, against Mr. Savimbi's 40 per cent, requiring a second round of voting. The Special Representative stated the same day that "with all deficiencies taken into account, the elections... can be considered to have been generally free and fair".

When the results were announced, UNITA launched a nationwide operation to seize municipalities by force and remove the Government's local administration. The Security Council called on both parties to abide by their commitments under the Peace Accords, and requested UNITA to respect the election results.

On 30 October, faced with further reports of hostilities in many parts of the country, the Security Council endorsed the statement of the Special Representative on the elections having generally been free and fair.

Barely 23 hours later, heavy fighting broke out between Government and UNITA forces in Luanda. The Secretary-General's efforts, supported by various Member States, resulted in a tenuous cease-fire which came into effect on 2 November.

Efforts by the Special Representative and others resulted in a 26 November meeting between senior delegations from the two sides, where they pledged to accept the Peace Accords and to reach a cease-fire. But this progress was followed by a set-back when, on 29 November, UNITA forces captured two cities.

As Angola plunged back into civil war, the Secretary-General and his Special Representative renewed their mediation. Talks were held in Addis Ababa, Ethiopia, to discuss prerequisites for relaunching the peace process. In January 1993, the parties reached agreement on a number of items, but some key issues remained to be solved before a cease-fire could be arranged. UNITA, citing concerns for its leadership's safety, failed to attend further talks scheduled for late February in Addis Ababa.

Following a demand by the Security Council for a cease-fire and the resumption of dialogue, peace talks resumed in April in Abidjan, Côte d'Ivoire, but broke down in May.

In spite of the difficulties created by the war, the United Nations intensified its humanitarian action to reach some 2 million people severely affected by the conflict. In May 1993, the United Nations issued an appeal for emergency assistance. The level of suffering, the appeal said, exceeded "anything seen in the previous 16 years". In June, about $70 million was pledged at a donors' meeting in Geneva.

In September, the Security Council condemned UNITA for its continuing military actions, and imposed an arms and oil embargo against the Angolan territory controlled by UNITA. The Council insisted that UNITA respect the 1991 Peace Accords, and that the parties make every effort to restart negotiations.

On 15 November, the Government and UNITA began talks in Lusaka, Zambia, chaired by the Special Representative. Agreement on the military questions on the agenda was reached in December 1993. Agreement on the police was reached in January 1994; on the completion of the electoral process in May; on the new United Nations mandate and the role of the three observer States (Portugal, the Russian Federation and the United States) in October. The question of national reconciliation proved to be the most difficult, since it involved matters such as the allocation of senior government posts to UNITA, including the governorships of provinces. After laborious negotiations, agreement was reached in October, and the Lusaka Protocol was signed on 20 November.

To help the Government and UNITA restore peace and achieve national reconciliation, the Security Council in February 1995 established UNAVEM III. The Mission's main task was to assist in the implementation of the Lusaka Protocol.

CONGO

A Belgian colony, the Republic of the Congo (Leopoldville), now the Republic of Zaire, became independent on 30 June 1960. Disorder broke out in the following days, and Belgium sent in troops, stating that the aim was to protect and evacuate Europeans.

On 12 July 1960, the Congolese Government asked for United Nations military assistance to protect the Congo against external aggression. Two days later, the Security Council called on Belgium to withdraw its troops and authorized the provision to the Congolese Government of military assistance, until the national security forces might be able, in the Government's opinion, to meet their tasks.

In less than 48 hours, contingents of the United Nations Force, provided by several countries (including Asian and African), began to arrive in the Congo. United Nations civilian experts were rushed to the country to help ensure essential public services.

Over the next four years, the task of the **United Nations Operation in the Congo (ONUC)** was to help the Government restore and maintain the country's independence and territorial integrity, to help maintain law and order, and to put into effect a wide programme of technical assistance.

To meet this task, an exceptionally large team was assembled. At its peak, the United Nations Force totalled nearly 20,000 officers and civilians. The instructions of the Security Council to this Force were strengthened early in 1961 after the assassination in Katanga of former Prime Minister Patrice Lumumba. The Force was to protect the Congo from outside interference, particularly by evacuating foreign mercenaries and advisers from the southern province of Katanga, and to prevent clashes and civil strife, by force as a last resort.

Following the reconvening of Parliament in August 1961 under United Nations auspices, the main problem was the attempted secession of Katanga, led and financed by foreign elements. In September and December 1961, and again in December 1962, the secessionist forces led by foreign mercenaries clashed with the United Nations Force. Secretary-General Dag Hammarskjöld lost his life on 17 September 1961 when his plane crashed on the way to Ndola (in what is now Zambia) where talks to end hostilities were to be held.

In February 1963, after Katanga had been reintegrated into the Congo, a phasing out of the Force began. At the request of the Government, the General Assembly authorized the stay of a reduced number of troops for a further six months. The Force was completely withdrawn by 30 June 1964.

Civilian aid continued in the largest single programme of assistance yet undertaken by the United Nations and its agencies, with some 2,000 experts at work in the Congo at the peak of the programme in 1963-1964.

ERITREA

The former Italian colony of Eritrea assumed federal status with Ethiopia in 1952, in accordance with a 1950 resolution of the General Assembly. Eritrea thus became an autonomous unit within the federation of Ethiopia and Eritrea. The federation became a unitary State on 14 November 1962, when Eritrea was fully integrated with Ethiopia. This development gave rise to a movement for the secession of Eritrea, which started a campaign of military resistance.

After the fall of Ethiopian President Mengistu Haile Mariam in May 1991, the Eritrean People's Liberation Front announced that it would form a provisional Government, pending a United Nations-supervised referendum to determine the wishes of the Eritrean people regarding their political status in relation to Ethiopia.

In May 1992, the Commissioner of the Referendum Commission of Eritrea invited the Secretary-General to send a delegation to observe and verify that the referendum process, scheduled from July 1992 to April 1993, was free, fair and impartial.

A United Nations Technical Team visited Eritrea in June 1992, holding discussion with the Referendum Commission, the Provisional Government and political, social and religious organizations. The Team made technical suggestions aimed at improving the organization of the referendum.

In October, the Secretary-General submitted to the General Assembly a proposal for an observer mission, and on 16 December the Assembly established the **United Nations Observer Mission to Verify the Referendum in Eritrea (UNOVER)**.

The Secretary-General appointed as Head of UNOVER and as his Special Representative for the referendum Mr. Samir Sanbar, who arrived in Asmara, the capital, on 15 February 1993. The Mission was carried out by 22 international staff, supported by local personnel. Their task was to observe all referendum activities, from the registration of voters to the announcement of the results.

During all stages, UNOVER observers maintained contact with community leaders and social organizations, visited municipalities and villages throughout the country, made random visits to registration centres to monitor voter registration, observed rallies and other referendum-related activities, and verified compliance by all parties with the referendum proclamation and with the code of conduct.

Voter registration started in December 1992. At the end of the process, about 1.1 million people had been registered. In April 1993, the number of UNOVER personnel was increased by some 100 election monitors.

Voting took place from 23 to 25 April 1993. On 27 April, the Special Representative declared the referendum process free and fair. The results showed 99 per cent of voters in favour of independence.

Eritrea was declared independent on 24 May, and on 28 May was admitted to the United Nations as the 182nd Member State.

LIBERIA

When the Government of President Samuel Doe was overthrown in 1990, civil war broke out, causing the breakdown of law and order in Liberia. In the following three years, the war claimed the lives of between 100,000 and 150,000 civilians, with some 700,000 refugees fleeing to neighbouring countries. Liberia remained divided: the Interim Government of National Unity administered the capital city of Monrovia; the National Patriotic Front of Liberia (NPFL) controlled nine counties; and the United Liberation Movement of Liberia for Democracy (ULIMO) controlled the remaining three counties.

From the outset of the conflict, the Economic Community of West African States (ECOWAS), a subregional organization made up of 16 countries, took initiatives towards a political settlement. These included creating a Military Observer Group (ECOMOG) in August 1990, and mediating agreements which became the basis for the peace plan of November 1990. On 30 October 1991, ECOWAS brokered the Yamoussoukro IV Accord, which provided for the disarmament of warring factions under ECOMOG supervision, and the establishment of transitional institutions to carry out free and fair elections.

The United Nations supported from the start the efforts of the ECOWAS member States. It also provided humanitarian assistance through its agencies and programmes. The United Nations Special Coordinator's office opened in 1990 to respond to the needs of Liberians throughout the country. Arrangements were made to assist those who fled to neighbouring countries, mainly Côte d'Ivoire, Guinea and Sierra Leone.

To establish peace and stability in the country, the Security Council on 19 November 1992 imposed a general and complete arms embargo on Liberia, and requested the Secretary-General to dispatch an envoy. The Secretary-General appointed a Special Representative for Liberia, who visited Liberia and eight other countries in the region.

In March 1993, the Secretary-General reported to the Security Council that the Special Representative's talks with the parties indicated a consensus for a larger United Nations role in the search for peace. The Council asked the Secretary-General to discuss with ECOWAS and the parties the contribution which the United Nations could make.

On 6 June 1993, nearly 600 Liberians, mainly people displaced by the war, were killed in an armed attack near the Liberian town of Harbel. The Security Council condemned the killings and asked the Secretary-General to launch an investigation.

The investigation panel concluded that the killings had been carried out by units of the Armed Forces of Liberia (one of the parties to the conflict), and that NPFL, to which the act of violence had initially been attributed, had had no role in it. The panel added that this finding did not diminish the responsibility of NPFL, ULIMO and others alleged to have engaged in similar atrocities, and recommended investigating such atrocities.

On 25 July 1993, after a three-day meeting in Cotonou, Benin, under the co-chairmanship of the Secretary-General's Special Representative, the envoy of the Organization of African Unity (OAU) and the Executive Secretary of ECOWAS, the parties signed the Cotonou Peace Agreement. The Agreement provided for a cease-fire, the disarmament and demobilization of military units, a transitional government, and general and presidential elections. A Joint Cease-fire Monitoring Committee was set up, comprising the three Liberian parties, ECOMOG and the United Nations.

On 22 September, the Security Council established the **United Nations Observer Mission in Liberia (UNOMIL)**, to assist in implementing the peace agreement. Under the agreement, ECOMOG had the primary responsibility for implementation; UNOMIL would monitor and verify the impartial application of the implementation procedures. UNOMIL was the first United Nations peace-keeping mission undertaken in cooperation with a peace-keeping operation already set up by another organization.

The task of UNOMIL comprised monitoring the cease-fire, the arms embargo and the disarmament and demobilization of combatants; assisting in humanitarian activities, including the return of refugees and displaced persons; and observing the election process, conducted by the transitional government.

In accordance with the Cotonou Agreement, ECOMOG was to be reinforced by troops from countries outside West Africa. On the basis of an ECOWAS appeal, the Secretary-General set up a Trust Fund to assist in the deployment and maintenance of the ECOMOG troops. In September 1993, the United States pledged $19.8 million to the Trust Fund, for the deployment and maintenance of the additional troops and for covering some maintenance costs of the existing troops. In January 1994, battalions from Tanzania and Uganda were deployed to Liberia.

After months of stalemate, the Liberian National Transitional Government (LNTG) was installed on 8 March 1994. Elections were to be held in September. But the demobilization proceeded slowly, and came to a halt with the emergence of two new armed factions and accusations that both NPFL and ULIMO had resumed hostilities. Increased fighting forced the UNOMIL observers to move from many of the rural areas to the more secure Monrovia, since the authority of the LNTG could not be extended beyond the capital. Both the NPFL and ULIMO experienced internal divisions, further adding to instability. The elections were postponed indefinitely.

In September, President Jerry Rawlings of Ghana, the ECOWAS Chairman, convened the NPFL, ULIMO and AFL for peace talks attended by the OAU and the United Nations at Akosombo, Ghana. The Akosombo Agreement, signed on 12 September, sought to reinforce and supplement the Cotonou Agreement, recognized as the framework for peace. On 21 December, all warring factions concluded in Accra, Ghana, a peace agreement calling for a cessation of hostilities, the seating of a new transitional government, disarmament of combatants and the eventual holding of elections.

In April 1995, the Secretary-General reported to the Security Council that the peace process remained at an impasse. The Council urged the parties to install a transitional government, re-establish a cease-fire and take steps to implement the Accra Agreement.

MOZAMBIQUE

Mozambique became independent from Portugal on 25 June 1975. But after only a few years of relative peace, the country was plunged into a devastating civil war waged against the Government by the Mozambican National Resistance (RENAMO), supported by the minority regime in South Africa.

On 4 October 1992, Joaquim Chissano, President of Mozambique, and Afonso Dhlakama, President of RENAMO, signed in Rome a General Peace Agreement. Under the Agreement, negotiated over a period of two years in the Italian capital, a cease-fire was to come into effect by 15 October. The cease-fire was to be followed by the separation of the two sides' forces and their concentration in 49 assembly areas. Demobilization of the troops who would not serve in the new Mozambican Defence Force was to be completed six months after the cease-fire. Meanwhile, preparations would be made for general elections.

The Agreement called for a major United Nations role in monitoring its implementation, and in providing technical assistance for and monitoring the elections. The implementation of the Agreement was to be overseen by a Supervisory and Monitoring Commission (CSC) chaired by the United Nations.

In October, the Security Council approved the dispatch to Mozambique of a team of military observers and the appointment by the Secretary-General of his Special Representative, Mr. Aldo Ajello.

The Special Representative and the team of observers arrived in the capital city of Maputo on 15 October, the day the Peace Agreement entered into force. Both parties had pledged to undertake specific action to start monitoring jointly the implementation of the Agreement. But no such action had started when the Special Representative arrived in Mozambique, and he immediately began discussions with the parties towards this end.

In November 1992, the CSC was established to guarantee the implementation of the Agreement, settle any dispute between the parties and coordinate its subsidiary Commissions. Chaired by the United Nations, it was composed of Government and RENAMO delegations, with representatives of Italy (the mediator State), France, Germany, Portugal, the United Kingdom, the United States (observer States at the Rome talks) and the Organization of African Unity (OAU).

In December, the Secretary-General submitted to the Security Council a plan for a **United Nations Operation in Mozambique (ONUMOZ)**. The Council established ONUMOZ on 16 December, and endorsed the Secretary-General's recommendation that the elections not take place until the military aspects of the Agreement had been implemented. At its peak, ONUMOZ numbered some 6,500 troops, including some 370 military observers, as well as civilian personnel.

The Peace Agreement provided for legislative and presidential elections one year after the signature of the Agreement, to be organized by the National Electoral Commission (NEC). ONUMOZ was to monitor the entire electoral process.

The military tasks of ONUMOZ included monitoring the cease-fire, the separation and assembly of forces, their demobilization, and the collection, storage and destruction of weapons; verifying the disbanding of irregular armed groups; and providing security for United Nations and other international activities.

The military aspects were closely linked with the humanitarian effort. A major goal of the humanitarian assistance programme of ONUMOZ was to help the 3.7 million Mozambicans displaced by the war to resettle in their communities.

In March 1993, the Government and the United Nations High Commissioner for Refugees (UNHCR) announced that the voluntary repatriation of 1.3 million refugees would begin in April. The three-year operation would be the biggest ever undertaken by UNHCR in Africa.

In April 1993, the Secretary-General reported to the Security Council that, despite positive developments, the elections originally planned for October would have to be rescheduled, due to delays in implementing the Peace Agreement. The Council urged the Government and RENAMO to finalize the timetable for the demobilization of troops, the formation of the new unified army and the holding of elections. But in July, continuing delays in implementing the Agreement prompted the Security Council to express its concern.

In August, President Chissano and RENAMO President Dhlakama met in Maputo in talks organized with the assistance of the United Nations. But a consultative conference involving all political parties to discuss a draft electoral law broke down over the composition of the NEC.

In September, the Security Council urged the parties to apply the revised timetable for implementing the Peace Agreement and to begin demobilizing.

In an attempt to break the stalemate, the Secretary-General visited Mozambique in October. After meeting with President Chissano and RENAMO President Dhlakama, the Secretary-General announced a breakthrough in the peace process. Major agreements had been reached on the assembly and demobilization of troops, the composition of the NEC, the system and timetable for finalizing the Electoral Law, and the creation of local committees to monitor the activities of the police.

The long-awaited assembly of troops began in November, while the Electoral Law was approved in December. President Chissano and Mr. Dhlakama met on a number of occasions, and several disagreements were overcome.

Demobilization started in March 1994, and was substantially concluded in August. More than 76,000 soldiers from both sides were demobilized, and ONUMOZ helped combine over 10,000 of them into the new national army. The transfer of authority, equipment and infrastructure from the former army to the new Mozambique Defence Force was formally completed on 16 August. By mid-October, ONUMOZ had collected about 155,000 weapons from the troops of both parties and from paramilitary forces.

In August, the Secretary-General reported that some 75 per cent of the estimated 3.7 million people internally displaced at the time of the signature of the Peace Agreement had been resettled. By the end of 1994, most refugees in the neighbouring countries had also returned to Mozambique.

Between 1 June and 2 September, some 6.3 million voters were registered—81 per cent out of an estimated eligible population of 7.8 million. The NEC accepted the application of 12 presidential candidates, and accredited 14 political parties and coalitions to participate in the legislative elections for the 250 seats of the National Assembly.

On the eve of the elections, alleging irregularities, Mr. Dhlakama announced his party's withdrawal from the polls. But following intensive negotiations, he agreed on RENAMO's continued participation in the elections and guarantees of close international monitoring.

The country's first multi-party elections, at which some

90 per cent of the registered electorate voted, were held on 27-29 October, monitored by some 2,300 international observers. No major incidents were registered at the some 7,500 polling stations.

On 19 November, the Special Representative declared the elections free and fair. Two days later, the Security Council endorsed the results.

Mr. Chissano won the presidential elections with 53 per cent of the vote, while Mr. Dhlakama obtained 34 per cent. FRELIMO obtained 129 parliamentary seats, and RENAMO 109. The new National Assembly was installed on 8 December, and on 9 December Mr. Chissano was inaugurated as President. On the same day, ONUMOZ's mandate formally came to an end. Its task successfully fulfilled, ONUMOZ completed its withdrawal from Mozambique in January 1995.

(On **Namibia**, see Chapter 6.)

RWANDA

Internal and cross-border conflict broke out in Rwanda in October 1990, with sporadic fighting between the armed forces of the Hutu-led Government of Rwanda and the Tutsi-led Rwandese Patriotic Front (RPF) operating from Uganda and areas in northern Rwanda. Despite a number of cease-fire agreements, hostilities resumed in February 1993, interrupting negotiations between the two parties in Arusha, Tanzania, which were supported by the Organization of African Unity (OAU) and facilitated by the Government of Tanzania.

Rwanda and Uganda called on the Security Council to station United Nations military observers along their common border to prevent the military use of the border area, in particular the transport of military supplies. After consulting with the Council, the Secretary-General sent a goodwill mission to Rwanda and Uganda in March 1993. A technical mission in April confirmed that observers could monitor the border and verify that no military assistance crossed it. It was decided to deploy observers only on the Uganda side of the border.

While the Government of Rwanda and the RPF met in Dar es Salaam and agreed to reinstate the cease-fire and resume the peace talks, the United Nations launched an appeal for

$78 million in emergency humanitarian assistance to address the needs of some 900,000 war-displaced people in Rwanda. By September, the international community had made contributions worth $100 million.

On 22 June 1993, the Security Council established the **United Nations Observer Mission Uganda-Rwanda (UNOMUR)**, which was fully operational by the end of September.

The peace talks were concluded successfully on 4 August. The Arusha Peace Agreement provided for a broad-based transitional government, to be in effect until elections leading to a democratically elected government. After the signing of the Agreement, the situation eased somewhat. An estimated 600,000 displaced persons returned to their homes. The remaining displaced persons continued to rely on emergency assistance provided in some 30 camps.

The Government and the RPF requested the United Nations to establish another international force to assist in implementing the Peace Agreement. On 5 October, the Council set up the **United Nations Assistance Mission for Rwanda (UNAMIR)**, to monitor implementation of the Agreement and assist in the establishment and maintenance of a transitional government. It was to stay in Rwanda until elections and the installation of a new government, scheduled for October 1995.

Delay in implementing the Agreement slowed the deployment and operation of UNAMIR. Diplomatic efforts sought to expedite the establishment of a transitional government, but the delay had already contributed to a deterioration in the security situation. In January and February 1994, the Security Council urged the parties to cooperate to assure prompt installation of the transitional institutions. Negotiations on the composition of transitional bodies continued, and 25 March was set as the date of their installation. But ceremonies had to be cancelled because of the many unresolved issues.

On 6 April, President Juvénal Habyarimana of Rwanda and President Cyprien Ntaryamira of Burundi were killed in a rocket attack on their plane while returning from peace talks in Tanzania. The incident set off a torrent of violence and killings which had political as well as ethnic dimensions.

Rwanda's Prime Minister, cabinet ministers, government officials and scores of civilians, as well as UNAMIR peace-keepers, were the first victims of the carnage. The RPF started to fight back, governmental authority collapsed and transitional institutions disintegrated.

An interim government proclaimed on 8 April failed to establish its authority and stop the massacres, which had assumed genocidal proportion. When the fighting intensified in and around the capital city of Kigali, the interim government fled into exile in Zaire. With the RPF's southward push from its northern bases, the number of displaced persons and refugees increased tremendously. On 28 April alone, 280,000 people fled to Tanzania to escape the violence. The mass exodus into Zaire added another devastating dimension to the conflict. United Nations agencies and humanitarian relief organizations provided emergency assistance on an unprecedented scale.

UNAMIR concentrated on efforts to arrange a cease-fire but without success, and UNAMIR personnel came increasingly under attack. Subsequently, the Security Council reduced UNAMIR's strength from 2,548 to 270. UNAMIR's mandate was changed to include working with the parties towards a cease-fire agreement and assisting in the resumption of relief operations.

Reports confirmed that the killings were mainly carried out by members of the armed forces, the Presidential Guard, and the youth militia of the governing party. In the face of the scope of the massacres and the human tragedy inflicted on the people of Rwanda, the Security Council called for urgent international action to alleviate the suffering of the Rwandese people and to help restore peace.

On 17 May, the Security Council determined that the situation in Rwanda constituted a threat to international peace and security, and imposed an arms embargo against Rwanda. The Council authorized UNAMIR's expansion to up to 5,500 troops, and recognized the potential need for the mission to take action in self-defence against persons or groups who threatened protected sites and populations.

On 22 June, at the initiative of France, the Security Council authorized under Chapter VII of the United Nations Charter a temporary multinational humanitarian operation to contribute to the security and protection of displaced persons, refugees and civilians at risk. French-led multinational forces carried out "Opération Turquoise", which established a safe humanitarian protection zone in the south-west of Rwanda. On 21 August, the operation was terminated according to plan, when UNAMIR took over its responsibilities in the zone.

Meanwhile, the United Nations Commission for Human Rights appointed a Special Rapporteur to investigate the human rights situation in Rwanda. A Commission of Experts established in July by the Security Council reported in September that "overwhelming evidence" proved that Hutu elements had perpetrated acts of genocide against the Tutsi group in a "concerted, planned, systematic and methodical way".

On 18 July, after RPF forces took control of Rwanda—except in the humanitarian protection zone—it unilaterally declared a cease-fire, effectively ending the civil war. The next day, a broad-based Government of national unity was installed for a transitional period of five years. The new Government declared its commitment to the principles of the Arusha Peace Agreement and to national reconciliation and reconstruction, and assured UNAMIR of its cooperation in efforts to encourage the return of refugees.

UNAMIR continued its efforts to ensure security and stability, encourage the return of refugees and displaced persons, provide security and support for humanitarian assistance, and promote reconciliation. In October, its troop strength stood at 4,270.

For its part, after the resumption of civil war in April, UNOMUR expanded its monitoring activities in Uganda from the areas controlled by the RPF to the entire border area between the two countries. It also played an instrumental part in building up and supporting UNAMIR operations in Rwanda. However, as decided by the Security Council in June, UNOMUR was gradually reduced through August and September. The last military observers left Uganda, and UNOMUR was closed down on 21 September.

By September, estimates suggested that Rwanda's pre-war population of 7.9 million had fallen to 5 million. The victims of genocidal slaughter could number as many as one million. Estimates of internally displaced persons ranged from 800,000 to 2 million. Some 2.1 million Rwandese refugees were still in Zaire, Tanzania, Burundi and Uganda. At the same time, more than 200,000 refugees returned to Rwanda from Burundi and Uganda.

In July 1994, the United Nations had launched a humanitarian appeal for $552 million. Contributions by Governments, organizations and individuals made it possible to respond immediately to the extraordinary humanitarian challenge. As of 1 September, contributions amounted to $384 million, covering 70 per cent of the total requirement. Bilateral and other direct contributions brought the total amount to $762 million.

In November, the Security Council established the International Tribunal for Rwanda to persecute persons responsible for genocide and other violations of international humanitarian law. The Council called on all States to cooperate with the Tribunal, which is located in Arusha.

The humanitarian situation remained serious in early 1995. Two fund-raising drives launched by the United Nations in January to raise more than $700 million for the rehabilitation and reconstruction of the country were only partially met.

The Security Council in February 1995 expressed concern over reports of intimidation and security problems in camps for Rwandese refugees, particularly in Zaire. The Council welcomed two agreements on refugees—one between Zaire and the UNHCR to deploy a 1,500-strong Zairian security force to assist in maintaining law and order in refugee camps in that country; the other one between Zaire and Rwanda on the return of refugees and property. The Council also endorsed the UNHCR efforts to put in place security arrangements in the Tanzanian camps.

SOMALIA

The downfall in January 1991 of President Siad Barre, the leader of Somalia for 21 years, resulted in a power struggle and clan clashes in many parts of the country. In November, intense fighting broke out in the capital, Mogadishu, between the faction supporting Interim President Ali Mahdi Mohamed and the faction supporting General Mohamed Farah Aidid, Chairman of the United Somali Congress.

Fighting spread to other regions of the country, with heavily armed elements controlling various parts of Somalia. Widespread death and destruction forced hundreds of thousands of people to flee their homes. Almost 5 million people—over half the population—were threatened by hunger and disease. Nearly one million people sought refuge outside the country.

Despite the turmoil, the United Nations continued its humanitarian effort, and by March 1991 was fully engaged in the country, in cooperation with several non-governmental organizations. The Secretary-General also became increasingly involved with the political aspects of the conflict, in cooperation with the Organization of African Unity (OAU), the League of Arab States (LAS) and the Organization of the Islamic Conference (OIC).

In December, the Secretary-General dispatched an envoy to Somalia in an effort to restore peace. During that visit, all faction leaders expressed support for a United Nations role in bringing about national reconciliation.

On 23 January 1992, the Security Council imposed an arms embargo on Somalia and urged all parties to cease hostilities.

On 31 January, the Secretary-General invited interim President Ali Mahdi and General Aidid, as well as the LAS, the OAU and the OIC, to send representatives to attend talks in February at United Nations Headquarters. The talks succeeded in getting the two factions to agree on a cease-fire, and to a visit by a delegation composed of the United Nations and the three regional organizations.

After intensive negotiations conducted by the delegation, the two parties signed in March an agreement on the implementation of the cease-fire. Further talks led to agreements on a cease-fire to be monitored by United Nations observers, and on the protection of humanitarian convoys by United Nations security personnel.

On 24 April, the Security Council established the **United Nations Operation in Somalia (UNOSOM)**, to facilitate the cessation of hostilities and the maintenance of a cease-fire, and to promote a political settlement.

The Secretary-General appointed a Special Representative for Somalia, who left for the region on 1 May. In early July, 50 United Nations military observers arrived in Mogadishu, followed by some 500 United Nations security personnel. Meanwhile, humanitarian efforts were being carried out by six United Nations organizations and more than 30 relief organizations.

In August, the Secretary-General reported to the Security Council that the United Nations and its partners were ready to provide much greater assistance, but were prevented from doing so by the lawlessness and lack of security prevailing throughout Somalia. He recommended deploying up to 3,000 security troops to protect the humanitarian efforts. This proposal was endorsed by the Council.

In October and November, the situation continued to deteriorate. As famine threatened some 1.5 million lives, Somalia remained without a central government, Mogadishu was divided by rival militias and the country by a dozen factions.

The delivery of humanitarian aid became more and more difficult. Relief ships were blocked from docking and even shelled. Ports and airports came under fire. Money and relief supplies were being extorted from donor agencies, and the lives of their personnel trying to distribute aid to starving people were being put in danger.

As a result, only a trickle of relief supplies was reaching the needy. According to some estimates, as many as 3,000 people a day were dying of starvation. Unless the security problems were solved, United Nations and relief agencies would be unable to provide the massive assistance needed. On 24 November, the Secretary-General reported to the Security Council on the deteriorating situation in Somalia and on the factors preventing UNOSOM from carrying out its mandate.

On 3 December, the Security Council accepted an offer, made on 25 November by the United States, to take the lead in organizing and commanding an operation to ensure the delivery of humanitarian relief. Acting under Chapter VII of the Charter, which deals with enforcement measures, the Council authorized the use of all necessary means to establish a secure environment for humanitarian relief operations.

The first elements of the Unified Task Force (UNITAF), consisting of military units from 24 countries led by the United States, were deployed in Mogadishu on 9 December. By 28 December, all major relief centres in the country had been secured, and humanitarian assistance was again flowing. UNOSOM worked in strict coordination with UNITAF, and remained responsible for humanitarian assistance and for efforts to arrive at a political solution of the crisis.

At a meeting convened by the Secretary-General at Addis Ababa in January 1993, 14 Somali political movements signed a cease-fire agreement and pledged to hand over all weapons to UNITAF and UNOSOM.

By March 1993, some 37,000 UNITAF troops were deployed in 40 per cent of Somali territory, greatly improving the security situation and the delivery of humanitarian assistance. As a result, the level of malnutrition and death from starvation fell dramatically.

Following recommendations by the Secretary-General, the Security Council on 26 March decided on a transition from UNITAF to UNOSOM II, and expanded UNOSOM's size and mandate. It authorized UNOSOM II to use force under Chapter VII of the Charter, so as to enable it to establish a secure environment throughout Somalia. It also mandated UNOSOM II to assist the Somalis in rebuilding their economy and social and political life.

In March, the United Nations launched an appeal for $166 million to cover the relief and rehabilitation programme in 1993; over $130 million was pledged at a United Nations conference on humanitarian assistance to Somalia, held in March in Addis Ababa.

On the initiative of the Secretary-General and his Special Representative, a Conference on National Reconciliation was held in March in Addis Ababa, attended by the leaders of 15 Somali political movements. All participants endorsed an Agreement on disarmament and security, rehabilitation and reconstruction, restoration of property and settlement of disputes, and the establishment of a transitional national council.

In June, an attack against UNOSOM II in Mogadishu left 25 Pakistani soldiers dead. Condemning the attack, the Security

Council stressed the crucial importance of disarming all parties, and demanded that all parties comply with the commitments undertaken. Subsequently, UNOSOM II forces engaged in military actions in south Mogadishu, resulting in casualties in the civilian population as well as among UNOSOM members.

In an operation in south Mogadishu in October, 18 United States soldiers lost their lives. The United States temporarily reinforced its presence with air, sea and ground forces; but subsequently announced its intention to withdraw from Somalia by 31 March 1994. Belgium, France and Sweden also announced their decision to withdraw.

Also in October, the Secretary-General travelled to the region for consultations on UNOSOM II's future strategy for humanitarian, political and security activities. He held talks with the Presidents of Egypt, Djibouti, Kenya and Ethiopia. He also visited Baidoa and Mogadishu, holding talks with Somali elders and UNOSOM officials.

Meanwhile, humanitarian work and political reconciliation efforts continued. More than 100,000 refugees returned from Ethiopia to the relatively peaceful north-western part of the country, which in May 1991 had proclaimed its "independence" as "Somaliland Republic". In August 1993, a Conference of Kismayo Elders sought to restore stability in that southern city. Similar reconciliation meetings were held in other parts of Somalia.

In February 1994, the Security Council revised the mandate of UNOSOM II, stressing assistance to the Somali people and their leaders in attaining political reconciliation, reconstruction and stability. The Council authorized a gradual troop reduction, and set a March 1995 deadline for the completion of UNOSOM's mission.

In March, following talks brokered by the Secretary-General's Acting Special Representative, Somalia's 15 major movements signed in Nairobi a Declaration on national reconciliation. The agreement called on participants to prepare for a National Reconciliation Conference to appoint a President, Vice-President and Prime Minister. It also set out the signatories' commitment to implementing a cease-fire and disarming their militias. But the preparatory meeting for the National Reconciliation Conference was postponed repeatedly.

Reporting to the Security Council in May, the Secretary-General noted that while all Somali political leaders had appealed to UNOSOM to continue supporting their reconciliation effort, the security situation had steadily deteriorated. In July, the Council noted the gains made on the humanitarian front and in re-establishing police and justice systems, but expressed concern at the slow pace of national reconciliation.

Also in July, the Secretary-General sent to Somalia a mission to discuss UNOSOM's troop reduction. Acting on the recommendations of the mission, he recommended in August to reduce the force to 15,000 troops. On 25 August, the Security Council, while expressing support for the proposed troop reduction, invited the Secretary-General to report on prospects for national reconciliation and on options for UNOSOM's future.

The Secretary-General reported in September that UNOSOM's ability to provide security had been reduced by troop withdrawals, Somali political and military actions and budget restrictions. The Security Council encouraged the Secretary-General to continue with the preparation of contingency arrangements for the possible withdrawal of UNOSOM II, on the basis of its decision to end the mission in March 1995. The level of the force was to be reduced from over 18,000 to 15,000 by the end of October.

In October, the Secretary-General reported that Somali leaders still had not carried out commitments entered into under the 1993 Addis Ababa Agreement and the 1994 Nairobi Declaration. "The international community cannot impose peace", he noted. "Peace can only come from the Somalis themselves". The Secretary-General recommended extending UNOSOM's mandate through March 1995 to give Somali leaders time to consolidate any progress towards reconciliation.

A Security Council mission visited Somalia at the end of October to convey to the Somali political parties the Council's views on the situation in Somalia. The mission reported that political reconciliation was far from certain. The mission's chairman stated that continuation of UNOSOM II beyond

March could not be justified because of the political impasse in the country.

On 4 November, the Security Council extended UNOSOM's mandate for a final period until 31 March 1995, affirmed that the primary purpose of the mission was to facilitate political reconciliation, and urged all Somali factions to negotiate a cease-fire and the formation of a transitional government of national unity.

However, no further progress was made towards reconciliation. The withdrawal of UNOSOM II was completed in March 1995, but the Secretary-General declared that United Nations assistance to Somalia would continue in both the political and humanitarian areas. Under difficult conditions, United Nations agencies continued to carry out emergency and rehabilitation activities in the country.

(On **South Africa** see Question of Apartheid in Chapter 4. On **Western Sahara** see Chapter 6.)

THE AMERICAS
♦ **Central America** ♦ **Haiti**

CENTRAL AMERICA

The United Nations has supported from the start the efforts of Central American Governments to bring peace to the region. The combined action of the Security Council, the General Assembly and the Secretary-General has helped to resolve several protracted conflicts.

In 1987, the Presidents of five Central American countries—Costa Rica, El Salvador, Guatemala, Honduras and Nicaragua—signed the Esquipulas II agreement, by which they undertook to launch a region-wide process of democratization and national dialogue, bring about a cease-fire, and promote free and fair elections.

In February 1989, the five Presidents decided to set up a mechanism to verify the agreement with United Nations participation. They agreed to draw up a plan for the voluntary demobilization of the members of the Nicaraguan resistance (also known as "contras"). And Nicaragua announced it would call general elections under international and United Nations supervision.

In August 1989, at Nicaragua's request, the **United Nations Observer Mission for the Verification of Elections in Nicaragua (ONUVEN)** started operations in the country. It monitored the entire preparation and holding of the elections—the first United Nations-monitored elections in an independent country.

On election day, 25 February 1990, ONUVEN observers visited polling stations in 141 of the country's 143 municipalities and monitored vote counting. ONUVEN concluded that the elections had been conducted "in a highly commendable manner".

On the request of both the President and President-elect, a United Nations team facilitated a peaceful political transition and played a role in various negotiations that followed the elections. The success of ONUVEN helped create conditions for the voluntary demobilization of the Nicaraguan resistance.

That demobilization was overseen by another United Nations mission, the **United Nations Observer Group in Central America (ONUCA)**, which had been established in November 1989 as a mechanism to verify the security aspects of Esquipulas II, following a request from the five Central American countries. ONUCA established a presence in all five countries to verify the end of assistance to irregular forces and insurrectionist movements, and the end of the use of one country's territory for attacks on other countries.

In March 1990, the Security Council enlarged ONUCA's mandate to include overseeing the voluntary demobilization of the Nicaraguan resistance. The operation was undertaken throughout Honduras and Nicaragua. By 29 June, some 22,000 resistance members had turned in their weapons to ONUCA.

The civilian aspects of the demobilization—repatriation, relocation or resettlement—were the responsibility of the International Commission for Support and Verification (CIAV), set up in September 1989 by the Secretaries-General of the United Nations and of the Organization of American States.

ONUCA remained in Central America, contributing to peace efforts in the region, until January 1992.

United Nations action also focused on El Salvador. Following December 1989 and January 1990 requests from the Government of El Salvador and the Farabundo Martí National Liberation Front (FMLN), the Secretary-General began assisting in talks aimed at ending the conflict in the country.

The first major accord was achieved in July 1990, when the Government and FMLN signed an Agreement on Human Rights. Under the accord, the Security Council set up in May 1991 the **United Nations Observer Mission in El Salvador (ONUSAL)** to monitor all agreements concluded between the Government and FMLN, starting with the Agreement on Human Rights. ONUSAL was officially inaugurated in July 1991.

Months of intense negotiations between the Government and FMLN, brokered by the Secretary-General and his personal representative, culminated in the Peace Accords of 16 January 1992, which put an end to a conflict in which an estimated 70,000 people had lost their lives. The Security Council enlarged ONUSAL's mandate to include monitoring all aspects of the Peace Accords.

In February, the United Nations began one of its most comprehensive operations as ONUSAL undertook the complex task of verifying the implementation of the many provisions of the peace agreements. These included the separation of military forces and their demobilization, the implementation of programmes for reintegrating former combatants, and other reforms needed to tackle the root causes of the civil war. ONUSAL continued to monitor the human rights situation and to recommend measures to improve human rights protection.

In December 1992, the formal end of the conflict was proclaimed as FMLN troops completed their demobilization. A 50 per cent reduction of the Salvadoran Armed Forces was completed in January 1993. In June 1993, recommendations by an ad hoc commission for the purification of the officer corps were carried out, more than eight months after the original deadline.

As the undertakings related to military issues were fulfilled, ONUSAL's attention focused on the implementation of the many reforms and programmes necessary for consolidating peace. Those included the phasing out of the national police and the training and deployment of the new civilian police, the transfer of land to former combatants and landholders, and the implementation of the recommendations of the Commission on the Truth, established to investigate human rights violations committed during the 12-year war.

At the request of the Government, ONUSAL's mandate was enlarged in May 1993 to observe the presidential, legislative and local elections, held in March-April 1994. The elections, held "under generally acceptable conditions" according to the United Nations, were won by the ruling ARENA party, with FMLN emerging as the main opposition party.

ONUSAL remained in El Salvador to continue its verification responsibilities for those aspects of the Peace Agreements—in particular the land-transfer programme, judicial reform and deployment of the new National Civil Police—which had not been fully implemented by the time of the elections. The operation's mandate ended in April 1995. In May, a small political office (the Mission of the United Nations to El Salvador, or MINUSAL) began its work of verification of the outstanding areas of the peace agreements and the provision of good offices.

United Nations efforts have also focused on Guatemala. From 1991, a United Nations representative observed talks between the Government of Guatemala and the Guatemalan National Revolutionary Unity (URNG) aimed at ending the conflict which had lasted more than 30 years and bringing about national reconciliation. The talks were suspended in May 1993.

When the talks resumed in March 1994, the parties agreed on a Framework Agreement they had signed in January 1994, which provided for the United Nations to moderate the negotiations and to verify all agreements reached. In March, in Mexico City, the parties signed an agreement on human rights, which called for the establishment of a United Nations mission in Guatemala. In June, after intense negotiations, the parties signed in Oslo an agreement on the resettlement of people uprooted by the conflict, outlining a strategy for resettling refugees and displaced persons, as well as an agreement on the establishment of a commission to verify past human rights violations. In March 1995, an agreement on the identity and rights of indigenous people was signed, and work began on socio-economic aspects and the agrarian situation.

As called for by the agreement on human rights, the Secretary-General recommended in August 1994 the establishment of a **United Nations Human Rights Verification Mission in Guatemala (MINUGUA)**, stressing that such a mission would help to end human rights abuses and would bolster the peace process. On 19 September, the General Assembly approved the establishment of MINUGUA, which formally opened in Guatemala City in November and was fully deployed throughout the country by February 1995. Meanwhile, United Nations officials continued their efforts to sustain the negotiations and facilitate the conclusion of a peace agreement.

HAITI

In February 1986, Jean-Claude Duvalier, the "President for Life" whose family had ruled Haiti since 1957, left the country following years of internal discontent and repression. After his departure, Haiti had a series of short-lived Governments. A constitution was approved by referendum, and elections were to be held.

In 1990, Haiti's Provisional Government requested the United Nations to observe the electoral process. In October, the General Assembly approved a plan for electoral assistance, and the Secretary-General established the **United Nations Observer Group for the Verification of the Elections in Haiti (ONUVEH)**.

ONUVEH maintained close cooperation with other international observers, monitored the electoral process and contributed to a climate of security.

The elections were held on 16 December 1990. ONUVEH and other international observers visited polling stations in many parts of the country, including those in the most remote areas. The head of ONUVEH described the elections as "highly successful", held in conditions of security and without intimidation.

Jean-Bertrand Aristide, candidate of the National Front for Change and Democracy (FNCD), won the presidential elections with 67 per cent of the vote, followed by Marc Bazin of the

National Democratic Popular Alliance (ANDP) with 14 per cent. Nine other candidates shared the remaining votes. Haiti's democratically elected President was inaugurated on 7 February 1991, and the last ONUVEH contingent left Haiti on 22 February.

On 30 September, a coup headed by Lieutenant-General Raoul Cédras ended democratic rule. President Aristide went into exile. On the same day, the Organization of American States (OAS) condemned the coup and began diplomatic efforts for the return to legality.

On 3 October, President Aristide addressed the Security Council. The Council condemned the coup, called for the restoration of the legitimate Government and expressed support for the efforts of the OAS.

On 11 October, the General Assembly demanded the restoration of the legitimate Government, the application of the Constitution and the respect of human rights.

In November 1992, the General Assembly asked the Secretary-General to assist, in cooperation with OAS, in solving the crisis. In December, the Secretary-General appointed Mr. Dante Caputo as his Special Envoy for Haiti. In January 1993, the OAS also appointed Mr. Caputo as its Special Envoy.

In response to the continuing deterioration of conditions in Haiti, and following a request from President Aristide, a joint United Nations/OAS mission, the future International Civilian Mission in Haiti (MICIVIH) authorized in April, was deployed in the country in February 1993 to monitor the human rights situation and investigate violations.

Meanwhile, the Special Envoy sought to reach agreement between all the parties on the return of the President, the appointment of a Prime Minister to head a Government of national unity, and the question of an amnesty. But despite mounting international pressure, the de facto authorities refused to accept the settlement proposed by the Special Envoy.

In an effort to restore constitutional rule, the Security Council on 16 June imposed an oil and arms embargo against Haiti. On 21 June, General Cédras agreed to begin a dialogue to resolve the crisis. Talks conducted in New York by the Special

Envoy and involving President Aristide and General Cédras culminated in the signing on 3 July of the Governors Island Agreement. Under the Agreement, President Aristide would return to Haiti on 30 October 1993 and appoint a new Chief Commander of the Armed Forces to replace General Cédras, who would take early retirement.

The parties agreed to hold a dialogue, under United Nations and OAS auspices, to create the conditions for a peaceful transition. Under the Pact of New York, signed on 14 July by political forces represented in the Haitian Parliament, the President would nominate a Prime Minister, to be confirmed by Parliament.

After the Parliament in August ratified the appointment by President Aristide of Mr. Robert Malval as Prime Minister, the Security Council suspended the embargo.

As provided for in the Governors Island Agreement, the Security Council in September established the **United Nations Mission in Haiti (UNMIH)** to provide assistance in modernizing the Haitian armed forces and in establishing a new police force. The Mission's advance team was deployed by October, but its mandate was undermined by the non-compliance of Haiti's military authorities with the 3 July Agreement.

Moreover, on 11 October, armed civilians prevented a UNMIH military contingent from disembarking in Port-au-Prince. Following this incident, UNMIH, MICIVIH and staff of other international agencies left Haiti.

On 18 October, the Security Council's oil and arms embargo resumed. On 30 October—the day President Aristide was to have returned—the Security Council condemned the de facto authorities for not having fulfilled their obligations. In December, the General Assembly reaffirmed its support for President Aristide, and condemned the violence and military coercion in Haiti.

In the same month, a meeting of the Friends of the Secretary-General for Haiti (Canada, France, the United States and Venezuela, joined later on by Argentina), attended by the Special Envoy, was held in Paris to determine steps to bring about a negotiated solution.

In January 1994, the joint UN/OAS International Civilian

Mission to Haiti (MICIVIH), which had been withdrawn to the Dominican Republic in October 1993 for security reasons, returned to Haiti to continue the monitoring of human rights. The Mission denounced the grave violations taking place in Haiti, and met with harassment and obstruction.

In May, the Security Council strengthened the sanctions by adding a trade embargo, with the exception of medical products and foodstuff, and listed specific conditions for their termination.

The humanitarian situation continued to deteriorate, in spite of efforts by the United Nations, the OAS and relief organizations. With the tightening of sanctions, more people had become dependent on foreign aid, with relief organizations feeding about one in seven Haitians.

In July, the military authorities declared the international staff of MICIVIH undesirable and gave them 48 hours to leave Haiti. The Secretary-General, taking into consideration their security, decided to evacuate the international staff.

Following recommendations adopted in Brazil by OAS Foreign Ministers and by the Security Council, the Secretary-General suggested in July that the mandate of UNMIH be modified. On 31 July, the Security Council authorized Member States to form a multinational force and to use all necessary means to facilitate the departure of the military leaders and the return of President Aristide.

On 25 August, the Secretary-General dispatched an envoy to seek the agreement of Haiti's military leaders to a visit by a high-level mission to discuss arrangements to that effect. However, the military leaders declined to meet the envoy.

On 18 September, the United States and the military authorities in Haiti reached an agreement aimed at avoiding further violence. The agreement, mediated by a delegation headed by former United States President Jimmy Carter, provided for the early retirement of certain military leaders, the lifting of the embargo, and free and democratic legislative elections.

The first contingents of the 20,000-strong multinational force led by the United States began deploying in Haiti on 19 September. They were followed shortly thereafter by a

UNMIH advance team, which started monitoring the operations of the multinational force and preparing the transition to a UNMIH operation.

General Cédras resigned on 10 October as Commander of the Armed Forces and left for Panama, accompanied by the Chief of Staff. President Aristide returned to Haiti on 15 October, and the Security Council lifted the sanctions the following day. The Secretary-General welcomed Mr. Aristide's return, noting that, with the departure of the military leaders and the convening of Parliament, the United Nations objectives were being implemented.

MICIVIH returned to Haiti in October 1994. Its mandate was to continue to monitor and promote respect for human rights by making recommendations to the Haitian authorities, implementing an education and civic information programme, and helping to solve problems such as those relating to detention, medical assistance to victims and the return of displaced persons. It was also to monitor preparations of the 1995 elections, and assist in observing the elections.

In January 1995, the Security Council determined that a secure and stable environment, appropriate to the deployment of UNMIH, existed in Haiti, and authorized the deployment of up to 6,000 troops and 900 civilian police officers.

UNMIH took over responsibilities from the multinational force in March 1995. Its mandate was to assist the Government to sustain the secure and stable environment established by the multinational force, as well as to facilitate free and fair elections.

ASIA
♦ **Afghanistan** ♦ **Cambodia** ♦ **Cyprus** ♦ **Iran-Iraq**
♦ **Iraq-Kuwait** ♦ **Korean Peninsula** ♦ **Middle East**
♦ **South Asia Subcontinent: India-Pakistan** ♦ **Tajikistan**

AFGHANISTAN

Following Soviet military intervention in late December 1979, 52 Member States requested on 3 January 1980 an urgent meeting of the Security Council on the situation in Afghanistan. Following a negative vote from the Soviet Union on a draft resolution deploring the intervention, the Security Council called an emergency special session of the General Assembly. The session in January deplored "the recent armed intervention in Afghanistan" and called for the withdrawal of the foreign troops.

The Secretary-General launched a process of talks involving Afghanistan, Pakistan, the Soviet Union, other neighbouring countries and Security Council members. The talks, conducted by the Secretary-General's Personal Representative, sought to reach a settlement based on four elements: non-interference, return of refugees, withdrawal of foreign troops and international guarantees.

Eight years of intensive negotiations based on those elements culminated in a comprehensive settlement in April 1988. A timetable was established for the withdrawal of the foreign troops.

On 14 April 1988, at a ceremony at the United Nations Office at Geneva, the Secretary-General presided over the signing of the settlement, known as the Geneva Accords. The Accords were signed by the Foreign Ministers of Afghanistan and Pakistan, as well as by those of the Soviet Union and the United States as guarantor States.

In line with the Accords, the signatories requested that United Nations military personnel be deployed in Afghanistan and Pakistan. The **United Nations Good Offices Mission in Afghanistan and Pakistan (UNGOMAP)** monitored the withdrawal of Soviet troops, which was completed in February 1989. UNGOMAP continued to monitor aspects of the Geneva Accords until March 1990.

In May 1988, in view of the gravity of the humanitarian situation, the Secretary-General called for establishing a United Nations common system to deal with the needs of the country. This led to the appointment of the Coordinator of the United Nations Humanitarian and Economic Assistance Programmes relating to Afghanistan (UNOCA). In June 1988, the Secretary-General issued an appeal for $1.1 billion in international assistance. At a pledging conference in New York in October, the Secretary-General and the Coordinator launched Operation Salam, an international effort for relief and rehabilitation in Afghanistan, for which UNOCA became responsible.

In 1989, UNOCA launched the first large-scale mine-clearance programme in the world, which to date has cleared more than 42 million square metres. More than 2.3 million people have received mine-awareness training.

With the continuing internal conflict in Afghanistan, the General Assembly in November 1988 asked the Secretary-General to encourage a comprehensive political settlement with a view to establishing a broad-based government.

In May 1989, the Secretary-General appointed a Personal Representative in Afghanistan and Pakistan, who has subsequently, through continuous contact with the various elements involved, sought to find a peaceful solution to the conflict.

In May 1991, the Secretary-General outlined principles for a political solution, which included the need to preserve the sovereignty, territorial integrity, political independence and non-aligned and Islamic character of the country; the recognition of the right of Afghans to determine their own form of government and choose their economic, political and social system; and the need for an intra-Afghan dialogue leading to the establishment of a broad-based government.

On 16 April 1992, following a period of intensifying conflict, the Government of President Najibullah was replaced by a *Majahidin* Government, which subsequently proclaimed the establishment of an Islamic State. A few days later, the Secretary-General travelled to the region and met with the leaders of Pakistan and Iran. He stated that peace and national unity were prerequisites for soliciting financial and humanitarian assistance from the international community, and reaffirmed that the United Nations was ready to assist the Afghan people in the reconstruction of their country.

On 24 April, an Agreement on forming an interim government was reached among most of the Afghan parties, in Peshawar, Pakistan. These events led to the return of more than 1.5 million refugees, increasing the need for humanitarian assistance. In June, the Secretary-General issued a $197 million appeal for emergency relief aid.

Serious fighting erupted in August, causing many casualties and large-scale damage to the capital city of Kabul, and forcing United Nations staff temporarily to evacuate the city. The

Secretary-General appealed for restraint and the resumption of dialogue, and the Security Council issued a statement of concern.

In spite of a cease-fire, which permitted several United Nations fact-finding and technical assistance missions to visit Kabul, fighting and rocketing of Kabul erupted again in December 1992. The hostilities put severe strains on the relief effort. By the end of the year, about $87 million had been received for humanitarian assistance required in 1992.

In January 1993, UNOCA became the United Nations Office for Coordination of Humanitarian Assistance to Afghanistan (UNOCHA), reflecting a new emphasis on emergency programmes. Throughout the year, United Nations agencies and non-governmental organizations continued to provide humanitarian assistance. A new appeal was launched, and by the end of the year close to $70 million had been pledged.

In February, three United Nations staff and a consultant were murdered on the road to Jalalabad. The Secretary-General expressed his shock and reiterated his concern at the continued fighting in Kabul, which was taking a heavy toll among civilians. Serious security problems forced the recall of the international staff from Jalalabad and from Kandahar. Later in the year, the security situation in Jalalabad improved and the international staff returned. From the beginning of 1994, they dealt with the influx of displaced persons from Kabul and established a camp east of Jalalabad. In mid-1994, as the situation improved, international staff also returned to Kandahar.

After renewed negotiations in Islamabad, attended by Saudi Arabia and Iran, most of the Afghan party leaders signed a peace accord on 7 March 1993. Welcoming the accord, the Secretary-General expressed the hope that the cease-fire would improve the security situation and permit the unhindered delivery of humanitarian assistance. But sporadic fighting continued during the spring of 1993, particularly in Kabul.

Most of the Afghan leaders met in Jalalabad on 29 April to resolve the issues arising from the Islamabad peace accord on which no agreement had been reached. In May, the leaders agreed on the composition of the Cabinet, paving the way for the swearing in of the Prime Minister and his Cabinet by the President of Afghanistan on 17 June.

In the second half of 1993, the political situation became more stable, and the United Nations international staff evacuated from Kabul in 1992 were able to return. The Personal Representative encouraged the President, the Prime Minister and other leaders to overcome their differences by providing informal proposals. In October, an appeal for $59 million was issued for humanitarian assistance during the six winter months, of which $34 million was received.

Violence flared up again in early 1994, when forces allied with the Prime Minister started rocketing Kabul and imposed a blockade on the city, and those allied with the President attacked their opponents in other areas of the country. Fierce fighting led to the deaths of an estimated 7,000 persons in the first nine months of the year. Up to half a million people were forced to leave Kabul, many of them fleeing to Jalalabad. In October 1994, over 200,000 displaced persons were living in camps near Jalalabad set up under the coordination of UNOCHA, with about the same number living in overcrowded conditions in the city.

In December 1993, the General Assembly requested the Secretary-General to dispatch a special mission to Afghanistan to solicit the views of Afghan leaders on how the United Nations could best facilitate national reconciliation and reconstruction.

In February 1994, a special envoy was appointed to head the Special Mission, with the Personal Representative as its deputy head. In March and April, the Special Mission travelled extensively inside Afghanistan, where it heard the views not only of the leaders but also of hundreds of Afghans and was received by large crowds who called for a revived United Nations role. The Mission also travelled to capitals of the region, and in July recommended that the United Nations begin consultations with Afghan leaders on a cease-fire and the establishment of a transitional authority.

On the instructions of the Secretary-General, who visited Islamabad in September, the Mission organized a gathering of 35 prominent Afghans in Quetta in September 1994. They were asked to advise the Mission on ways to bring about a cease-fire, the transfer of power through a transitional government, and the creation of a neutral security force.

Subsequently, the Mission and a working group of four independent Afghan personalities focused on finalizing a mechanism to bring about a peaceful transfer of power. Following consultations, all Afghan faction leaders in February 1995 agreed in principle to the mechanism. But this was followed by renewed fighting among the factions in Kabul and other parts of the country.

CAMBODIA

After the intervention in Cambodia by Viet Nam in December 1978, the General Assembly in 1979 called for the withdrawal of foreign forces, non-interference in the country's internal affairs and self-determination for the Cambodian people. It also appealed for humanitarian relief to the civilian population.

As requested in 1981 by the General Assembly, the Secretary-General began to exercise his good offices among the Governments and parties involved. After a visit to the region in 1985, he listed a series of objectives on which there was convergence, thus detailing for the first time the elements of a comprehensive political settlement. In 1988, he formulated ideas for a settlement framework, which were presented by his Special Representative to the four Cambodian parties and the States concerned during a mission to the region.

The Secretary-General's proposals gave momentum to the negotiations. In 1988, the first face-to-face talks among the four Cambodian parties took place in Jakarta. In April 1989, Viet Nam announced the withdrawal of its troops from Cambodia, which was completed in September. In July-August 1989, the Paris Conference on Cambodia was attended by 18 countries, the four Cambodian parties and the Secretary-General.

Throughout this period, the United Nations ran a programme of humanitarian assistance to the Cambodian people. In operation since 1980, it consisted of three major components—within Cambodia, at the border, and within Thailand. Assistance was provided by the United Nations High Commissioner for Refugees (UNHCR) and by the United Nations Border Relief Operations (UNBRO), set up in 1982. Other United Nations agencies also contributed.

In January 1990, the five permanent members of the

Security Council started a series of high-level meetings on Cambodia. In August, they reached agreement on the main elements of a political settlement, calling for United Nations control and supervision of the country's administrative structures, followed by United Nations-supervised elections. In September, the plan was endorsed by the Security Council and was accepted by all Cambodian parties and by Viet Nam.

On 1 May 1991, following an appeal by the Secretary-General and the Foreign Ministers of France and Indonesia (the Co-Chairmen of the Paris Conference), a cease-fire went into effect. In October, the Security Council established the **United Nations Advance Mission in Cambodia (UNAMIC)** to assist the Cambodian parties in maintaining the cease-fire.

On 23 October, the parties signed in Paris the Agreements on Cambodia—a peace treaty to end the conflict and prepare for elections. The Agreements assigned to the United Nations an unprecedented role. A large operation, the **United Nations Transitional Authority in Cambodia (UNTAC)**, would supervise the cease-fire, the end of foreign military assistance and the withdrawal of foreign forces; regroup, canton and disarm all armed forces of the Cambodian parties, and ensure a 70 per cent level of demobilization; control and supervise the administrative structures, including the police; ensure the respect of human rights; and organize and conduct elections.

The Security Council established UNTAC in February 1992. The deployment of UNTAC officially began in March, with the arrival in the capital city of Phnom Penh of Mr. Yasushi Akashi, the Secretary-General's Special Representative for Cambodia and Head of UNTAC. At its peak, UNTAC's strength was over 21,000 military and civilian personnel from more than 100 countries.

Also in March, the United Nations started a programme of repatriation and resettlement of some 360,000 Cambodian refugees and displaced persons, with UNHCR as the lead agency. The programme was successfully completed in April 1993. In June 1992, several Governments pledged $880 million for the reconstruction of Cambodia.

Under the Paris Agreements, the Supreme National Council of Cambodia (SNC) was to be "the unique legitimate body and source of authority" throughout the transitional period. The SNC, comprised of the four Cambodian parties under the chairmanship of Prince Norodom Sihanouk, delegated to the United Nations "all powers necessary" to ensure implementation of the Agreements.

In July 1992, as specified in the Paris Agreements, UNTAC began to exercise control over foreign affairs, defence, security, finance and information in order to establish a neutral environment in which to hold the elections.

Registration of political parties began in August 1992; by January 1993, 20 parties had applied for registration. Of the four Cambodian parties who were signatories of the Paris Agreements, three took part in the electoral process: the Party of the State of Cambodia (through the Cambodian People's Party (CPP)), the Front uni national pour un Cambodge indépendant, neutre, pacifique et coopératif (FUNCINPEC) and the Khmer People's National Liberation Front/Buddhist Liberal Democratic Party (KPNLF/BLDP). The fourth signatory, the Party of Democratic Kampuchea (PDK), representing the Khmer Rouge, failed to register as a political party and took no part in the election.

When registration of voters ended in January 1993, over 4.6 million Cambodians had been registered, representing nearly all the estimated eligible voters in the zones to which UNTAC had access. UNTAC was not given full access to the areas controlled by PDK.

The elections were held from 23 to 28 May 1993 in all of Cambodia's 21 provinces. Some 1,400 fixed polling stations and 200 mobile teams were employed. UNTAC military personnel and civilian police ensured tight security. Aside from a few incidents, polling was conducted in a peaceful and often festive atmosphere, with voters sometimes walking several miles to cast their ballots, undaunted by threats of violence or banditry, rough terrain or the heavy rain that swept most of the country.

Over 4.2 million Cambodians, representing more than 89 per cent of the registered voters, cast ballots. FUNCINPEC won 45 per cent of the vote, CPP 38 per cent and KPNLF/BLDP 3 per cent. In the Constituent Assembly, 59 seats were won by

FUNCINPEC, 51 by CPP, 10 by KPNLF/BLDP and 1 by the MOLINAKA party.

At a 10 June meeting of the SNC presided over by Prince Sihanouk, the Special Representative declared the elections free and fair. On 15 June, the Security Council endorsed the results of the elections and expressed support for the newly elected Constituent Assembly.

On 24 September, Prince Sihanouk promulgated the Constitution, which had been drawn up by the Constituent Assembly, and was elected King of Cambodia. In accordance with the Constitution, he appointed the heads of the new Government. On the same day, UNTAC's mandate terminated and by mid-November its withdrawal was virtually completed.

United Nations agencies have remained in Cambodia to assist in its development. The Secretary-General appointed a Representative to Cambodia to maintain close liaison and dialogue with the Government in accordance with the spirit and principles of the Paris Agreements. The international community, through the International Committee on the Reconstruction of Cambodia, continues to support the Government's recovery efforts.

CYPRUS

Cyprus became independent in 1960, with a Constitution which was intended to balance the interests of the island's Greek Cypriot and Turkish Cypriot communities. In August 1960, Cyprus, Greece, Turkey and the United Kingdom entered into a treaty which guaranteed the basic provisions of the Constitution and the territorial integrity and sovereignty of Cyprus.

Since the outbreak of fighting between the two communities in December 1963, the United Nations has sought to secure a peaceful settlement. The Security Council met on 27 December 1963 to consider a complaint by Cyprus charging intervention in its internal affairs and aggression by Turkey. Turkey maintained that Greek Cypriot leaders had tried for more than two years to nullify the rights of the Turkish Cypriot community and denied all charges of aggression.

In March 1964, the Security Council established the **United Nations Peace-keeping Force in Cyprus (UNFICYP)**, to prevent fighting, help maintain law and order, and promote a return to normal conditions.

The efforts of the Secretary-General and his Special Representative in Cyprus led, beginning in 1968, to talks between the two communities, which were held intermittently until early in 1974.

A *coup d'état* in Cyprus on 15 July 1974 by Greek Cypriot and Greek elements favouring union with Greece was followed by military intervention by Turkey, whose troops established Turkish Cypriot control over the northern part of the island.

The Security Council called for a cease-fire and laid the basis for negotiations between Greece, Turkey and the United Kingdom, which were held until mid-August, when they broke down. A further Turkish military operation extended the area under Turkish Cypriot control in the north. A cease-fire came into effect on 16 August.

Four days later, the Secretary-General appointed the United Nations High Commissioner for Refugees as Coordinator of United Nations Humanitarian Assistance for Cyprus. More than 200,000 people needed assistance as a result of the hostilities. The High Commissioner continues to aid displaced persons, and UNFICYP provides support to the humanitarian effort.

In November 1974, the General Assembly called on all States to respect the sovereignty, territorial integrity, independence and non-alignment of Cyprus. It urged the withdrawal of all foreign armed forces, a halt to foreign interference, and the return of refugees to their homes. The Assembly stated that constitutional issues were to be resolved by the two communities, and urged the continuation of contacts which were taking place between the two communities with the help of the Secretary-General.

These contacts broke off after the unilateral announcement by the Turkish Cypriot leadership in February 1975 that a part of the island would become the "Turkish Federated State of Cyprus". In March, the Security Council expressed regret regarding this move, and stated that the decision did not prejudge the final political settlement.

Talks started in April under the auspices of the Secretary-

General. Agreement was reached that the Turkish Cypriots in the south of the island would be allowed to proceed north with UNFICYP assistance, and that a number of Greek Cypriots would be transferred to the north to be reunited with their families. Greek Cypriots in the north would be free to go south or to remain.

The transfer of Turkish Cypriots to the north was completed by September 1975. But other provisions of the agreement were only partially implemented. During the following years, the talks continued without making any decisive progress.

In November 1983, the Turkish Cypriot authorities unilaterally proclaimed a "Turkish Republic of Northern Cyprus". The Security Council considered the declaration invalid, called for its withdrawal, and requested the Secretary-General to pursue his good offices mission.

In 1984, the Secretary-General held "proximity talks" with the leaders of the two communities, and presented elements for a comprehensive solution through the establishment of a Federal Republic of Cyprus. At a joint meeting in New York in January 1985, the Turkish Cypriot side accepted the elements; the Greek Cypriot side stated that it could accept them only as a basis for negotiations.

The Secretary-General tried to overcome the differences by preparing a consolidated draft statement, which was accepted by the Greek Cypriot side in April 1985, but not by the Turkish Cypriot side.

Talks continued in the following years, but differences between the two sides remained.

In 1990, the Security Council reiterated that it foresaw a solution based on the existence of one State comprising two communities, and that the objective was a new Constitution regulating the relations between the two communities on a federal, bicommunal and bi-zonal basis. Both sides affirmed their commitment to the Council's views.

By March 1991, the Secretary-General was able to report to the Security Council that discussions held by his representatives with both sides in Cyprus and a senior official of the Ministry of Foreign Affairs of Turkey in exploring a set of ideas for an overall framework agreement had been useful. He noted that the clarifications that had emerged should make it possible to bring the two sides within range of agreement, particularly under three of the eight headings of an overall framework agreement, namely, Overall Objectives, Guiding Principles, and Security and Guarantees. The Secretary-General felt that an agreement should be within reach if it was possible to move forward on the issues of Territorial Adjustments and Displaced Persons.

The Secretary-General conferred separately with the leaders of the two communities in New York in January and March 1992. Reporting to the Security Council in April, the Secretary-General stated that the set of ideas would offer a fair basis on which an agreement could be concluded. A week later, the Council endorsed the set of ideas as an appropriate basis for reaching agreement.

In June, the Secretary-General began proximity talks in New York with the two leaders. After a three-week intermission, the talks resumed in July. Joint meetings between the two leaders continued in New York in October-November, focusing on the set of ideas.

At a joint meeting in March 1993, the two leaders agreed to resume negotiations in May, using the set of ideas to reach an overall framework agreement. In April-May, the Secretary-General's Deputy Special Representative undertook preparatory meetings in Cyprus. Both leaders indicated their willingness to pursue agreement on 14 proposed confidence-building measures. The most significant were the transfer of the vacant city of Varosha to United Nations administration and its becoming a special area for bicommunal contact and commerce; and the reopening of Nicosia International Airport, under United Nations administration, for unhindered traffic with both sides.

On the basis of these preparations, joint negotiations resumed in New York in May, chaired by the Secretary-General. The meetings recessed on 1 June to allow the Turkish Cypriot side to undertake consultations in Nicosia and Ankara. The purpose of these consultations was to promote acceptance of the Varosha/Nicosia International Airport package of confidence-building measures. It was agreed that the joint meetings would resume in New York no later than 14 June. However, the leader of the Turkish Cypriot community did not promote acceptance of the package and did not return to New York.

In July, the Security Council members shared the Secretary-General's disappointment that the Turkish Cypriot leader had not adhered to the agreement by which he had undertaken to promote acceptance of the package, and that he had failed to return to New York, preventing the resumption of the joint meetings.

The Special Representative visited Cyprus in July, where he met with both leaders and with political and business figures; then travelled to Greece and Turkey for talks with those Governments. Further discussions with the parties in Cyprus did not lead to any agreement.

The Secretary-General reported to the Security Council in September that the Turkish Cypriot side had not yet shown the goodwill and cooperation required to achieve an agreement on the package. It was apparent, he noted, that the Turkish Cypriot community was interested in considering the package seriously, but should be made fully aware of Turkey's support for it. The Secretary-General stressed that Turkey could play an important role, and he sought its cooperation. Two technical missions confirmed the benefits offered by the package.

The Secretary-General and his Special Representative resumed in January 1994 intensive contacts to achieve an agreement on the package of confidence-building measures. After further meetings in January-February with the Secretary-General's Representatives, both sides accepted in principle the package and agreed on an agenda for proximity talks on the modalities for implementing it.

In March-April 1994, the Representatives worked intensively with both sides to find ways to implement the package. The proposals, presented to the parties on 21 March, were accepted by the Greek Cypriot leader provided that they were accepted by the Turkish Cypriot leader. But despite several extensions, the proximity talks did not result in an agreement.

Reporting to the Security Council in May, the Secretary-General concluded that the absence of agreement was due essentially to a lack of political will on the Turkish Cypriot side and presented the Council with five options. Further consultations between the Deputy Special Representative and the Turkish Cypriot leader resulted in clarifications of the 21 March proposals.

In June, the Secretary-General indicated to the Security Council that sufficient progress had been made for the United Nations to implement the package on the basis of the 21 March proposals and subsequent clarifications. He planned to address to each leader an identical letter expressing his intention to proceed on this basis, describing the clarifications and seeking their cooperation.

The 21 March proposals and the Secretary-General's letter to the two leaders would have been submitted simultaneously to the Security Council for endorsement. However, the Greek Cypriot leader informed the Secretary-General that he would have difficulty in accepting this manner of procedure, reiterating that he was not prepared to contemplate any change to the 21 March proposals or any further negotiation on the confidence-building measures. The Turkish Cypriot leader had already declined to accept the proposed procedure.

In July, the Security Council requested the Secretary-General to launch consultations to undertake a fundamental and far-reaching reflection on ways of approaching the Cyprus problem. The Secretary-General in August sought the views of the Security Council members, Greece, Turkey and the United Kingdom. In September, his Special Representative held consultations in the United Kingdom, Greece, Cyprus and Turkey. He then reported to the Secretary-General that matters were close to an impasse both on the confidence-building measures and on the substance of the Cyprus problem.

At the invitation of the Secretary-General, the two community leaders met informally at the Nicosia residence of the Deputy Special Representative on five occasions in October. They discussed the essential elements of a federation in Cyprus as well as the implementation of the confidence-building measures.

In November and December, the Secretary-General met separately with the two leaders. He told them that the elements discussed during their meetings offered the possibility of a significant step forward both on the substance of the Cyprus question and on the confidence-building measures. He also encouraged the Turkish Cypriot leader to respond in a commensurate manner to the ideas that had been broached. The Special Representative and the Special Deputy Representative were instructed to continue their contacts with the parties in order to establish the basis for further discussion.

UNFICYP continues to supervise the cease-fire, maintain surveillance over the buffer zone between the cease-fire lines and promote a return to normal conditions through intercommunal humanitarian activities.

IRAN-IRAQ

United Nations efforts to end the conflict between Iran and Iraq began at the very onset of hostilities in September 1980. On 22 September, the Secretary-General appealed to both countries to act with restraint, and proposed his good offices to reach a negotiated settlement. On 28 September, the Security Council called on Iran and Iraq to refrain from further use of force and urged them to accept mediation.

Between 1980 and 1986, the Security Council repeatedly called for a cease-fire and for the withdrawal of forces to internationally recognized boundaries; cessation of military operations against civilian targets; respect for the right of free navigation and commerce in international waters; restraint from actions endangering peace, security and marine life in the Persian Gulf region; and an exchange of prisoners of war. The Council supported the efforts of the Secretary-General and his Special Representative to achieve a comprehensive settlement.

In April 1985, the Secretary-General travelled to Teheran and Baghdad, where he discussed with the two Governments a plan he had presented to them the month before. Through his mediation, the Secretary-General sought to end the conflict, and also tried to mitigate its effects in areas such as attacks on population centres, the use of chemical weapons, the treatment of prisoners of war, and the safety of navigation and civil aviation.

Between March 1984 and August 1988, the Secretary-General dispatched seven missions to investigate allegations by

Iran or Iraq on the use of chemical weapons. The missions indicated that chemical weapons had been used. The Security Council and the Secretary-General condemned the use of such weapons, and called for strict observance of the 1925 Geneva Protocol against the use of poison gas and bacteriological weapons. The Secretary-General dispatched to the region other fact-finding missions in connection with allegations of attacks on civilian areas and the treatment of prisoners of war and civil detainees.

In January 1987, the Secretary-General called on Security Council members to work together to explore steps to end the conflict. In an unprecedented meeting in his office later that month, he suggested to the 15 members elements of a peace plan. On 20 July 1987, the Security Council adopted resolution 598 (1987), which a year later would become the framework for reaching a cease-fire agreement.

The resolution called for a cease-fire and for the withdrawal of forces to internationally recognized boundaries; provided for the dispatch of observers to verify, confirm and supervise the cease-fire and withdrawal; urged the release of prisoners of war; and called on Iran and Iraq to cooperate with the Secretary-General in implementing the resolution and in settling all outstanding issues.

On 23 July 1987, Iraq accepted the resolution. The Secretary-General conducted intensive diplomatic activity, which included his visit to Iran and Iraq in September 1987, during which he presented an implementation plan to the two Governments. High-level contacts continued in 1987 and 1988. In March 1988, the Secretary-General invited the Presidents of Iran and Iraq to send emissaries for consultations on implementing resolution 598 (1987).

On 17 July 1988, Iran informed the Secretary-General that it accepted the resolution. After discussions in New York with the Foreign Ministers of the two countries, a formula was devised by the Secretary-General. On that basis, he was able to announce on 8 August that a cease-fire would go into effect on 20 August. Direct talks between the two Ministers under the Secretary-General's auspices were to follow.

On 9 August, the Security Council set up the **United Nations Iran-Iraq Military Observer Group (UNIIMOG)**.

The first elements of UNIIMOG were dispatched to Iran and Iraq on 10 August.

Ministerial-level talks in August and September, under the auspices of the Secretary-General and a Personal Representative, sought to reach a common understanding on the implementation of resolution 598 (1987). Further talks were held in October and November.

In November, Iran and Iraq signed memoranda of understanding with the International Committee of the Red Cross on the release and repatriation of sick and wounded prisoners of war. Exchanges of war dead also took place.

Talks continued in 1989 and 1990, including meetings of the Secretary-General with the two Foreign Ministers. In August 1990, bilateral efforts of the two Governments helped resolve some of the outstanding issues. Communications the Secretary-General received from the Governments indicated that implementation of resolution 598 would be carried out in accordance with the Treaty and Conventions to which both were parties.

By November 1990, both sides had nearly completed a troop withdrawal to the internationally recognized boundaries. UNIIMOG supervised and verified the withdrawal, and defused any local tension.

In February 1991, with the withdrawal of forces completed, the Security Council terminated UNIIMOG's mandate. That same month, small civilian offices of the Secretary-General were established in Baghdad and Teheran. A few military officers attached to these offices allowed the United Nations to continue to respond promptly to requests by either Government to investigate matters for which military expertise was required. The offices were also important in the Secretary-General's efforts to complete the implementation of resolution 598.

In December 1991, the Secretary-General commented on the issue of responsibility for the conflict, which was referred to in resolution 598. He added, however, that no useful purpose would be served in pursuing the matter further. Rather, in the interest of peace, he suggested it would be imperative to move on with the settlement process.

By the end of 1992, the offices in Baghdad and Teheran were phased out, and the Permanent Missions of Iran and Iraq became the channels of communication between those countries and the United Nations for matters related to resolution 598.

IRAQ-KUWAIT

On 2 August 1990, Iraqi forces invaded Kuwait. On the same day, the Security Council condemned the invasion and demanded Iraq's withdrawal. On 6 August, the Council imposed comprehensive mandatory sanctions against both Iraq and occupied Kuwait.

A series of Security Council resolutions adopted between August and October 1990 demanded Iraqi withdrawal from Kuwait, declared the annexation "null and void", banned air transport to and from Iraq and Kuwait, and endorsed a naval blockade to enforce the sanctions.

The United Nations undertook many initiatives to avert war. The Secretary-General met with the Iraqi Foreign Minister in Amman in August 1990, and with the President of Iraq in Baghdad on 12-13 January 1991. He also met with several political leaders concerned with the crisis, and was in constant contact with all parties.

In November 1990, the Security Council set 15 January 1991 as the deadline for Iraqi compliance with the Council's resolutions. The Council authorized Member States cooperating with Kuwait to use "all necessary means" to uphold and implement these resolutions "and to restore international peace and security in the area".

The deadline passed with Iraq not complying with the Council's resolutions. On 16 January, coalition forces allied to restore Kuwait's sovereignty began air attacks against Iraq, followed by a ground offensive. The coalition forces acted in accordance with the Council's authorization, but not under the direction or control of the United Nations. Hostilities were suspended on 27 February, by which time the Iraqi forces had left Kuwait.

On 3 April, the Security Council, in resolution 687, set terms for a cease-fire, demanded that Iraq and Kuwait respect the inviolability of the border, requested the Secretary-General to submit plans for the deployment of a United Nations observer unit, and decided that Iraq's weapons of mass destruction should be destroyed.

On the same day, the Security Council established a demilitarized zone (DMZ) along the Iraq-Kuwait border and set up an observer mission to monitor the DMZ. The **United Nations Iraq-Kuwait Observation Mission (UNIKOM)** monitored the withdrawal of the remaining armed forces. Following a series of incidents, the Security Council in February 1993 expanded the mandate of UNIKOM from an unarmed observation mission to an armed force capable of preventing or redressing small-scale violations. To that end, the military observers were reinforced by one mechanized infantry battalion.

In October 1994, in response to reports that substantial numbers of Iraqi troops were being redeployed towards the border with Kuwait, the Security Council President issued a statement of concern. On 15 October, the Council demanded the withdrawal of all military units deployed to southern Iraq to their original positions. Iraq was requested not to redeploy them to the south or take any other action to enhance its military capacity in southern Iraq.

Resolution 687 also deals with the elimination of Iraq's weapons of mass destruction and ballistic missiles with a range greater than 150 kilometres together with related items and facilities. To implement these provisions, the Security Council established the **United Nations Special Commission (UNSCOM)**, with powers of no-notice inspections. Iraq was required to cooperate with UNSCOM. The Director-General of the International Atomic Energy Agency (IAEA) was asked to undertake similar tasks in the nuclear area, with UNSCOM assistance.

In the first two years, Iraq challenged the mandate of UNSCOM and IAEA, sought to obstruct ground and aerial inspections and logistical support for their operations, and did not provide the required information.

Politically, Iraq's obstruction also took the form of rejection of two Security Council resolutions—resolutions 707 and 715. Resolution 707 reiterated the demand that Iraq make "full, final and complete disclosures" of all aspects of its banned programmes. Resolution 715 approved the plans for the ongoing monitoring and verification of Iraq's compliance with its obligation not to reacquire the banned weapons capabilities. The plans were due to enter into effect immediately, that is, 11 October

1991, and required Iraq to make disclosures about its dual-purpose capabilities by 11 November 1991 and thereafter biannually.

While Iraq never formally recognized resolution 707, it did finally provide UNSCOM in June 1992 with what it called "reports". These were far from "full, final and complete disclosures", neither providing a complete understanding of the programmes nor the means to verify the data contained in the reports. Furthermore, the reports omitted whole classes of information. As late as March 1995, the Commission was still requesting, and receiving piecemeal, data which should have been provided by 15 April 1991. IAEA experienced similar problems.

Nevertheless, through their own efforts, UNSCOM and IAEA uncovered much of Iraq's banned programmes. Identified capabilities to produce banned weapons were eliminated. These included: programmes to enrich uranium for weapons purposes, work on plutonium for the same purpose, and a full-scale project to develop nuclear weaponry; a major chemical weapons programme to produce thousands of tonnes of five different chemical warfare agents; some 151 ballistic missiles, including chemical and conventional missile warheads and auxiliary materials; superguns; and a biological warfare research programme.

Iraq objected that the ongoing monitoring and verification mandated by resolution 715 would infringe indefinitely its sovereignty, national security, independence and dignity. Despite UNSCOM's assurances, given as early as March 1992, that Iraq's legitimate concerns would be taken into account, efforts to implement monitoring and verification were delayed until November 1993, when Iraq finally accepted the resolution. UNSCOM did not receive declarations about Iraq's dual-purpose capabilities until January 1994.

Upon Iraq's acknowledgement of resolution 715, UNSCOM and IAEA proceeded to establish the system of ongoing monitoring and verification. In April 1995, UNSCOM reported to the Security Council that the system was operational.

Meanwhile, the United Nations Secretariat and Iraq held talks between 1991 and 1993 on the question of resuming limited export of Iraq's oil and oil products to pay for essential civilian needs, as well as to provide payments to the fund to compensate victims of Iraq's aggression and to support other United Nations activities related to Iraq. Iraq refused to accept the Security Council resolutions concerned, viewing plans for their implementation as an infringement of its sovereignty, and demanded that the Council allow it to export its oil in a normal manner. In response to Iraq's refusal to cooperate, the Council in October 1992 allowed States to deposit Iraqi frozen assets representing the proceeds of the sale of Iraqi oil into a United Nations escrow account. It also decided that no further Iraqi assets should be released for humanitarian purposes, except to the sub-account of the escrow account or directly to the United Nations for humanitarian activities in Iraq. The account was designated to pay for the Compensation Fund, UNSCOM, the Boundary Demarcation Commission, humanitarian aid, and the return of Kuwaiti property (see below).

In April 1995, the Security Council authorized States to permit the import of up to $1 billion worth of Iraqi oil every 90 days as a means by which to generate resources to meet humanitarian needs in Iraq. However, Iraq rejected this offer, claiming infringement of its sovereignty.

As called for in resolution 687, the **Iraq-Kuwait Boundary Demarcation Commission** was established in May 1991. It included one representative of Iraq, one of Kuwait, and three independent experts appointed by the Secretary-General. The Commission was to demarcate the boundary as set out in the "Agreed Minutes" signed by the two countries at Baghdad in 1963. The Minutes reaffirmed the delimitation of the boundary as stated in a 1932 exchange of letters between the Prime Minister of Iraq and the Ruler of Kuwait.

All Commission members participated in the first five sessions held between May 1991 and April 1992. Iraq did not attend the subsequent six sessions between July 1992 and May 1993, but was sent all relevant Commission material.

The Commission did not reallocate territory, but carried out the technical work necessary to demarcate, for the first time, the precise coordinates of the boundary reaffirmed in the 1963 Agreed Minutes. In conjunction with the establishment of geographic coordinates and the emplacement of boundary pillars and markers, the Commission undertook new surveying and mapping of the entire length of the border area.

In April 1992, the Commission ruled that the border running through the disputed Rumaila oilfield should be moved 570 yards northward. Kuwait was also given control of a part of the town of Umm Qasr. In July, the Commission completed demarcation of the boundary between Batin and Samfan, indicating that the oilfields between the two points fell in Kuwait's territory.

The physical demarcation of the land part of the boundary was completed in November 1992. In March 1993, the Commission decided on the marking of the boundary along the low-water line in the Khowr Zhobeir and decided on the geographical coordinates which define the median line from a point nearest to the junction of Khowr Zhobeir and Khowr Abd Allah waterways to a point at the eastern end of the Khowr Abd Allah where there is marked change in the general direction of the coast.

The Commission viewed navigational access for both States to the various parts of their territories bordering the demarcated boundary as important for ensuring an equitable character and for promoting stability, peace and security along the border. The Commission noted that this right of navigational access is provided for under the rules of international laws as embodied in the 1982 United Nations Convention on the Law of the Sea, ratified by both Iraq and Kuwait.

At its final session in May 1993, the Commission approved the coordinates for the final demarcation of the boundary. On 27 May, the Security Council reaffirmed that the Commission's decisions were final, demanded that Iraq and Kuwait respect the inviolability of the boundary, and reaffirmed its decision to guarantee such inviolability.

With the demarcation of the boundary, a number of Iraqi citizens and their assets would be located on the Kuwaiti side of the border in the town of Umm Qasr and in the farming area of Al-Abdaly. In December 1992, the Secretary-General informed the Security Council that he had been in touch with Iraq and Kuwait to determine how the United Nations might help to bring about a settlement.

In January 1993, Kuwait informed the Secretary-General that the Iraqi nationals would not be permitted to remain in Kuwait, but would be compensated for their property and assets on the basis of an assessment by a neutral party nominated by the United Nations. Iraq responded that it would "take no action that might tend to recognize the injustice deliberately inflicted on Iraq", but would "take no action that might provoke dispute or contention with the United Nations".

In accordance with a September 1993 arrangement between the United Nations and Kuwait, the Secretary-General appointed an independent contractor to carry out an assessment of the property and assets, on the basis of which he would decide the compensation which Kuwait would be asked to pay into a United Nations trust fund for disbursal to the Iraqi citizens. The Secretary-General made his decision in early 1994. The Iraqi citizens refused to accept compensation, and the Secretary-General deposited the compensation into a United Nations escrow account at their disposal. By February 1994, all Iraqi nationals had been relocated to Iraq.

In November 1994, Iraq informed the Secretary-General that it recognized Kuwait's sovereignty, territorial integrity and international boundaries.

Also under resolution 687, the Security Council established a Fund to compensate any direct loss, damage or injury to foreign Governments, nationals or corporations resulting from Iraq's invasion of Kuwait. Iraq was required to contribute to the Fund an amount not exceeding 30 per cent of the annual value of its oil exports. In 1993, the Fund's Governing Council appointed nine jurists and experts as Commissioners, to examine claims and recommend compensation. The first payments, concerning humanitarian cases, were awarded in June 1994.

Resolution 687 also required Iraq to cooperate with the International Committee of the Red Cross (ICRC) in the repatriation of displaced persons and in the search for those still unaccounted for. In November 1992, the Security Council stated that the ICRC had not received information as to the whereabouts of those reported missing in Iraq, nor had it received permission to visit Iraqi prisons and detention centres. Few missing persons and detainees had been released since

March 1992, while hundreds were believed still to be inside Iraq. In July and September 1994, Iraq participated for the first time since October 1991 in meetings of the Tripartite Commission. The Commission, which meets periodically under ICRC auspices, seeks to resolve issues of missing Kuwait and third-country nationals, and is composed of France, Iraq, Kuwait, Saudi Arabia, the United Kingdom and the United States. The ICRC has also transmitted the cases of Iraqi missing persons to Kuwaiti authorities.

The modalities of the return of Kuwaiti property seized by Iraq, pursuant to a Security Council resolution, were arranged through the Office of the Secretary-General, in consultation with the parties. A Coordinator was appointed by the Secretary-General, and the return of property began in August 1991. By the end of 1994, property belonging to a number of Ministries and offices of the Government of Kuwait had been returned. However, while claims were submitted, no private property was returned to Kuwait.

In September 1994, Iraq informed the Secretary-General that upon completion of the return of property, slated for late 1994, Iraq would have returned all the property in its possession. In response, Kuwait submitted a partial list of property that had yet to be returned, which, it said, demonstrated that the claims of Iraq to have returned all property were false.

Humanitarian assistance to Iraq

In March 1991, in the aftermath of the Persian Gulf conflict, the Secretary-General sent to Iraq a United Nations mission to assess humanitarian needs. Following that mission's report, the Secretary-General launched the United Nations Humanitarian Programme for Iraq. In April 1991, he appointed an Executive Delegate to coordinate the work of the United Nations programmes and agencies, as well as those of non-governmental organizations (NGOs), in promoting the return of those displaced and providing humanitarian assistance to the civilian population.

In April 1991, the Security Council, concerned by · the repression of the Iraqi population in many parts of Iraq, including the massive flow of Kurdish refugees into Iran and Turkey, expressed the hope that a dialogue would take place to ensure the respect of the human and political rights of all Iraqi citizens.

In July 1991, a mission to Iraq provided a thorough assessment of humanitarian needs. The Inter-agency Programme in Iraq has focused on the needs of the most vulnerable groups. In 1992, this operation became the responsibility of the newly created Department of Humanitarian Affairs. Its work has continued to focus on the provision and monitoring of humanitarian assistance in Iraq, undertaken by United Nations agencies and programmes together with local and international NGOs, under the overall coordination of a senior United Nations official.

A Memorandum of Understanding between the United Nations and Iraq provides the legal framework for humanitarian assistance in Iraq. A one-year Plan of Action, agreed upon in April 1993, was subsequently extended until March 1995.

In 1994, the United Nations Humanitarian Programme in Iraq was severely affected by a lack of funds.

The situation in Iraq called for continued humanitarian action. Emphasis was placed on relief assistance, with increasing importance given to rehabilitation. The general economic and public health situation declined further throughout 1994. The drastic deterioration of public health in all parts of the country saw a critical shortage of life-saving drugs and an increase in the incidence of malaria and water-borne diseases. A household survey conducted in northern Iraq in 1994 documented a drastic fall in living standards and a sharp increase in the number of destitute persons.

KOREAN PENINSULA

The question of Korea came before the General Assembly in 1947. United Nations efforts to re-establish a unified Korean State through nationwide elections were not successful, and separate governments came into being in north and south Korea in 1948—the Democratic People's Republic of Korea (DPRK) and the Republic of Korea, respectively.

That same year, the General Assembly created the United Nations Commission on Korea to seek the objectives laid out by the Assembly in November 1947, namely the re-establishment of the national independence of Korea, and the withdrawal of all occupying forces.

On 25 June 1950, the United States and the United Nations Commission on Korea informed the United Nations that the Republic of Korea had been attacked by DPRK's forces. The same day, the Security Council called for a cease-fire and withdrawal of DPRK forces to the 38th parallel. Two days later, as fighting continued, the Security Council recommended that United Nations Member States furnish the necessary assistance to the Republic of Korea to repel the attack and restore stability on the peninsula. In the mean time, the United States announced that it had ordered its air and sea forces to give cover and support to the troops of the Republic of Korea, and later authorized the use of ground forces.

In July, the Security Council asked Member States providing military forces in accordance with earlier resolutions to make them available to a unified command under the United States. Sixteen nations made troops available to the unified command; this force was not, however, a United Nations peace-keeping operation placed under the command of the Secretary-General, but an international force acting under the unified command.

The Soviet Union, which had been absent from the Security Council for six months in protest against the representatives of Chiang Kai-shek representing China at the United Nations, considered the Council's decision illegal. The Soviet Union stated that the resolutions were invalid because they were adopted in the absence of two permanent members. The People's Republic of China also rejected the Council's decisions as invalid, and in November 1950, a Chinese volunteer force entered the fighting on the side of the DPRK. Fighting continued until 27 July 1953, when an Armistice Agreement was signed. A Military Armistice Commission was established to supervise the implementation of the Agreement and to settle any violations through negotiations.

The **United Nations Commission for the Unification and Rehabilitation of Korea** replaced the United Nations Commission on Korea in 1950, and remained in the country until it was dissolved by the General Assembly in 1973. The Assembly, in a unanimous decision, considered the Commission's mandate fulfilled when a joint communiqué was issued by the DPRK and the Republic of Korea in July 1972, stating that their common aim was to promote national unity and seek reunification through peaceful means.

In 1974, the General Assembly urged the DPRK and the Republic of Korea to further their dialogue to expedite reunification. The DPRK and the Republic of Korea became Members of the United Nations in September 1991.

In December 1991, two agreements were signed: "The Agreement on Reconciliation, Non-Aggression, Cooperation and Exchange between the North and the South", and the Joint Declaration on the Denuclearization of the Korean Peninsula — an agreement to ensure a nuclear-weapons-free peninsula through inter-Korean inspections.

In March 1993, the DPRK announced its intent to withdraw from the Nuclear Non-Proliferation Treaty (NPT) (see Arms Regulation and Disarmament in this Chapter) to which it had acceded in 1985. The Safeguards Agreement which it signed in December 1991 with the International Atomic Energy Agency (IAEA) permitted IAEA to inspect the DPRK's nuclear facilities. But an IAEA request to inspect two additional sites was denied, leading to the DPRK's announcement. The DPRK maintained that the United States and the Republic of Korea had instigated IAEA officials and certain member States to adopt an unjust resolution demanding that the DPRK open military sites having no relevance to nuclear activities.

According to the terms of the NPT, withdrawal from the Treaty could become effective only three months after such an intent was declared. In May 1993, the Security Council called upon the DPRK to reconsider its withdrawal.

On 11 June, following negotiations with the United States, the DPRK announced that it had suspended its withdrawal. In June and August, IAEA was able to conduct limited safeguard activities at the DPRK's declared nuclear sites. IAEA reported in October that the DPRK did not agree to requests for ad hoc and routine inspections at the facilities as required by the Safeguards Agreement. In November, the General Assembly urged the DPRK to cooperate with IAEA in the full implementation of the Safeguards Agreement. In December, the DPRK stated that the issue would be resolved through further talks with the United States and IAEA.

Also in December, the Secretary-General visited the Republic of Korea and the DPRK to discuss the situation in the Korean peninsula, including the nuclear inspections issue. In February 1994, the DPRK and IAEA reached agreement on inspection of the country's seven declared facilities. The inspections were completed in May.

At about the same time, a new issue emerged. IAEA urged the DPRK not to initiate the discharge of an experimental reactor without enabling IAEA inspectors to take specific safeguards activities. However, the DPRK informed IAEA on 12 May that it had already begun refuelling the reactor. IAEA said the step violated the Safeguards Agreement and would maintain the uncertainty about the amount of nuclear material in the DPRK. The DPRK maintained that it had a unique status with regard to the NPT because it had only temporarily suspended its withdrawal from the Treaty and was not duty-bound to fully implement the obligations of the Safeguards Agreement.

On 30 May, the Security Council urged the DPRK to proceed with the discharge operations in a manner which preserved the possibility of fuel measurements, in accordance with IAEA requirements. In early June, IAEA reported that the opportunity to ascertain whether nuclear material from the reactor had been diverted was lost. On 10 June, IAEA reported that the DPRK was preventing IAEA from verifying the history of the reactor, and suspended non-medical assistance to the DPRK. On 14 June, the DPRK withdrew from IAEA, stating that the Agency's inspections could not be allowed until the DPRK had decided whether to return to the NPT or completely withdraw.

Subsequently, the DPRK and the United States resumed negotiations, and in October arrived at an "Agreed Framework" on an overall resolution of the issue. By its terms, the DPRK would freeze and then dismantle its nuclear programme, monitored by IAEA. It would continue to be a party to the NPT and would cooperate with IAEA in fulfilling its obligation for full-scope inspections. In return, arrangements would be made to provide alternative reactors and interim energy sources, as well as to normalize commercial and diplomatic relations between the DPRK and the United States.

From October 1994, commercial and communications links between the United States and the DPRK were developed, as called for by the Framework Agreement. The DPRK accepted the concept, proposed by the United States, regarding the provision of new and safer reactors to the DPRK. It also agreed to continue to freeze the use of its own reactors as long as talks continued.

MIDDLE EAST

The United Nations has been concerned with the question of the Middle East from its earliest days. In response to conflicts which have broken out at various times during five decades, the Organization has established peace-keeping missions and formulated principles for a peaceful settlement. It continues its efforts to find a just and lasting solution to the underlying political problems.

The Middle East question has its origin in the issue of the future of Palestine, which was brought before the United Nations in 1947. At the time, Palestine was a Territory administered by the United Kingdom under a Mandate from the League of Nations. It had a population of about 2 million, two thirds Arabs and one third Jews.

In 1947, the General Assembly endorsed a plan, put before it by the United Nations Special Committee on Palestine, for the partition of the Territory, providing for the creation of an Arab and a Jewish State, with Jerusalem under international status. The plan was not accepted by the Palestinian Arabs or by the Arab States.

On 14 May 1948, the General Assembly appointed a United Nations Mediator, Count Folke Bernadotte, to promote a peaceful settlement of the situation in Palestine. On the same day, the United Kingdom relinquished its Mandate over Palestine, and the State of Israel was proclaimed.

On the following day, the Palestinian Arabs, assisted by Arab States, opened hostilities against the new State. The hostilities were halted through a truce called for by the Security Council and supervised by the United Nations Mediator, with the assistance of a group of military observers which came to be known as the **United Nations Truce Supervision Organization (UNTSO)**.

When Count Bernadotte was assassinated on 17 September 1948 in Jerusalem, Ralph J. Bunche was appointed Acting Mediator. Under his auspices, armistice agreements were signed in 1949 by Israel and four Arab countries—Egypt, Jordan, Lebanon and Syria. UNTSO assisted the parties, through Mixed Armistice Commissions, in supervising the application of the agreements.

Following Egypt's nationalization of the Suez Canal Company in July 1956, Israel and, later, France and the United Kingdom intervened militarily against Egypt. The General Assembly, meeting in an emergency special session, called for a cease-fire and withdrawal of those forces from Egyptian territory, and established the **United Nations Emergency Force (UNEF)**—the first United Nations peace-keeping force. UNEF supervised the troop withdrawals and was then deployed on Egyptian territory, with Egypt's consent, to act as a buffer between Egyptian and Israeli forces. It patrolled the Egypt-Israel armistice demarcation line and the frontier south of the Gaza Strip, and brought relative quiet to the area. The Canal, blocked as a result of the conflict, was cleared by the United Nations.

UNEF was withdrawn in May 1967, at Egypt's request.

Fighting broke out again on 5 June 1967 between Israel and Egypt, Jordan and Syria. The Security Council on 6 June called for a cease-fire. By the time hostilities ended six days later, Israel had occupied the Sinai and the Gaza Strip, the West Bank of the Jordan River, including East Jerusalem, and part of the Syrian Golan Heights. The Secretary-General, acting on decisions of the Council, stationed UNTSO observers in the Golan and Suez Canal sectors to supervise the cease-fire. Meeting in emergency special session, the General Assembly in July called on Israel not to alter the status of Jerusalem.

On 22 November 1967, the Security Council unanimously adopted resolution 242, which defined principles of a just and lasting peace in the Middle East. The principles were:

♦ withdrawal of Israeli armed forces from territories occupied in the 1967 conflict; and

♦ termination of all claims or states of belligerency and respect for and acknowledgement of the sovereignty, territorial integrity and political independence of every State in the area and their right to live in peace within secure and recognized boundaries, free from threats or acts of force.

The resolution also affirmed the need to settle the refugee problem.

The Council requested the Secretary-General to designate a Special Representative for the Middle East to help achieve a peaceful settlement in accordance with resolution 242. Ambassador Gunnar Jarring, who was appointed to that post, started talks in 1967 with Egypt, Israel and Jordan (Syria did not accept resolution 242). The talks continued intermittently until 1973, but despite Mr. Jarring's efforts no significant progress could be made.

Fighting broke out again on 6 October 1973, when Egypt and Syria attacked Israeli positions. The Security Council, by resolution 338 of 22 October 1973, called on the parties to cease hostilities and start full implementation of resolution 242. It also decided that, concurrently with the cease-fire, negotiations should start to establish a just and lasting peace in the Middle East. As fighting continued, the Council demanded again an immediate cease-fire and the return of the parties to the positions they had occupied on 22 October, and set up a new **United Nations Emergency Force (UNEF II)**. The Force was stationed in the Egypt-Israel sector.

In December, a Peace Conference on the Middle East was convened at Geneva under United Nations auspices and the co-chairmanship of the Soviet Union and the United States, with Egypt, Israel and Jordan attending. Before adjourning, the

Conference decided to continue its work through a Military Working Group, which would discuss the disengagement of forces.

Those discussions led to a disengagement agreement between Egypt and Israel, signed in January 1974 at a meeting of the Military Working Group chaired by the UNEF Commander. The agreement covered a partial Israeli withdrawal from occupied territory in the Sinai, the establishment of a buffer zone controlled by UNEF and areas of limited forces and armaments on both sides of the zone. The disengagement was completed in March 1974 with UNEF assistance.

Israel and Egypt signed a second disengagement agreement in September 1975, providing for further Israeli withdrawals. These were completed in February 1976, and a new, larger buffer zone was set up under UNEF control.

UNEF's mandate was renewed by the Security Council until June 1979, when it was not extended. UNTSO observers remain stationed in various areas of the Middle East.

An agreement on the disengagement of Israeli and Syrian forces was signed at a meeting of the Military Working Group in May 1974. The agreement also provided for an area of separation, and for zones of limited forces and armaments on both sides of the area, and called for the establishment of a United Nations observer force to supervise its implementation. The Security Council therefore set up the **United Nations Disengagement Observer Force (UNDOF)**. The disengagement was completed in June 1974. UNDOF observers remain stationed in the area.

Meanwhile, the General Assembly had increasingly turned its attention to other aspects of the Middle East question. In 1968, it established a Special Committee to Investigate Israeli Practices Affecting the Human Rights of the Palestinian People and Other Arabs of the Occupied Territories (as it was later renamed), which reports to the Assembly. In 1974, the Assembly reaffirmed "the inalienable rights of the Palestinian people in Palestine" to self-determination, independence and sovereignty, and recognized the Palestinian people as a principal party in the establishment of a just and lasting peace in the Middle East. It also invited the Palestine Liberation Organization (PLO) to participate in the work of the Assembly and United Nations international conferences as an observer.

In 1975, the General Assembly established the Committee on the Exercise of the Inalienable Rights of the Palestinian People. In 1977, the Assembly called for the annual observance of 29 November as the International Day of Solidarity with the Palestinian People.

A new element in the Middle East situation was introduced in November 1977, when Egyptian President Anwar Sadat visited Jerusalem. Direct negotiations between Egypt and Israel led in September 1978 to two agreements known as the Camp David accords—one on a framework for peace in the Middle East, and the other on a framework for concluding a peace treaty between Egypt and Israel, which was signed in March 1979. Under the peace treaty, Israel withdrew from the Sinai, over which Egypt then took control.

In 1983, the General Assembly endorsed the Geneva Declaration on Palestine that had been adopted by the International Conference on the Question of Palestine (Geneva, August-September 1983). The Assembly has stated repeatedly that the question of Palestine is the core of the Middle East conflict, and that peace must be based on a comprehensive, just and lasting solution, under United Nations auspices. The Assembly has also reaffirmed the need for Israeli withdrawal from the territories occupied since 1967, including Jerusalem, and has determined that Israel's decision to impose its laws and administration on Jerusalem and the occupied Golan Heights is null and void.

At subsequent sessions, the General Assembly called for an International Peace Conference on the Middle East, under United Nations auspices, based on Security Council resolutions 242 and 338.

In December 1987, the Palestinian uprising (*intifadah*) began. Palestinians in the occupied territories declared that the uprising would continue until Palestinian independence and statehood were achieved. The General Assembly called on Israel to rescind its action against detainees and imprisoned Palestinians and to release them immediately.

In January 1988, the Secretary-General recommended the adoption of several measures to protect Palestinian civilians living in the occupied areas. For its part, the Security Council has repeatedly affirmed the applicability of the Fourth Geneva Convention, which deals with protection of civilians in time of war, to all territories occupied by Israel since 1967, and has called on Israel to abide by its obligations under the Convention.

In November, the Palestine National Council (PNC) called for an International Peace Conference on the Middle East under United Nations auspices, based on resolutions 242 and 338, with the participation of all involved and interested parties. This proclamation provided the basis for a Palestinian peace initiative announced before the General Assembly by PNC Chairman Yasser Arafat, who invited Israel to begin a dialogue with the PLO.

In December, the General Assembly acknowledged the PNC's call for an international peace conference. The Assembly also acknowledged the proclamation of the State of Palestine by the PNC on 15 November 1988, and decided to designate the PLO as "Palestine".

In April 1989, Israeli Prime Minister Yitzhak Shamir put forward his own plan calling for elections to select a Palestinian delegation to negotiate for an interim self-governing administration.

In December 1990, in a Presidential statement, the Security Council reaffirmed its support for a negotiating process in which all parties would participate, based on resolutions 242 and 338, which would take into account the right to security of all States in the region, including Israel, as well as the legitimate political rights of the Palestinian people.

In 1991, the Secretary-General decided to reactivate the mission of the Special Representative to the Middle East, as called for in resolution 242. In March, he appointed Ambassador Edouard Brunner to that post.

In October, a Peace Conference on the Middle East opened in Madrid, co-sponsored by the Soviet Union and the United States. The Secretary-General reported in November that although the Conference was being conducted outside the United Nations framework, that process had the support of the parties and had as its basis resolutions 242 and 338.

In December, the Assembly reaffirmed a set of principles for achieving a comprehensive peace, including:

♦ withdrawal of Israel from the Palestinian territory occupied since 1967, including Jerusalem, and from the other occupied Arab territories;

♦ dismantlement of the Israeli settlements in those territories;

♦ arrangements guaranteeing the security of all States in the region within secure and internationally recognized boundaries;

♦ resolution of the problem of Palestine refugees in conformity with General Assembly resolutions; and

♦ guarantee of freedom of access to holy places, religious buildings and sites.

Also in December, the General Assembly revoked the determination in its 1975 resolution that "Zionism is a form of racism and racial discrimination".

In October 1992, the co-sponsors of the Madrid process invited the United Nations to attend, as a full participant, the peace talks on the Middle East. The Secretary-General appointed a Special Representative to the talks, with the task of coordinating the role of the United Nations in the working groups on arms control and regional security, water, environment, economic and regional development, and refugees.

Following several months of Norwegian-mediated secret negotiations, Israel and the PLO on 10 September 1993 exchanged letters of mutual recognition. The PLO recognized Israel's right to exist, and Israel recognized the PLO as the representative of the Palestinian people.

Three days later, at a ceremony in Washington, D.C., attended by Israeli Prime Minister Yitzhak Rabin, PLO Chairman Yasser Arafat, United States President Bill Clinton and Russian Foreign Minister Andrei Kozyrev, Israel and the PLO signed the Declaration of Principles on Interim Self-Government Arrangements. The historic agreement opened the way to Palestinian self-rule, providing for Israeli withdrawal and the establishment of an interim Palestinian self-government, first in the Gaza Strip and the West Bank town of Jericho and later in the rest of the West Bank. Other sensitive issues, such as Israeli settlements, Jerusalem, the return of Palestinian refugees and future boundaries, were to be addressed in further negotiations.

Warmly welcoming the agreement, the Secretary-General said that the United Nations was ready to assist in its implementation, and that it would coordinate assistance from its agencies and programmes. A task force to focus on the social and economic development of Gaza and Jericho was formed in response to a request from Israel and the PLO.

In December 1993, the General Assembly expressed its support for the agreement and stressed the need for rapid progress in the negotiations.

On 4 May 1994, Israel and the PLO signed the Agreement on the Gaza Strip and the Jericho Area, which marked the beginning of the transfer of powers from Israel to the Palestinian Authority.

Also in May, the Secretary-General appointed a Special Coordinator in the Occupied Territories. The Coordinator provides overall guidance to and facilitates coordination among the programmes and agencies of the United Nations system, so as to assist in implementing the Declaration of Principles.

On 25 July, Israel and Jordan signed the Washington Declaration, which terminated the state of war between them. Warmly welcoming this development, the Secretary-General expressed his hope that it would accelerate the process of achieving a comprehensive, just and lasting peace in the Middle East.

In September, Israel and the PLO signed an "early empowerment" agreement according to which the transfer of civilian authority had to be progressively extended within the West Bank.

Progress was also achieved in the negotiations on Middle East regional issues carried out in the working groups, which began to focus on specific projects. The United Nations has continued to play an active role as a full participant in these tasks.

Lebanon

Tension along the Israel-Lebanon border increased in 1972. Israel, which stated that it was acting in reprisal for raids carried out in its territory by Palestinian commandos, attacked Palestinian camps in Lebanon. In April 1972, at Lebanon's request and in accordance with a Security Council decision, the United Nations Truce Supervision Organization (UNTSO) set up a cease-fire observation operation in the Israel-Lebanon sector. UNTSO observers have remained in the area.

Another United Nations peace-keeping force was set up in March 1978 after Israeli forces invaded southern Lebanon following a Palestinian commando raid in Israel. The Security Council called on Israel to cease its military action against Lebanon's territorial integrity, and established the **United Nations Interim Force in Lebanon (UNIFIL)** to confirm the withdrawal of Israeli forces, restore international peace and security and assist the Lebanese Government in re-establishing its authority in the area.

When Israeli forces completed their withdrawal from Lebanon in June 1978, they handed over their positions in the border area not to UNIFIL but to Lebanese irregular forces (Christian and associated militias), which they supported and supplied. The area remained tense, with frequent exchanges of fire between those irregular forces and the Israel Defence Forces (IDF), on the one hand, and armed elements (mainly of the PLO and Lebanese National Movement) on the other. In July 1981, a de facto cease-fire came into effect, and the area remained generally quiet until mid-1982.

On 6 June 1982, after two days of intense exchanges of fire in southern Lebanon and across the Israel-Lebanon border, Israeli forces moved into Lebanese territory in strength. UNIFIL positions were overrun or bypassed, and Israeli forces reached and surrounded Beirut.

Meeting in June, July and August as hostilities continued, the Security Council called for a halt to military activities, and demanded that Israel withdraw to the internationally recognized boundaries of Lebanon and lift the blockade of Beirut.

In August, the Security Council authorized the deployment of United Nations military observers, the Observer Group Beirut, to monitor the situation in and around Beirut. A cease-fire went into effect on 12 August.

Later that month, France, Italy and the United States concluded an agreement with Lebanon for participation of their troops in a multinational force to assist Lebanese armed forces in carrying out an orderly and safe departure from Lebanon of Palestinian armed personnel in the Beirut area. The evacuation of the Palestinian forces from Beirut was completed on 1 September. The last elements of the multinational force were withdrawn on 13 September.

Tension greatly increased the day after, when President-elect Bashir Gemayel and several others were killed in a bomb explosion. The following day, IDF units took up new positions in the area. The Security Council condemned the Israeli incursions into Beirut in violation of the cease-fire agreements and Council resolutions; demanded that Israel return to its pre–15 September positions; and called again for the respect for Lebanon's sovereignty, territorial integrity, unity and political independence under the sole authority of the Lebanese Government.

On 16 September, Lebanese Christian militias entered the Sabra and Shatila Palestinian refugee camps in the suburbs of Beirut, killing large numbers of refugees. The Security Council condemned the massacre, as did the General Assembly, which called for respect for and application of the Fourth Geneva Convention relative to the Protection of Civilian Persons in Time of War. Shortly afterwards, at the request of the Lebanese Government, British, French, Italian and United States contingents of the multilateral force returned to Beirut.

The withdrawal of the IDF from the Beirut area began in July 1983. This set the stage for fighting in the evacuated area between Lebanese Government forces and Christian Phalangists on the one hand, and Shi'ite and Druse militias on the other. As hostilities intensified, French and United States contingents of the multilateral force became involved in the fighting.

The situation in the Beirut area remained unstable, with continuing killings and destruction, throughout the rest of 1983 and 1984. The multilateral force encountered serious obstacles in its task, and suffered heavy casualties. Italy, the United Kingdom and the United States withdrew their forces in early 1984, followed by France in March, thus ending the 19-month multinational effort.

In 1984, the Secretary-General convened at UNIFIL headquarters a conference of military representatives of Lebanon and Israel, which met intermittently between November 1984 and January 1985, to expedite the withdrawal of Israeli forces.

Starting in February 1985, Israel carried out its own three-phase plan for unilateral redeployment and withdrawal of its forces, which was completed by mid-1985. During the third phase, the IDF deployed along the Israel-Lebanon border, while keeping a "security zone" in southern Lebanon, where "local forces"—the so-called South Lebanese Army (SLA)—functioned with IDF backing.

After the withdrawal, attacks by Lebanese resistance groups against Israeli forces and Lebanese irregulars armed and controlled by them increased sharply. The Israeli-controlled area, which overlaps parts of UNIFIL's area of deployment, remained a focus of hostilities between Lebanese groups on the one hand and the Israeli and associated de facto forces (SLA) on the other.

The Secretary-General continued his efforts to persuade Israel to leave the security zone, but without success. Israel, while maintaining that the zone is a temporary arrangement governed by its security concerns and reaffirming that it has no territorial designs in Lebanon, has argued that the Lebanese Government does not exercise authority in the area and that UNIFIL, being a peace-keeping force, is not mandated to take the forceful action necessary to control cross-border attacks. Lebanon insists that Israel withdraw, stating that the occupation is illegal and contrary to United Nations resolutions.

UNIFIL has attempted to contain the conflict and shield the inhabitants of the area. From time to time, this has involved the Force in confrontations and it has suffered casualties. UNIFIL has continued to cooperate with the Lebanese authorities, United Nations agencies and other organizations in providing humanitarian assistance, treating Lebanese at medical centres and repairing buildings damaged by firing.

In 1988, a serious Government crisis led to bitter fighting. In August 1989, the hostilities reached such a level that the Secretary-General conveyed to the Security Council his anxiety about the violence in and around Beirut. The Council appealed for an immediate cease-fire.

In October 1989, Lebanese leaders worked out a peace formula at an Arab League–sponsored meeting in Taif, Saudi Arabia. Under the Taif accord, Lebanese members of parliament elected in November a new President, René Mouawad. He was assassinated 17 days after his election, and was succeeded by Elias Hrawi, who formed a new Government. The Security Council expressed support for the Taif agreement and the Government's efforts to extend its authority over all the territory.

In October 1990, President Hrawi invited Syrian forces to move into East Beirut. Syrian forces took control of the city, and the President set about implementing a security plan for Beirut which was part of the peace formula worked out at Taif. The withdrawal of the militias from the Beirut area went forward with relative ease. By December, the Lebanese army, with Syrian support, was in control of the capital.

In 1991, the United Nations stepped up its efforts for Lebanon's reconstruction and development. In July, 14 United Nations agencies and programmes conducted a needs-assessment mission. In December, the General Assembly called on the international community to provide technical and financial assistance to the country.

Also in 1991, an intensive process of quiet diplomacy by the Secretary-General and his envoy led to the release of several hostages and prisoners. In August-September, three Western hostages held in Lebanon and 51 Lebanese prisoners held by Israel were released; in October-December, six more hostages and 40 more prisoners were released.

In 1992-1994, the situation along the Israel-Lebanon border remained volatile. Lebanese armed elements who proclaimed their resistance to Israeli occupation continued to mount attacks on the IDF and SLA forces in the "security zone", causing retaliatory artillery fire and air raids.

In July 1993, in response to rocket attacks against northern Israel, the IDF launched massive air strikes against south Lebanon. As a result of the fighting, hundreds of thousands of civilians were displaced, dozens of Lebanese villages were destroyed or damaged, and scores of homes, schools, hospitals, roads and bridges were demolished. After the hostilities ceased, a Lebanese army unit was deployed in parts of UNIFIL's area of operation to maintain public order.

A United Nations needs-assessment mission was dispatched to Lebanon at the request of the Government. In August, on the basis of the mission's findings, the Secretary-General launched an appeal for $28 million in humanitarian assistance.

UNIFIL has continued to be deployed in the area, contributing to stability and providing protection to the population.

United Nations Relief and Works Agency for Palestine Refugees in the Near East (UNRWA)

The United Nations Relief and Works Agency for Palestine Refugees in the Near East was established by the General Assembly in 1949. UNRWA's mandate has been periodically renewed, most recently until 30 June 1996.

UNRWA initially provided emergency relief to some 750,000 Palestine refugees who had lost their homes and livelihood as a result of the 1948 Arab-Israeli conflict. By 1994, UNRWA was providing essential health, education, relief and social services to over three million registered Palestine refugees. Of this number, about one million lived in 59 refugee camps served by the Agency in Jordan, Lebanon, the Syrian Arab Republic, the Gaza Strip and the West Bank.

UNRWA's operations are supervised and supported by its Headquarters in Vienna, Austria; Amman, Jordan; and Gaza. The Commissioner-General, who reports to the General Assembly, heads all UNRWA operations, assisted by an Advisory Commission comprised of Belgium, Egypt, France, Japan, Jordan, Lebanon, Syria, Turkey, the United Kingdom and the United States. In addition to its international staff, UNRWA employs nearly 20,500 local staff, mainly Palestine refugees.

In 1994/95, UNRWA's major programmes of education, health, and relief and social services accounted for over 82 per cent of total funds.

Forty-eight per cent of the Agency's funds were devoted to education. In the 1994/95 school year, there were over 409,500 pupils in UNRWA's 643 elementary and preparatory schools, employing more than 11,400 teachers. The Agency ran eight vocational and technical training centres for some 5,000 students. It also awarded 872 university scholarships during the year.

Health services accounted for nearly 21 per cent of the 1994/95 budget. As of June 1995, the Agency ran 122 health units and mother-and-child health clinics, 32 specialist clinics, 107 diabetes clinics and 107 hypertension clinics. There were over 6.4 million patient visits to all UNRWA health services units and clinics during the year.

Relief and social services amounted to nearly 14 per cent of UNRWA's 1994/95 budget. UNRWA ran 75 women's centres for over 11,000 participants and 25 rehabilitation centres. By January 1995, the Agency had provided 396 loans to 610 income-generation projects, totalling over $6.4 million, in Jordan, Lebanon, Syria, the Gaza Strip and the West Bank, in addition to sponsoring a vast number of grant-based and mini-loan poverty-alleviation projects.

UNRWA's humanitarian role has been reinforced by recurrent conflicts in the Middle East, such as the civil war in Lebanon, the Palestinian uprising (*intifadah*) and the Persian Gulf crisis, which led to the displacement of over 300,000 Palestinians into the UNRWA area of operations.

The historic developments which took place in 1993 and 1994 (see above) had a profound impact on the work and responsibilities of the Agency. With the establishment of the Palestinian Authority in the Gaza Strip and the Jericho Area and the anticipated extension of self-rule to the rest of the West Bank, UNRWA entered a new era in its relationship with the Palestinian people. In October 1993, the Agency launched a $100 million Peace Implementation Programme to support the peace process, develop the socio-economic infrastructure and improve the lives of Palestinian refugees.

UNRWA depends almost entirely on voluntary contributions for its regular and emergency operations. The Agency's regular budget for the biennium 1994/95 included $532.8 million in cash and $79.5 million in-kind, for a total of $632.3 million.

SOUTH ASIA SUBCONTINENT: INDIA-PAKISTAN

For over four decades, the United Nations has been concerned with the dispute between India and Pakistan over Kashmir. In addition, the United Nations mounted a large humanitarian operation during and after the conflict over Bangladesh in 1971.

The State of Jammu and Kashmir was one of the princely states which became free, under the partition plan and the Indian Independence Act of 1947, to accede to India or Pakistan. The Hindu Maharajah of this State, with a largely Muslim population, at first sought to avoid joining either India or Pakistan. However, when Pathan tribesmen invaded from Pakistan he acceded to union with India on 24 October 1947, and Indian army units were dispatched to his assistance.

In January 1948, India complained to the Security Council that tribesmen and others, with Pakistan's support and participation, were invading Kashmir and that extensive fighting was taking place. Pakistan denied the charges, and declared Kashmir's accession to India illegal. The Security Council set up a United Nations Commission for India and Pakistan to investigate the facts and exercise mediation.

The Security Council recommended various measures, including the use of observers, to stop the fighting and to create conditions for a plebiscite. To assist in carrying out these measures, it dispatched the Commission to the region to place its good offices at the disposal of the parties.

The Commission made proposals on a cease-fire and troop withdrawals, and proposed that the accession of Jammu and Kashmir be decided by plebiscite. Both sides accepted. The cease-fire came into effect on 1 January 1949, and United Nations military observers were deployed in the area to supervise it. In July 1949, a cease-fire line was established in Jammu and Kashmir, under an agreement between India and Pakistan reached in Karachi under the auspices of the United Nations Commission.

The two countries also accepted the proposal for a plebiscite, but the Commission was unable to reach agreement with the parties on the terms of demilitarization of the State before a plebiscite could be held. Despite mediation by various United Nations representatives, differences remained and the problem came before the Security Council at various times between 1957 and 1964.

Hostilities between India and Pakistan broke out again in August 1965. The Security Council called for a cease-fire, and the fighting was brought to a stop in September, with the assistance of the **United Nations Military Observer Group in India and Pakistan (UNMOGIP)**, which had been set up under the Council's 1948 resolution establishing the United Nations Commission for India and Pakistan. The Secretary-General organized observers to supervise the cease-fire along the India-Pakistan border, as the **United Nations India-Pakistan Observation Mission (UNIPOM)**.

At a series of meetings between Indian and Pakistani officials, convened by the representative of the Secretary-General in January 1966, a plan and ground rules for withdrawals were worked out. On 10 January, the Prime Minister of India and the President of Pakistan had agreed, in a joint Declaration at Tashkent—where they met under the auspices of the Soviet Union—to withdraw their troops to positions held before 5 August 1965. The withdrawal was carried out in February 1966 under the supervision of UNMOGIP and UNIPOM military observers.

Another conflict broke out between India and Pakistan in 1971 in connection with civil strife in East Pakistan, which later became Bangladesh. As millions of refugees streamed into India, tension increased. With the consent of India and Pakistan, the Secretary-General set up two large-scale humanitarian programmes—one, under the United Nations High Commissioner for Refugees, for the relief of East Pakistan refugees in India, and the other, under a United Nations representative, for assistance in East Pakistan.

In December 1971, when full-scale hostilities broke out between the two countries, the Secretary-General notified the Security Council that the situation constituted a threat to international peace and security. The Council, unable to reach agreement on the situation, referred the matter to the General Assembly, which called on both countries to institute a cease-fire and withdraw their forces to their own sides of the borders.

After the cease-fire had put an end to the fighting on 17 December, the Security Council demanded its strict observance until withdrawal of all armed forces to their territories and to positions respecting the cease-fire line in Kashmir supervised by UNMOGIP. The Council also authorized the Secretary-General to appoint a Special Representative to aid in solving humanitarian problems. In 1972, with United Nations assistance, refugees returned to their homeland, while the United Nations relief operation aided the war-shattered economy of Bangladesh, which became a Member of the United Nations in 1974.

In July 1972, India and Pakistan signed at Simla an agreement defining a Line of Control in Kashmir which, with minor deviations, followed the course of the cease-fire line established in the 1949 Karachi agreement. In the Simla agreement, both sides undertook to "settle their differences by peaceful means" and committed themselves to "a final settlement of Jammu and Kashmir".

In July 1990, India and Pakistan started talks to discuss various bilateral issues, including Jammu and Kashmir. By January 1994, seven rounds of talks at the Foreign Secretary level were held, but without visible progress.

Tension in Jammu and Kashmir has increased in recent years. The Secretary-General has stated his readiness to facilitate the search for a lasting solution. India has expressed its preference for a strictly bilateral framework for its talks with Pakistan. Pakistan has welcomed the Secretary-General's offer.

In the absence of an agreement, UNMOGIP observers continue to be deployed along both sides of the cease-fire line established under the Simla agreement. Although India provides UNMOGIP with the same administrative facilities as before, it has restricted the activities of the observers on its side of the Line of Control on the grounds that the Karachi agreement has ceased to be operative and UNMOGIP's mandate has, therefore, lapsed.

As of December 1994, UNMOGIP had a strength of 39 military observers.

TAJIKISTAN

One of the 15 republics of the Soviet Union, Tajikistan became an independent State in 1991. In May 1992, the Tajik opposition—a coalition of Islamic and other groups—seized power after two months of demonstrations, plunging the central Asian country into civil war. After suffering defeat in December 1992, most of the opposition forces crossed the border into Afghanistan. Although the civil war ended in early 1993, the continued armed insurgency of the opposition forces, in particular across the Tajik-Afghan border, continued to destabilize the country. The civil war resulted in more than 20,000 deaths and some 400,000 refugees and displaced persons.

The United Nations became involved early on in the peace effort. At the invitation of the Government, a United Nations fact-finding mission visited Tajikistan in September 1992, followed by a goodwill mission in November. The Secretary-General in April 1993 appointed a Special Envoy for Tajikistan, who visited the country and held talks with Government and opposition leaders. Also in April, the World Food Programme launched a $4 million emergency relief operation.

Meanwhile, cross-border infiltration by armed opposition groups from Afghanistan continued, leading to fighting between them and Government forces. In July 1993, Afghan fighters launched a large-scale attack which resulted in 27 deaths.

In August, the Security Council stressed the urgent need for the cessation of all hostile actions on the Tajik-Afghan border, and urged the Government and all opposition groups to participate in negotiations towards a cease-fire.

In September 1993, an accord was reached in Moscow on placing peace-keeping forces of the Commonwealth of Independent States (CIS) in Tajikistan. But in November, the Secretary-General reported to the Council that infiltration by Afghan fighters continued, as did fighting between them and Government and CIS forces. Armed confrontation was also intensifying within the country.

In March 1994, Tajik parties reached agreement to begin a political dialogue on national reconciliation. The first round of talks was held in Moscow in April under United Nations auspices, focusing on a political settlement, solutions to the problem of refugees and internally displaced persons, fundamental institutional issues and consolidation of the statehood of Tajikistan. Also in April, the United Nations launched a humanitarian appeal for $37 million.

A second round of talks, held under United Nations auspices and led by the Special Envoy, took place in June in

Teheran, Iran. A cease-fire agreement between the Government and the opposition was signed in Teheran on 17 September. Talks in October-November in Islamabad, Pakistan, led to the signing of a protocol on a Joint Commission, made up by both parties, for implementation of the cease-fire agreement.

To assist the Joint Commission in monitoring the cease-fire, the Security Council on 16 December 1994 established the **United Nations Mission of Observers in Tajikistan (UNMOT)**. Also in December 1994, the United Nations launched an appeal for $42 million to meet the emergency needs of some 600,000 persons affected by the conflict.

By January 1995, some 55 UNMOT personnel, including 22 military observers, had been deployed in the country. Meanwhile, the Special Envoy and other United Nations officials continued consultation in the region towards a peaceful solution of the conflict.

EUROPE
♦ **Georgia-Abkhazia** ♦ **Former Yugoslavia**

GEORGIA-ABKHAZIA
The conflict in Abkhazia, located on the Black Sea in the northwestern region of the Republic of Georgia, has historic roots. Abkhazia has been for centuries the home of a people possessing a distinctive language and culture, whose descendants more recently have constituted only a minority of the territory's population. In 1931, Abkhazia became an autonomous republic within the Soviet Socialist Republic of Georgia. The political turmoil in the Soviet Union in the late 1980s and its formal dissolution in 1991 were accompanied by the rise of nationalist feelings among both Georgians and Abkhazians, and by growing demands from Abkhazians for greater autonomy.

In 1992, amid social unrest, the local authorities in Abkhazia attempted to separate from Georgia. Armed confrontation erupted in the summer of 1992, when the Government of Georgia deployed 2,000 troops in Abkhazia to secure rail and other communication links. On 14 August, as Georgian troops entered Abkhazia, fierce fighting resulted in some 200 dead.

The Abkhaz leadership left Sukhumi, the Abkhaz capital, and retreated to the town of Gudauta.

A cease-fire agreement was reached on 3 September in Moscow by the Republic of Georgia, the leadership of Abkhazia and the Russian Federation. Under the agreement, the territorial integrity of Georgia was to be ensured, and a cease-fire was to go into effect on 5 September, monitored by a commission made up of the three signatories. The United Nations was called upon to assist in implementing the peace settlement.

The agreement was never fully implemented and the situation remained tense, as confirmed in September by a United Nations mission to the region. On 1 October, the cease-fire collapsed. The Abkhaz forces, supported by fighters from the North Caucasus, quickly captured major towns. An estimated 30,000 civilians fled to the Russian Federation.

Seeking to revive the peace process, the United Nations sent a second mission in October to explore ways of supporting the implementation of the cease-fire agreement. In November, a United Nations office opened in the Georgian capital of Tbilisi to coordinate the work of the Organization in Georgia.

Following a request from the Government of Georgia, a United Nations humanitarian assessment mission visited Georgia in early 1993. The United Nations then issued a $20 million appeal for emergency humanitarian assistance.

In May 1993, the Secretary-General appointed a Special Envoy for Georgia, who visited Georgia and reported that all parties supported a United Nations role in reaching a solution. Georgia fully supported the subsequent proposal of the Secretary-General for a peace conference under United Nations auspices and the deployment of United Nations military observers. The Abkhaz side favoured a conference but opposed the deployment of observers.

Following renewed fighting, a cease-fire was finally established as of 28 July. On 24 August, the Security Council established the **United Nations Observer Mission in Georgia (UNOMIG)**, with the mandate of monitoring the cease-fire.

While UNOMIG was still being deployed, the cease-fire broke down when Abkhaz forces on 16 September launched attacks on Sukhumi and later on Ochamchira. The Georgian authorities appealed for assistance to the Russian Federation and to the United Nations. The Abkhaz side took over Sukhumi on 27 September.

The fighting resulted in a massive displacement of civilians, with an estimated 100,000 people affected. The United Nations made an appeal for emergency supplies and organized a relief flight.

On 7 October, the Secretary-General reported to the Security Council that the mandate of UNOMIG had been invalidated as a result of the breakdown of the cease-fire and the collapse of the machinery responsible for implementing it. He proposed to maintain the observers in Sukhumi, as he continued negotiations with the parties to end the conflict, with the Russian Federation acting as facilitator.

In October, the Security Council condemned the violation of the cease-fire agreement and of international humanitarian law by Abkhaz forces. It also condemned the killing of the Chairman of the Defence Council and Council of Ministers of the Autonomous Republic of Abkhazia.

On 2 December, the Secretary-General's Special Envoy announced the signing the previous day of a Memorandum of Understanding between the Georgians and the Abkhazians. The Memorandum included a pledge not to use force or threat of force during the negotiation period, an exchange of prisoners of war, and the return of refugees. On 22 December, the Security Council authorized the deployment of additional UNOMIG military observers to assist in implementing the Memorandum of Understanding.

Further negotiations on the political status of Abkhazia resulted in a declaration by both parties on 4 April 1994 that Abkhazia should have its own Constitution, legislation and state symbols. Subsequent talks concentrated on proposals for establishing a unified State of Georgia, which would include a number of republics.

A cease-fire agreement was reached in Moscow on 14 May, establishing a security zone along the Inguri river and outlining details of troop withdrawal from the zone of conflict. The parties agreed that a peace-keeping force of the Commonwealth of Independent States (CIS) would be deployed to monitor compliance with the agreement, and appealed to the Security Council to provide for UNOMIG's participation in the operation. On 21 July, the Security Council requested UNOMIG to monitor the implementation of the agreement and to observe the operation of the CIS peace-keeping force.

A programme for the voluntary return of refugees and displaced persons to Abkhazia commenced in October 1994, overseen by the Office of the United Nations High Commissioner for Refugees (UNHCR), but little progress was registered in this area. The Special Envoy continued negotiations towards a comprehensive settlement, focusing on the question of the political status of Abkhazia, and the return of refugees and displaced persons.

FORMER YUGOSLAVIA

A founding Member of the United Nations, the Socialist Federal Republic of Yugoslavia was comprised of six republics—Bosnia and Herzegovina, Croatia, Macedonia, Montenegro, Serbia, and Slovenia. At the end of the 1980s, following a period of political and economic crisis, the republics of Slovenia and Croatia began to separate themselves from the rest of the country. Efforts by the collective federal presidency and the six Presidents to end conflicts and negotiate a revised structure for the country failed.

Hostilities began in June 1991, when Croatia and Slovenia declared themselves independent from Yugoslavia. Serbs living in Croatia, supported by the Yugoslav People's Army, opposed the move. By September, fighting had escalated into an all-out war between Croatia and Serbia. In March 1992, Bosnia and Herzegovina also declared its independence—an act supported by Bosnian Croats and Bosnian Muslims, but opposed by Bosnian Serbs. The European Community sought to resolve the Yugoslav crisis in the framework of the Conference on Yugoslavia, but its efforts proved unsuccessful.

The United Nations became involved in the situation in Yugoslavia on 25 September 1991, when the Security Council imposed an arms embargo on Yugoslavia and invited the Secretary-General to offer his assistance in support of the peace efforts of the European Community. In October, the Secretary-General appointed Mr. Cyrus Vance as his Personal Envoy for Yugoslavia.

The Personal Envoy undertook negotiations with all parties, which resulted in agreements on a cease-fire in Croatia, and on establishing a United Nations peace-keeping operation.

On 21 February 1992, even though some political groups in Yugoslavia were still objecting to the United Nations plan, the Security Council established the **United Nations Protection Force (UNPROFOR)**, to create conditions of peace and security for negotiating a settlement in the framework of the European Community's Conference on Yugoslavia.

UNPROFOR was deployed in Croatia in four "United Nations Protected Areas" in which Serbs were the majority or a substantial minority of the population, and where ethnic tensions had led to armed conflict. UNPROFOR's mandate was to ensure that such areas were vacated by the Yugoslav People's Army and demilitarized, and that all persons living in them were protected from armed attacks. UNPROFOR was also to assist the United Nations humanitarian agencies and facilitate the return of displaced persons to their homes.

As the conflict in Bosnia and Herzegovina broke out and rapidly intensified, humanitarian problems increased dramatically. Under difficult circumstances, various United Nations agencies and several humanitarian organizations continued their work.

From April 1992, the situation in Bosnia and Herzegovina deteriorated rapidly. The Security Council appealed for a cease-fire, and demanded that interference by the Yugoslav and Croatian armies cease immediately. But in spite of all efforts by the European Community, the Secretary-General and UNPROFOR, the conflict continued to worsen.

On 30 May, the Security Council imposed wide-ranging economic sanctions on Yugoslavia (which by then consisted of Serbia and Montenegro). It also demanded that all parties allow the delivery of humanitarian supplies to the Bosnian capital of Sarajevo and other areas of Bosnia and Herzegovina.

Bosnia and Herzegovina, Croatia and Slovenia had become Members of the United Nations on 22 May. The former Yugoslav Republic of Macedonia joined the United Nations on 8 April 1993.

By June 1992, there were widespread reports of "ethnic

cleansing"—elimination by the ethnic group controlling a territory of members of other ethnic groups—mostly conducted by Bosnian Serb forces. The number of refugees and displaced persons had risen to more than 2.2 million—the largest refugee crisis in Europe since the Second World War.

In August, the United Nations Commission on Human Rights appointed a Special Rapporteur to investigate the situation in the former Yugoslavia. Meeting in a two-day extraordinary session on Yugoslavia, the Commission condemned human rights violations and ethnic cleansing, especially in Bosnia and Herzegovina.

As Serbian forces continued fierce fighting around Sarajevo and in other areas, the Security Council in September expanded UNPROFOR's mandate and strength in Bosnia, authorizing the Force to protect the convoys of released civilian detainees and the delivery of humanitarian assistance. Deployment of additional troops in five new zones was also authorized.

In September, the General Assembly decided that the Federal Republic of Yugoslavia (Serbia and Montenegro) could not continue automatically the membership of the former Yugoslavia in the United Nations. Acting on the recommendation of the Security Council, the Assembly decided that the Federal Republic should not participate in the work of the Assembly and should apply for membership.

In October, the Security Council banned all military flights over Bosnia and Herzegovina, instituting a "no-fly zone". To monitor implementation of the ban, the Council in November authorized the deployment of observers on the borders of Bosnia and Herzegovina.

In November, the former Yugoslav Republic of Macedonia requested the deployment of United Nations observers, due to concerns about the possible impact of fighting in the former Yugoslavia. In December, the Security Council established an UNPROFOR presence at the borders of the country with Albania and Yugoslavia. The mandate of the Force was essentially preventive—to monitor developments in the border areas which could threaten the country's territory.

In its second extraordinary session on Yugoslavia, the Commission on Human Rights in December condemned all human rights violations there, and demanded that the "Republic of Serbia" use its influence with the self-proclaimed Serbian authorities in Bosnia and Herzegovina and Croatia to end ethnic cleansing. The Commission condemned the indiscriminate shelling of cities, the systematic murder of civilians, the destruction of vital services and the use of military force against relief operations.

In December, the General Assembly condemned Serbia, Montenegro and Serbian forces for violating the sovereignty, territorial integrity and political independence of Bosnia and Herzegovina.

Diplomatic efforts to bring peace to Bosnia and Herzegovina continued. In January 1993, Mr. Vance and the European Community mediator, Lord David Owen—Co-Chairmen of the Steering Committee of the International Conference on the Former Yugoslavia (ICFY)—held talks in Geneva with the President of the Bosnian Government, the leader of Bosnian Serbs, the leader of Bosnian Croats, and the Presidents of Croatia and Yugoslavia (Serbia and Montenegro).

The Bosnian Serb "parliament" rejected in April the so-called Vance-Owen plan for a settlement of the conflict in Bosnia and Herzegovina. The Bosnian Government and the Bosnian Croats, as well as the President of Serbia, had agreed with the outlines of the Vance-Owen plan.

In February, the Security Council established an International Criminal Tribunal for the former Yugoslavia, to prosecute persons responsible for having committed or ordered serious violations of international humanitarian law. It was the first time the United Nations established an international criminal court with jurisdiction to prosecute crimes committed during armed conflict. The Tribunal is located in The Hague, the Netherlands.

In March, fighting intensified in eastern Bosnia and Herzegovina, with Bosnian Serb units attacking several cities and threatening Bosnian Muslims. In April, the Security Council demanded the withdrawal of Bosnian Serbs units, the end of armed attacks and the unimpeded delivery of humanitarian assistance. In May, the Council declared Sarajevo, Tuzla, Zepa,

Gorazde, Bihac and Srebrenica as "safe areas" which should be free from armed attacks and other hostile acts.

Intensive peace talks continued in New York and Geneva, under the auspices of Lord Owen and Mr. Thorvald Stoltenberg, the new Special Representative of the Secretary-General after Mr. Vance's resignation in April 1993. In the field, the United Nations continued its efforts to prevent further atrocities, alleviate human suffering, expedite delivery of humanitarian assistance and curtail military activities.

In June, the Security Council authorized UNPROFOR to use force, including air power, in reply to attacks against the safe areas by any Bosnian side. UNPROFOR's strength was increased by a further 7,600 troops.

In December 1993 and January 1994, Lord Owen and Mr. Stoltenberg held further rounds of inconclusive consultations. Fighting between Bosnian Muslims and Bosnian Croat forces continued to rage in central Bosnia and the Mostar area.

On 6 February, the Secretary-General stated that an attack against civilian targets in Sarajevo made it necessary to prepare for the use of air strikes to deter further attacks. He requested that the North Atlantic Council of the North Atlantic Treaty Organization (NATO) authorize air strikes, at the request of the United Nations, against artillery positions in or around Sarajevo which UNPROFOR had determined to be responsible for attacks against civilian targets. On 9 February, the North Atlantic Council authorized such air strikes.

In March, following negotiations under United States auspices, the Bosnian Government, the Bosnian Croats and the Republic of Croatia reached a Framework Agreement establishing a Federation in the areas of Bosnia and Herzegovina with a majority Bosnian and Croat population, as well as an outline of a preliminary agreement for a confederation between Croatia and Bosnia and Herzegovina.

While the political and military provisions of the Agreement proved difficult to implement, a 23 February cease-fire led to a halt in the year-long fighting between Bosnian and Croat forces in central Bosnia and the Mostar area, and to an improvement of the delivery of humanitarian aid to major cities through Bosnia and Herzegovina.

Also in March, the Secretary-General appointed a Special Coordinator for Sarajevo to develop a plan of action to restore essential public services in and around the city.

On 29 March, following negotiations under the auspices of the United States and the Russian Federation, the Government of Croatia and local Serb authorities in the United Nations Protected Areas concluded a cease-fire agreement. The implementation of the agreement implied the interposition of UNPROFOR in a zone of separation, as well as its monitoring of the withdrawal of heavy weapons.

In April, a "Contact Group", composed of France, Germany, the Russian Federation, the United Kingdom and the United States, was constituted to define a peaceful settlement in Bosnia and Herzegovina.

In May, the Foreign Ministers of the European Union Troika (Belgium, Germany and Greece) and of France, Russia, the United Kingdom and the United States met in Geneva, together with the Co-Chairmen of the Steering Committee of the ICFY. They urged the Bosnian parties to reach an agreement on the concept of a territorial compromise based on 51 per cent for the Bosnian-Croat Federation and 49 per cent for the Bosnian Serb entity.

In July, the Contact Group presented its territorial proposal, which was accepted by the Bosnian Federation, Croatia and the Federal Republic of Yugoslavia, but rejected by the Bosnian Serb party. In August, the Federal Republic of Yugoslavia severed economic and political relations with the Bosnian Serb leaders and closed its border with the Bosnian Serb-controlled territory in Bosnia and Herzegovina, except for the transport of food, clothing and medicine.

A UNHCR humanitarian airlift to Sarajevo marked the second anniversary of its operations there on 3 July 1994. It was the longest humanitarian airlift in history, the agency reported, with an average of 14 flights a day.

In September, the Security Council strengthened sanctions against the Bosnian Serbs, in view of their refusal to agree to the Contact Group's territorial proposal. The Council also suspended certain sanctions against the Federal Republic of Yugoslavia, after the Co-Chairmen of ICFY certified that it was meeting its commitment to close the border with Bosnia and Herzegovina.

In November-December, the Secretary-General went to Sarajevo and other European capitals, continuing high-level diplomatic efforts to reach a negotiated settlement to the conflict in the former Yugoslavia. On 31 December, the parties to the Bosnian conflict signed a four-month cessation of hostilities agreement. The agreement broke down in March and expired on 1 May.

In March 1995, the Secretary-General recommended that UNPROFOR be replaced by three operations in Bosnia and Herzegovina, Croatia and the former Yugoslav Republic of Macedonia, stating that such an arrangement would respond to the wishes of the three countries, without compromising the cost-effectiveness and efficiency of an integrated United Nations peace-keeping presence.

On 31 March, the Security Council replaced UNPROFOR with three separate but interlinked peace-keeping operations: UNPROFOR in Bosnia and Herzegovina, the **United Nations Confidence Restoration Operation in Croatia (UNCRO)**, and the **United Nations Preventive Deployment Force (UNPREDEP)** in the former Yugoslav Republic of Macedonia.

ARMS REGULATION AND DISARMAMENT

Since its foundation, the United Nations has dealt with arms limitation and disarmament as one of the priority issues in international relations. The basic objectives of disarmament have remained constant through the years, but the approaches to the issue and the scope of deliberations have changed, reflecting varying political realities and international conditions.

At the outset, the approach was broad. Throughout the 1950s, the objective was the regulation, limitation and balanced reduction of all armed forces and armaments through a coordinated, comprehensive programme. In 1959, the concept of general and complete disarmament was first included in the General Assembly's agenda as a separate item. In the early 1960s, plans to achieve general and complete disarmament were submitted by the United States and the Soviet Union.

With little progress towards agreement on such a programme, starting in the late 1950s impetus was given to a "partial approach". It was felt that the achievement of some first, limited steps would increase confidence and create a more favourable atmosphere for comprehensive agreements. Devoting parallel and, at times, primary attention to "collateral" measures, it was hoped, would facilitate the achievement of general and complete disarmament.

But by the mid-1960s, it became widely accepted that general and complete disarmament was not attainable in any short or specific period. Since then, it has been accepted that general and complete disarmament should be regarded as the ultimate goal, with an increasing concentration on partial objectives.

A new disarmament strategy was developed in the late 1970s. At the initiative of the non-aligned countries, which sought to give new impetus to multilateral disarmament efforts, the General Assembly in 1978 held its first special session devoted to disarmament. The session's Final Document, adopted unanimously, set out a new strategy comprising agreed goals, principles and priorities in arms limitation and disarmament, as well as a programme of action leading towards the realization of the ultimate objective of general and complete disarmament. It also specified measures to strengthen the multilateral machinery that dealt with disarmament issues within the United Nations system.

The General Assembly met again in 1982 and 1988 in special sessions devoted to disarmament, but was unable to reach agreement on implementing the programme of action. It did agree, however, in 1982 to formalize the dissemination of information on disarmament issues as a distinct activity of the United Nations, and established the United Nations Disarmament Information Programme. Efforts continued to find ways of advancing a comprehensive programme of disarmament and of achieving specific measures of arms limitation, disarmament and confidence-building.

United Nations machinery. The United Nations machinery dealing with disarmament and related international security issues was established by the Charter and subsequent decisions of the General Assembly and the Security Council. Over the years, it has undergone changes which have reflected the prevailing circumstances in international relations.

The General Assembly is the chief deliberative organ of the United Nations in this field. It works through two subsidiary bodies open to all Members: the Disarmament and International Security Committee (First Committee), which meets while the Assembly is in session and deals with all disarmament items on its agenda, and the United Nations Disarmament Commission, a specialized deliberative body which meets outside of the Assembly session and focuses on a few specific issues at a time.

The Conference on Disarmament, which has a limited number of members, is the single global disarmament negotiating forum of the international community. It considers items related to nuclear and other weapons of mass destruction as well as, more recently, transparency in conventional weapons. After long negotiations, it concluded the 1993 Chemical Weapons Convention. It is currently negotiating a comprehensive nuclear-test-ban treaty.

The Conference has a unique relationship with the United Nations: it defines its own rules of procedure and develops its own agenda, taking into account the recommendations of the General Assembly, and reports to the Assembly annually.

Disarmament efforts. In the past decades, a wide variety of ideas and initiatives were put forward, particularly in the field of nuclear disarmament, both within and outside the United Nations. By and large, they reflected the perceptions of their proponents of what constituted the main challenges to international peace and security and were designed to cope with them accordingly, either as integral parts of the comprehensive approach or as "partial" measures on their own. These perceptions as a rule reflected the military-strategic thinking of the major alliances and political groups, including some individual States not belonging to these groups. For instance, the non-aligned countries were concerned largely with the dangers stemming from nuclear weapons and the nuclear arms race. Members of the Warsaw Treaty Organization underlined the issue of nuclear disarmament and called for a range of measures. Members of the North Atlantic Treaty Organization (NATO), on the other hand, in advocating disarmament measures, stressed the need to maintain the overall military balance and stability in international relations through credible deterrence.

Reflecting this wide spectrum of positions, the disarmament agenda of the international community contained diverse and often contentious measures. Most of them dealt with various aspects of nuclear weapons; the cessation of the nuclear arms race and nuclear disarmament; the cessation of the improvement and development of nuclear weapons and of their production; a comprehensive programme for the phased reduction of nuclear weapons leading to their complete elimination; a "nuclear freeze"; and a cut-off in the production of fissile material.

Other proposals ranged from a general prohibition of the use or threat of use of nuclear weapons to a prohibition of their first use and the prohibition of certain types of nuclear weapons. Over the years, prominence was given to initiatives aimed at prohibiting all nuclear weapons tests. The question of giving to non-nuclear-weapon States security guarantees against the use or threat of use of nuclear weapons has been the subject of continuing discussion, most recently in the framework of the Security Council.

Besides seeking to reduce the nuclear weapons threat, the international community also made efforts to deal with other weapons of mass destruction. Various proposals aimed at banning the use of chemical weapons and called for their global and comprehensive prohibition. Further areas of concern related to biological weapons, new types of weapons of mass destruction, radiological weapons, limitation and reduction of conventional weapons and international arms transfers, the prevention of an arms race in outer space, curbing the naval arms race, naval armaments and disarmament, and reduction of military budgets.

Although few proposals led to actual negotiations and concrete agreements, such agreements as were concluded commit Governments to significant arms limitation and disarmament measures.

♦   In the nuclear field, among the most important multilateral agreements were the 1963 Treaty Banning Nuclear Weapon

Tests in the Atmosphere, in Outer Space and under Water (Partial Test-Ban Treaty) and the 1968 Treaty on the Non-Proliferation of Nuclear Weapons (Non-Proliferation Treaty). At the regional level, the 1959 Antarctic Treaty, the 1967 Treaty for the Prohibition of Nuclear Weapons in Latin America and the Caribbean (Treaty of Tlatelolco) and the 1985 South Pacific Nuclear Free Zone Treaty (Treaty of Rarotonga) keep large areas of the globe free of nuclear weapons.

♦ A number of bilateral treaties were concluded between the United States and the Soviet Union. These comprise the 1972 Treaty on the Limitation of Anti-Ballistic Missile Systems (ABM Treaty) and Interim Agreement on Certain Measures with respect to the Limitation of Strategic Offensive Arms (SALT I); the 1973 Agreement on the Prevention of Nuclear War; the 1974 Treaty on the Limitation of Underground Nuclear-Weapon Tests (Threshold Test-Ban Treaty); the 1976 Treaty on Underground Explosions for Peaceful Purposes (PNE Treaty); the 1979 Treaty on the Limitation of Strategic Offensive Arms (SALT II); and the 1987 Treaty on the Elimination of Intermediate- and Shorter-Range Missiles (INF Treaty).

♦ Several multilateral agreements were concluded on weapons of mass destruction, the demilitarization/denuclearization of some areas, and activities affecting the environment. Agreements included the 1967 Treaty Governing the Activities of States in the Exploration and Use of Outer Space, including the Moon and Other Celestial Bodies (Outer Space Treaty); the 1971 Treaty on the Prohibition of the Emplacement of Nuclear Weapons and Other Weapons of Mass Destruction on the Sea-bed and the Ocean Floor and in the Subsoil Thereof (Sea-bed Treaty); the 1972 Convention on the Prohibition of the Development, Production and Stockpiling of Bacteriological (Biological) and Toxin Weapons and on Their Destruction (BW Convention); the 1977 Convention on the Prohibition of Military or Any Other Hostile Use of Environmental Modification Techniques (ENMOD) Convention; and the 1979 Agreement Governing the Activities of States on the Moon and Other Celestial Bodies (Agreement on Celestial Bodies).

♦ In the area of conventional weapons, the only global agreement was the 1981 Convention on Prohibitions or Restrictions on the Use of Certain Conventional Weapons Which May Be Deemed to Be Excessively Injurious or to Have Indiscriminate Effects (Inhumane Weapons Convention, dealing with land-mines, booby-traps, incendiary weapons and others). At the regional level, progress was achieved, specifically in Europe, with the 1975 Helsinki confidence-building measures, the 1986 Stockholm Document, and the 1990 Treaty on Conventional Armed Forces in Europe (CFE Treaty) and Vienna Document on confidence-building measures.

Since 1990, arms limitation and disarmament efforts have been pursued in a greatly altered international environment marked by contradictory trends. With the dissolution of the Soviet Union and profound political changes in Eastern Europe, more than four decades of adverse ideological and military competition came to an end, creating unprecedented opportunities for progress in disarmament. The end of the cold war, however, has by no means removed the risk of armed conflict in a world newly characterized by potential regional arms races and the accumulation of ever more destructive weaponry by a growing number of countries. Regional instabilities, the emergence of ethnic and religious tensions and the continuing risk of proliferation of both weapons of mass destruction and conventional weapons have created a serious challenge to international stability. This has rendered disarmament a more urgent and necessary element of the system of international peace and security.

Since the end of the cold war, substantial progress towards disarmament has been made on various long-standing issues. With regard to nuclear weapons, the two major nuclear Powers concluded two treaties on the reduction of their strategic offensive arms (START I in 1991 and START II in 1993). The 1995 Conference of parties to the Treaty on the Non-Proliferation of Nuclear Weapons reviewed the operation of the Treaty and decided on its indefinite extension. In 1994, multilateral negotiations began on a comprehensive nuclear-test-ban treaty and a committee was established to negotiate a cessation of the production of fissionable material for weapons purposes.

With regard to other weapons of mass destruction, the Chemical Weapons Convention, which prohibits the production, use and spread of chemical weapons and provides for the destruction of existing stockpiles, was signed in 1993. In 1994, a special Conference of States parties to the Biological Weapons Convention established an Ad Hoc Group to draft proposals, including possible verification measures, to strengthen the Convention.

With regard to conventional weapons, a group of experts of States parties to the Inhumane Weapons Convention concluded preparations for a review conference of that treaty, giving priority to the question of anti-personnel land-mines. The review conference of the Convention is to be held in Vienna in 1995.

New disarmament issues have been gaining prominence. Among them are the exchange of objective information on military matters and the transparency of military expenditures and of arms transfers. In connection with transfers, the General Assembly in 1992 established a Register of Conventional Arms to which Member States may report transfers of certain categories of weapons. Other new issues are conversion and the safe and cost-effective destruction of weapons. The question of verifying compliance with the wide range of existing agreements has also taken on many new aspects.

United Nations Institute for Disarmament Research (UNIDIR)

The United Nations Institute for Disarmament Research (UNIDIR) is an autonomous institution within the framework of the United Nations. It was established by the General Assembly in 1980 to undertake independent research on disarmament and related problems, particularly international security. It is mainly financed by voluntary contributions from States and public and private organizations. UNIDIR aims to:

♦ provide the international community with more diversified and complete data on problems relating to international security, the arms race and disarmament, particularly in the nuclear field, so as to facilitate progress, through negotiations, towards greater security and economic and social development;

♦ promote informed participation by all States in disarmament efforts;

♦ assist negotiations on disarmament and efforts to ensure greater international security at a progressively lower level of armaments, particularly nuclear armaments, by means of objective and factual studies and analyses; and

♦   carry out research on disarmament so as to provide insight into the problems involved and stimulate initiatives for new negotiations.

UNIDIR organizes conferences, publishes papers and implements projects. Cooperation with research institutes continues with the development of UNIDIR's computerized information and documentation database service, the UNIDIR Newsletter, and regional conferences. A fellowship programme enables scholars from developing countries to do research at the Institute.

OUTER SPACE

United Nations interest in the peaceful uses of outer space was first expressed in 1957, soon after the launching of the first man-made satellite, and has grown steadily with the advance of space technology. The Organization's concern is that space be used for peaceful purposes and that the benefits from space activities be shared by all nations.

The focal point of United Nations action is the General Assembly's **Committee on the Peaceful Uses of Outer Space**, set up in 1959. Reflecting its interest in both the legal and other aspects of international cooperation regarding outer space, the Committee has a Legal Subcommittee and a Scientific and Technical Subcommittee.

Discussions in the Legal Subcommittee have resulted in five legal instruments, all of which have entered into force:

♦   the 1966 Treaty on Principles Governing the Activities of States in the Exploration and Use of Outer Space, including the Moon and Other Celestial Bodies provides that space exploration shall be carried out for the benefit of all countries, irrespective of their degree of economic or scientific development; that outer space shall be the province of all humankind, free for exploration and use by all States on a basis of equality and in accordance with international law, and not subject to national appropriation; and that celestial bodies shall be used exclusively for peaceful purposes. Parties to the Treaty undertake not to place nuclear weapons or other weapons of mass destruction in orbit. The Treaty also provides for the international responsibility of States parties for all national activities in outer space, whether carried out by governmental agencies or by non-governmental entities;

♦ the 1967 Agreement on the Rescue of Astronauts, the Return of Astronauts and the Return of Objects Launched into Outer Space provides for aiding the crews of spacecraft in the event of accident or emergency landing, and establishes procedures for returning a space object or its components found beyond the territory of the launching authority to that authority;

♦ the 1971 Convention on International Liability for Damage Caused by Space Objects provides that the launching State is liable for damage caused by its space objects on the earth's surface or to aircraft in flight and also to space objects of another State or persons or property on board such objects;

♦ the 1974 Convention on Registration of Objects Launched into Outer Space provides that launching States shall maintain registries of space objects and furnish specified information on each space object launched, for inclusion in a central United Nations Register;

♦ the 1979 Agreement Governing Activities of States on the Moon and Other Celestial Bodies elaborates the principles relating to the Moon and other celestial bodies set out in the 1966 Treaty, and sets up the basis for the future regulation of exploration and exploitation of natural resources thereof.

In 1982, the General Assembly adopted Principles governing the use by States of artificial earth satellites for international direct television broadcasting, taking into consideration that such use has international political, economic, social and cultural implications. In 1986, it adopted Principles relating to remote sensing of the earth from outer space, which stated that such activities were to be conducted for the benefit of all countries, in accordance with international law, with respect for the sovereignty of all States and peoples over their own natural resources, and for the rights and interests of other States. Remote sensing was to be used to preserve the environment and to protect humankind from natural disasters.

Other legal work of the Committee has included elaborating principles on the use of nuclear power sources in outer space, the definition and delimitation of outer space and the character and utilization of the geostationary orbit, and examining the legal application of the principle that outer space should be used for the benefit of all countries.

In the scientific and technical fields, the Committee has given priority to implementing the United Nations Programme on Space Applications, which started in 1969. The Programme carries out training courses and seminars on space science and technology, often co-sponsored by Governments and international organizations; fellowship programmes for training of space technologists and applications specialists, sponsored by Governments and national space agencies; and technical advisory services to Member States, particularly the developing countries, and to the specialized agencies.

The General Assembly, in 1990, endorsed the Committee's recommendation that the United Nations should lead an effort to establish regional centres for space science and technology education. The centres aim at developing skills and knowledge of university educators and research and application scientists in those aspects of space science and technology that contribute to sustainable development.

The Committee has also given priority to the coordination of outer space activities within the organizations of the United Nations system, several of which carry out projects using space technology for the economic and social development of countries. Activities are carried out in remote sensing, communications, meteorology, basic space science, and use of space technology for maritime communications and air navigation.

In addition, the Committee makes recommendations to the General Assembly on questions relating to remote sensing of the earth by satellites, the use of nuclear power sources in outer space, space transportation systems and their implications for future activities in space, the physical nature and technical attributes of the geostationary orbit, life sciences (including space medicine), planetary exploration and astronomy, space communications for development, and spin-off benefits of space technology.

Two major world conferences on outer space have been organized by the United Nations—the First and Second United

Nations Conference on the Exploration and Peaceful Uses of Outer Space, held in Vienna in 1968 and 1982. The first conference examined the practical benefits deriving from space research and exploration, and the extent to which non-space countries, especially developing countries, might enjoy them. The second conference, known as UNISPACE 82, reflected the growing involvement of all nations in outer space activities; assessed the state of space science and technology; considered the applications of space technology for economic and social development; and discussed international cooperative programmes related to space and the role of the United Nations.

UNISPACE 82 made recommendations, endorsed in 1982 by the General Assembly, on matters such as the use of space technology, remote sensing of the earth by satellites, the use of the geostationary orbit, and direct television broadcasting by satellites. The Committee on Outer Space has directed the implementation of these recommendations.

In 1989, the General Assembly endorsed the international initiative to celebrate 1992 as International Space Year (ISY) and agreed that the United Nations should play a role. Activities focused on management of the resources of the Earth and its environment, education programmes and public education.

Recent scientific, technical and political developments could further promote international cooperation related to outer space. In the light of these developments, the convening of a third UNISPACE conference is being discussed by the Committee and its subsidiary bodies.

CHAPTER 3

ECONOMIC AND SOCIAL DEVELOPMENT

Most of the work of the United Nations, excluding peace-keeping operations, goes into programmes aimed at carrying out the pledge of the Charter to "promote higher standards of living, full employment and conditions of economic and social progress and development". The vast bulk of this endeavour is concentrated in the developing countries, where two thirds of the world's people live.

Since 1960, the General Assembly has proclaimed four United Nations Development Decades to focus international action on policies and programmes for development. The Assembly has also adopted a number of declarations, programmes of action and development strategies designed to strengthen international cooperation for development.

Giving practical expression to these broad strategies and concerns has been largely the responsibility of programmes directly under the responsibility of the Economic and Social Council, such as the United Nations Development Programme and the World Food Programme (see below) and the family of specialized agencies (see Chapter 8).

Over the past 50 years, these efforts have profoundly affected the lives and well-being of millions of people throughout the world. While every Development Decade has emphasized certain issues of particular concern at that time, the United Nations has invariably stressed the need to ensure overall progress to meet its goals of reducing poverty and redressing inequalities between rich and poor—both between and within countries.

STRIVING FOR A DEVELOPMENT CONSENSUS

Before the end of the First United Nations Development Decade (1961-1970), the need for a world plan of action or "strategy" for development became evident. The General Assembly therefore adopted, in 1970, an International Development Strategy for the Second United Nations Development Decade (1971-1980), an important step in promoting international economic cooperation on a just and equitable basis.

In 1974, the General Assembly adopted the Declaration and Programme of Action on the Establishment of a New International Economic Order (NIEO), which was based on "equity, sovereignty, interdependence, common interest and cooperation among States, irrespective of their economic and social systems". To further the NIEO, the General Assembly adopted, in 1974, the Charter of Economic Rights and Duties of States, stipulating that every State has the right to exercise full permanent sovereignty over its wealth and natural resources.

In 1979, the General Assembly called for the launching of global negotiations on international economic cooperation for development. The following year, the Assembly adopted unanimously an International Development Strategy for the Third United Nations Development Decade (1981-1990).

At its special session in 1990, the General Assembly adopted unanimously the Declaration on International Economic Cooperation, in particular the Revitalization of Economic Growth and Development of the Developing Countries.

The Declaration emphasized the importance of a supportive international economic environment, appropriate domestic policies and human resources development. It introduced new concerns such as the integration of Eastern Europe in the world economy, protection of the environment, reduction of military expenses and regional economic integration.

The adoption of the Declaration laid the foundation for the adoption by the General Assembly later in 1990 of the International Development Strategy for the Fourth United Nations Development Decade (1991-2000).

The Strategy focuses on the mutually reinforcing relationship between reactivation of growth and development on the one hand, and the improvement of the human condition on the other. Regarding the latter, the Strategy singles out four priority areas: poverty and hunger, human resources and institutional development, population, and environment. For the reactivation of growth and development, the Strategy identifies four issues that need to be addressed urgently: external debt, development finance, international trade, and commodity markets. The Strategy also recognizes the need for developing countries to modernize and transform their industry and agri-culture and make use of advances in science and technology.

Strengthening the relationship between economic growth and human welfare has become the principal theme of develop-ment for the 1990s.

The United Nations has long recognized the centrality of social development. Hence the many United Nations pro-grammes focusing on social issues, such as population, crime prevention and drug control, or on special groups, such as women, children, youth, the elderly, disabled persons and the family (see below.)

The centrality of social development has been combined with a growing concern on the environmental dimension of human progress, and the urgent need to adopt sustainable development strategies which ensure that current policies do not endanger resources for future generations.

To advance a global consensus on development priorities and to give political momentum to action programmes in specific areas, the United Nations has initiated a round of international conferences focusing on children (1990), environ-ment and development (1992), population and development (1994), social development (1995), the advancement of women (1995), and human settlements (1996).

AN AGENDA FOR DEVELOPMENT

Stating that the international community needed a new, com-pelling vision of the future, the Secretary-General issued in May 1994 *An Agenda for Development*,* a blueprint for a new conceptualization of development and a re-energized drive to improve the human condition. The request for such a report, recommending ways of enhancing the United Nations role in international cooperation for development, had been made by the General Assembly in December 1992.

In the Secretary-General's formulation, each of the five dimensions of development—peace, economy, environment, so-cial justice and democracy—are an integral part of the whole.

---

*An Agenda for Development, DPI/1622/DEV, E.95.I.16, 1995.

Economic growth is the engine of development, and to ensure this growth the Secretary-General argues for pragmatic policies which take advantage of the efficiency of markets, since Governments can no longer be assumed to be paramount economic agents. But Governments must continue to provide regulatory frameworks to economic activity. Economic growth requires investment in human development, which is "investment in long-term competitiveness." And economic growth can only be sustainable if it promotes employment, poverty reduction and improved patterns of income distribution.

Peace, justice and democracy are essential for development, the Secretary-General states. Without peace, human energies cannot be productively employed. Without social justice, mounting inequalities will threaten social cohesion. And without political participation in freedom, development will remain fragile and always at risk.

The United Nations, and in particular the Economic and Social Council, has an important role to play in setting development priorities and coordinating activities and assistance, the Secretary-General says. The revitalized Council could significantly contribute to greater policy coordination within the United Nations system as a whole.

In November 1994, in response to comments and views by Member States, the Secretary-General submitted to the General Assembly a set of *Recommendations*** on *An Agenda for Development.*

The *Recommendations* are based on four broad concepts: development should be recognized as the foremost and most far-reaching task of our time; development must be seen in its many dimensions—peace, the economy, environmental protection, social justice and democracy; the emerging consensus on the priority and dimensions of development should find expression in a new framework for international cooperation; and within this new framework, the United Nations must play a major role in both policy leadership and operations.

The General Assembly in December 1994 established a working group to further elaborate an action-oriented Agenda for Development.

**An Agenda for Development, DPI/1622/DEV, E.95.I.16, 1995.

WORLD SUMMIT FOR SOCIAL DEVELOPMENT, 1995

The awareness of the social dimensions of development led the General Assembly in 1992 to convene a World Summit for Social Development at the level of Heads of State or Government. The Assembly decided that the summit should address the core issues, affecting all societies: enhancing social integration, particularly of the disadvantaged and marginalized groups; alleviating and reducing poverty; and expanding employment.

At the Summit, held in March 1995 in Copenhagen, Denmark, leaders from 117 countries pledged themselves to confront "profound social problems" facing the world's disadvantaged, particularly poverty, unemployment and social exclusion. The meeting adopted a Declaration and a Programme of Action recommending measures aimed at eliminating inequalities within and among countries and fostering social development policies and programmes.

In the Declaration, world leaders agreed on a set of commitments to:

♦ eradicate absolute poverty by a target date to be set by each country:

♦ support full employment as a basic policy goal;

♦ promote social integration based on the protection of all human rights;

♦ achieve equality and equity between women and men;

♦ accelerate the development of Africa and the least developed countries;

♦ ensure that structural adjustment programmes include social development goals;

♦ increase the resources allocated to social development;

♦ create an environment enabling people to achieve social development;

♦ attain universal access to education and primary health care; and

♦ strengthen cooperation for social development through the United Nations.

Enhancing international cooperation for the betterment of living conditions in the world was a central topic. Major emphasis was on the importance of finding a durable solution to the external debt problems of developing countries, and on the need to reallocate resources in line with social development priorities.

AFRICA—A UNITED NATIONS PRIORITY

Concern by the United Nations system and the Member States over the critical economic situation in Africa led to the convening in 1986 of a General Assembly special session on Africa. The Assembly adopted the United Nations Programme of Action for African Economic Recovery and Development, 1986-1990, which sought to mobilize political and financial support for economic reforms. Reviewing the Programme of Action in 1991, the Assembly concluded that the critical economic situation in Africa continued, and called for a New Agenda for the Development of Africa in the 1990s.

The General Assembly unanimously adopted the New Agenda in December 1991. Its objective is an average real growth rate in gross domestic product of at least 6 per cent a year throughout the 1990s, in order for Africa to achieve economic growth and equitable development, to increase income and to eradicate poverty.

The New Agenda accords special attention to human development and increased employment, and to programmes which promote rapid progress in life expectancy, the integration of women in development, child and maternal health, and nutrition, water and sanitation, education and shelter.

ECONOMIC AND SOCIAL ACTIVITIES

The United Nations family of organizations facilitates the work of development in a multitude of ways, under the overall coordination of the Economic and Social Council.

To help Governments establish a more effective framework for development, the United Nations and its specialized agencies offer support in the preparation of national development plans with the aim of ensuring balanced economic and social progress and the best use of available human, physical and financial resources. The Organization and its agencies help developing countries mobilize the funds needed to pay for development programmes, both by increasing their export earnings and by attracting outside capital under terms they can afford.

Increasing priority is being given to programmes dealing with human resource development, eradication of poverty, population activities, the advancement of women, drug abuse control, crime prevention, the application of science and technology to development, and protection of the environment. Major programmes of the United Nations system are geared to population groups—children, youth, the elderly, disabled persons, migrants and refugees.

Development programmes for individual countries are carried out at the request of the Governments concerned. Other programmes are implemented on a regional basis by the United Nations Economic and Social Commissions—for Africa, for Asia and the Pacific, for Western Asia, for Latin America and the Caribbean, and for Europe.

In 1993, expenditures on operational activities for development (development grants) of the United Nations system amounted to $4.9 billion. Of this amount, 40.4 per cent went to Africa, 20.1 per cent to Asia and the Pacific, 12.3 per cent to the Americas, 4.7 per cent to Europe and 4.4 per cent to Western Asia; 18 per cent was interregional. The least developed countries received 43 per cent of such assistance. By sector, the largest share went to health, followed by humanitarian assistance and disaster management, agriculture, forestry and fisheries, and general development.

Coordinating machinery. Under the Charter, the Economic and Social Council (ECOSOC) is the principal body coordinating the economic and social work of the United Nations and its specialized agencies and institutions. The Council is also the central forum for discussing international economic and social issues and for formulating policy recommendations.

The 32-member **Commission on Social Development**, a functional commission of ECOSOC, was established to advise ECOSOC on social policies. Meeting biennially, it focuses on policies designed to promote social progress, setting goals, programme priorities and social research in areas affecting social and economic development.

Within the United Nations Secretariat, the Department for Policy Coordination and Sustainable Development provides support for the coordinating and policy-making functions of

ECOSOC and its subsidiary bodies. Its activities include policy development, integration of the economic, social and environmental dimensions of such major policy issues as economic growth and adjustment, poverty, hunger and malnutrition, the rights of women, the elderly, children, disabled persons and migrant workers.

The Department for Economic and Social Information and Policy Analysis serves as the lead unit for economic and social information within the United Nations. It focuses on the compilation and dissemination of economic and social statistics; the analysis of long-term trends, including population trends; the elaboration of projections; the global monitoring and assessment of economic and social policies; and the identification of new and emerging issues requiring attention by the international community.

The Department for Development Support and Management Services serves as a focal point for providing management services for technical cooperation. It also acts as an executing agency, placing emphasis on the development of institutions and enterprises and the development of human resources. Technical cooperation focuses particularly on the requirements of the least developed countries, as well as those of economies in transition.

The following pages outline the various programmes of the United Nations in support of economic and social development. The activities of the intergovernmental agencies related to the United Nations are described in Chapter 8.

United Nations Development Programme (UNDP)

The United Nations Development Programme (UNDP) is the United Nations' main source of grants for sustainable human development—development that is both people-centred and respects the environment. It was created in 1965 through a merger of two programmes for United Nations technical cooperation. Funds come from the voluntary contributions of Member States of the United Nations and its agencies, which provide about $1 billion yearly to UNDP's central resources. A 36-member Executive Board composed of both developed and developing countries approves major programmes and policy decisions.

UNDP has three overriding goals:

♦ to help the United Nations become a powerful and cohesive force for sustainable human development;

♦ to focus its own resources on a series of objectives central to sustainable human development: poverty elimination, environmental regeneration, job creation, and advancement of women;

♦ to strengthen international cooperation for sustainable human development and serve as a major substantive resource on how to achieve it.

Through a worldwide network of 136 offices, UNDP works with Governments, organizations of civil society and people in some 175 developing countries and territories. To execute the projects and programmes it supports, it draws upon developing countries' national technical capacities, as well as the expertise of over 30 international and regional agencies and non-governmental organizations (NGOs).

People are at the centre of all UNDP activities, which promote growth with equity. The focus is on building countries' capacity for poverty elimination and grass-roots development; environmental conservation and sustainable use of natural resources; management development; technical cooperation among developing countries; transfer and adaptation of technology; and the advancement of women. Entrepreneurship is promoted as a means of creating jobs and reducing poverty. Global and interregional programmes address worldwide issues, such as food security, safe motherhood, and HIV/AIDS.

A yearly *Human Development Report*, prepared for UNDP by an independent team of consultants, assists the international community in developing new, practical and pragmatic concepts, measures and policy instruments for promoting people-oriented development.

UNDP normally plays the chief coordinating role for operational development activities undertaken by the whole United Nations system. This includes administering special-purpose funds such as the United Nations Capital Development Fund (UNCDF), the United Nations Volunteers (UNV), and the United Nations Development Fund for Women (UNIFEM) (see page 168.).

UNDP assists developing countries in preparing for major

United Nations conferences—for example the 1992 Conference on Environment and Development, the 1995 World Summit for Social Development and the 1995 World Conference on Women. It then assists those countries in carrying out the action plans of those conferences, and in mobilizing the additional resources needed to do so.

With the World Bank and the United Nations Environment Programme, UNDP is one of the managing partners of the Global Environment Facility (GEF), through which it is helping countries translate global concerns about ozone layer depletion, biodiversity loss, international water pollution and global warming into local action plans (see page 154).

In emergency situations, UNDP works closely with other United Nations agencies to ensure a relief-to-development continuum. (See also Humanitarian Assistance in Chapter 6.) Its "preventive development" programmes in such areas as poverty elimination, good governance and human rights protection help to create conditions for lasting peace.

United Nations Volunteers (UNV)

Established in 1970 by the General Assembly, the United Nations Volunteers programme (UNV) is administered by UNDP and funded by UNDP and United Nations agencies, as well as by donations from Governments.

Some 4,000 UNV specialists, field workers and national volunteers serve annually in over 130 countries. They work in development programmes of Governments, assisted by UNDP and United Nations specialized agencies, or in programmes initiated and executed by UNV itself. A hallmark of the UNV programme is its support to community-based initiatives. Today, more than 20 per cent of all UNVs are involved in grass-roots projects. UNVs are also active in humanitarian relief work, and are increasingly involved in United Nations operations for peace-building and democracy, especially in electoral work and human rights promotion.

Administered by UNV, the UNISTAR programme (United Nations Short-Term Advisory Resources) assigns executives and technical experts to advise private and public sector entrepreneurs. The TOKTEN programme (Transfer of Knowledge

Through Expatriate Nationals) enables expatriates to assist in their countries of origin.

United Nations Volunteers are drawn from more than 120 nationalities; three quarters come from developing countries, thus underlining UNV's emphasis on South-South cooperation. Fifty-five per cent of all UNVs work in Africa, another 25 per cent in Asia, while the remaining UNVs serve in Latin America and the Caribbean, Europe and the Commonwealth of Independent States and the Arab States.

Professional qualification is a precondition for UNVs: not only do they all hold degrees or diplomas from technical institutions or universities, but they must also have several years of working experience. More than half have worked for more than ten years before joining UNV, and the average age is 40. Their contracts are normally for two years, with shorter assignments for electoral or humanitarian missions. UNVs receive a modest living allowance, sufficient to cover expenses in their country of assignment, rather than a salary at market rate.

In recognition of volunteer activities worldwide, 5 December is observed annually as International Volunteer Day.

TRADE AND DEVELOPMENT

United Nations Conference on Trade and Development (UNCTAD)

The first United Nations Conference on Trade and Development (UNCTAD), held at Geneva in 1964, led to the establishment of UNCTAD as a permanent organ of the General Assembly in December 1964. Subsequent sessions of the Conference were held in 1968 (New Delhi), 1972 (Santiago), 1976 (Nairobi), 1979 (Manila), 1983 (Belgrade), 1987 (Geneva) and 1992 (Cartagena).

UNCTAD has 188 member States, including the 185 Members of the United Nations. The UNCTAD secretariat is located in Geneva.

UNCTAD is the principal organ of the General Assembly in the field of trade and development. Its mandate is to promote international trade, particularly that of the developing countries in order to accelerate their economic development. UNCTAD's functions comprise policy analysis; intergovernmental deliberations, consensus building and negotiation; monitoring, implementation and follow-up; and technical cooperation.

At the eighth session of UNCTAD in 1992, the Conference adopted the "Cartagena Commitment", which outlines a fresh approach to both long-standing and emerging development issues.

The thrust of UNCTAD's endeavours, as embodied in the Cartagena Commitment, is based on the recognition of the mutual interests among countries from different regions and at different levels of development. Emphasis is placed on the need both for effective national policies and for international cooperation aimed at improving the external economic environment. Policy recommendations incorporate novel concepts in the development dialogue which have come to the fore at the United Nations, particularly "good management" at both the national and international levels, the role of the market, the emphasis on poverty alleviation and human development, and the importance of democracy and human rights as factors of development. The Commitment provides guidelines to expand UNCTAD's work on sustainable development, focusing on issues such as the interaction between trade matters and environmental policies, and the impact of patterns of production and consumption on sustainable development.

Negotiations under UNCTAD auspices have resulted in:
♦ agreement on a Generalized System of Preferences (GSP), thanks to which over $70 billion worth of developing countries' exports receive preferential treatment in most developed country markets every year (1971);
♦ agreement on a Global System of Trade Preferences among developing countries (1989);
♦ agreement on a set of principles and rules for the control of restrictive business practices (1980);
♦ international commodity agreements, including those for cocoa, sugar, natural rubber, jute, tropical timber, tin, olive oil and wheat;
♦ intergovernmental commodity study groups, involving consumers and producers, including those for iron ore, tungsten, copper and nickel;
♦ the Common Fund for Commodities, established to provide

financial backing for the operation of international stocks and for research and development projects in the area of commodities (1989);

♦   alleviation of low-income developing country debt: more than 50 of the poorer developing countries have benefited from debt relief of over $6.5 billion since 1978, when a resolution on the retroactive adjustment of terms of the Official Development Assistance (ODA) debt of low-income developing countries was approved;

♦   guidelines for international action in the area of debt rescheduling (1980);

♦   agreement on a Substantial New Programme of Action for the Least Developed Countries (1981) and on the Programme of Action for the Least Developed Countries for the 1990s (1990); and

♦   United Nations Conventions in the area of maritime transport: on a Code of Conduct for Liner Conferences (1974), on International Carriage of Goods by Sea (1978), on International Multimodal Transport of Goods (1980), on Conditions for Registration of Ships (1986), and on Maritime Liens and Mortgages (1993).

UNCTAD's intergovernmental machinery comprises the Conference, which is the organization's highest policy-making body, the Trade and Development Board and its subsidiary bodies serviced by a permanent secretariat.

UNCTAD's executive body is the Trade and Development Board. It meets twice a year, in autumn and spring. At the first part of its annual session it addresses a topic relating to the international implications of macro-economic policies and issues concerning interdependence, using UNCTAD's annual *Trade and Development Report* as background; at the other part, it considers a topic relating to trade policies, structural adjustment and economic reforms. The Board also examines UNCTAD's contribution to the United Nations New Agenda for the Development of Africa in the 1990s (see page 138), and reviews implementation of the Programme of Action for the Least Developed Countries for the 1990s. The Board has 138 member States and is open to all UNCTAD members.

UNCTAD VIII in 1992 established four Standing Committees: on Commodities, on Poverty Alleviation, on Economic Cooperation among Developing Countries, and on Developing Services Sectors: Services, Shipping and Insurance.

In 1994, the Board established three new Ad Hoc Working Groups on Trade, Environment and Development; the Role of Enterprises in Development; and Trading Opportunities in the New International Trading Context. Other main bodies include the Special Committee on Preferences and the Intergovernmental Group of Experts on Restrictive Business Practices.

All UNCTAD member States are eligible to participate in the work of these bodies. In line with the Cartagena Commitment, external actors such as enterprises, trade unions, the academic community and NGOs are closely associated with UNCTAD's work.

The General Assembly has assigned to the UNCTAD secretariat responsibility for the substantive servicing of two bodies:

The **Commission on International Investment and Transnational Corporations** (a Commission of UNCTAD's Trade and Development Board), which is the focal point within the United Nations system on foreign direct investment and transnational corporations. Meeting annually, the Commission seeks to further understanding of the nature of transnational corporations; to secure international agreements; and to strengthen the capacity of developing countries in their dealings with transnational corporations through an integrated approach including research, information and technical assistance. A subsidiary body of the Commission, the Intergovernmental Working Group of Experts on International Standards of Accounting and Reporting, works to improve the availability and comparability of information disclosed by transnational corporations. (See also Investment and Transnational Corporations, below).

The **Commission on Science and Technology for Development**, which is the focal point within the United Nations system on issues related to science and technology for development. Meeting every two years, the Commission focuses on: technology for small-scale economic activities to address the basic needs of low-income countries; the gender implications of science and technology for developing countries; science and technology and the environment; the contribution of new and emerging technologies to industrialization in developing countries; and information technologies and their role in science and technology, particularly in relation to the needs of developing countries. (See also Science and Technology for Development, below.)

INVESTMENT AND TRANSNATIONAL CORPORATIONS

Transnational corporations are key organizers of economic activity in today's increasingly borderless world. Stretching across national borders, their activities are important for the competitiveness of both home and host countries.

There are more than 37,000 parent firms with over 200,000 foreign affiliates around the world. The sales of foreign affiliates worldwide surpass world exports as the principal means to deliver goods and services to global markets. Since the mid-1980s, direct foreign investment by transnational corporations has grown at unprecedented rates, reaching $225 billion in outflows in 1990 and a stock of over $2.1 trillion. Investment flows to developing countries have increased five-fold, amounting to about $80 billion in 1993 or about the same as total world inflows in 1986. This investment has been accompanied by a transfer of technology and managerial know-how, as well as greater access to global markets through increased inter-firm trade.

To help developing countries and the economies in transition better understand transnational corporations and benefit from their relations with them, the United Nations has offered since 1974 a range of technical and advisory assistance, as well as research and information services through its Programme on Transnational Corporations. The Programme has been carried out since May 1993 by UNCTAD, through its Division on Transnational Corporations and Investment.

With the emergence of foreign direct investment in the 1990s as a dynamic force in the world economy, and increasing attention by Governments to opening up their economies, the Programme has been counselling Governments on broadening and deepening the deregulatory process and on procedures to attract and promote foreign investment. Recent projects include the establishment of investment promotion institutions, the launching of entrepreneurship programmes and the development of strategies to implement privatization schemes. The Division not only assists in formulating legal frameworks for foreign investment; it is also involved in the design of broader economic infrastructure, encompassing company and contract laws and the national charter of accounts, which are vital for creating an environment conducive to marketization and international business operations.

In addition, the Division undertakes:

♦   research on international investment trends, their determinants and implications for host and home countries. Other areas of research include the role of transnational corporations in primary commodities, manufacturing and service sectors, technology transfer and trade, as well as their impact on the environment and the workplace. This work is reported in the annual *World Investment Report* and other studies;

♦   technical cooperation to developing countries and economies in transition seeking to attract international investment and improve their dealings with transnational corporations. Advisory assistance is offered on drafting and revising policies, laws and regulations, and in evaluating and formulating foreign investment and technology projects. The Division also conducts training workshops, seminars and roundtables for country officials, enterprise managers and entrepreneurs; and

♦   information services to Governments and NGOs on all aspects of international investment and transnational corporations.

SCIENCE AND TECHNOLOGY FOR DEVELOPMENT

Since the 1960s, the United Nations has been promoting the practical application of science and technology for the development of its Member States. The United Nations Conference on the Application of Science and Technology for the Development of the Less Developed Areas (Geneva, 1963) focused world attention on accelerating development through the application of advances in science and technology, and on the need to reorient research towards the needs of developing countries. The United Nations Conference on Science and Technology for Development (Vienna, 1979) adopted a Programme of Action designed to put science and technology to work for the economic development of all countries, particularly developing countries.

The programme on science and technology for development has been carried out since May 1993 by UNCTAD, through its Division for Science and Technology, in cooperation with the Department for Policy Coordination and Sustainable Development of the United Nations Secretariat. The Division also acts as the secretariat to the 53-member Commission on Science and Technology for Development, a functional commission of ECOSOC, which provides policy options and recommendations to ECOSOC within the framework of the Vienna Programme of Action and subsequent General Assembly resolutions.

The United Nations Fund for Science and Technology for Development, a trust fund of UNDP, finances a broad range of activities for strengthening the capacities of developing countries.

Within UNDP, the Division for Science, Technology and the Private Sector deals with science and technology related projects. FAO, ILO, UNESCO and UNIDO also address scientific and technological issues within their specific mandates.

The main thrust of the current work on science and technology for development within the United Nations system is in three areas:

♦ **Capacity-building and resource mobilization**. Priority is on fostering endogenous capacity-building in science and technology at the national level, in particular strengthening capacities regarding the acquisition, development, application and diffusion of science and technology;

♦ **Technology assessment and information services**. This area emphasizes networking among institutions to assess the potential and risks of new technologies for use in developing countries;

♦ **Investment and technology**. The main focus is on the interrelationship between technology, trade in goods and services, investments, finance and the environment.

SUSTAINABLE DEVELOPMENT

The United Nations has played a major role in defining and promoting the concept of "sustainable development"— development which "meets the needs of the present without compromising the ability of future generations to meet their own needs," in the words of the World Commission on Environment and Development, established by the General Assembly in 1983. The goal of sustainable development guides the overall action of the United Nations for economic and social progress.

United Nations Environment Programme (UNEP)

Established as a result of the United Nations Conference on the Human Environment (Stockholm, 1972), the United Nations Environment Programme (UNEP) was the first United Nations agency to be based in a developing country. It has its headquarters in Nairobi, Kenya.

UNEP's mission is to provide leadership and encourage partnerships in caring for the environment by enabling nations and peoples to improve their quality of life without compromising that of future generations. UNEP's catalytic and coordinating role was reinforced in 1992, when the United Nations Conference on Environment and Development (see below) adopted Agenda 21—a comprehensive blueprint for global sustainable development. Major priorities include environmental monitoring, assessment and early-warning; promoting environmental activities throughout the United Nations system; raising public awareness; facilitating information exchange on environmentally sound technologies; and providing technical, legal and institutional advice to Governments for capacity building and sustainable development initiatives.

UNEP has three main components: the 58-member Governing Council, which reports to the General Assembly through the Economic and Social Council; the Environment Fund, a voluntary fund used to finance environmental initiatives; and the Secretariat, headed by the Executive Director, which supports the Governing Council, coordinates elements of the environment programme and administers the Environment Fund.

UNEP derives 7 per cent of its resources from the United Nations regular budget; the rest comes from voluntary governmental contributions to the Environment Fund, which amounted to $65 million in 1994, and project-specific trust funds.

In addition to its basic global and regional responsibilities, UNEP's work programme addresses the sustainable management and use of natural resources; sustainable production and consumption; a better environment for human health and well-being; globalization trends and the environment. Activities cover a wide range of environmental problems, such as atmosphere and climate change, depletion of the ozone layer, freshwater resources, oceans and coastal areas, deforestation and desertification, biological diversity, biotechnology, health and chemical safety.

UNEP's Global Environment Monitoring System (GEMS) and Global Resource Information Database (GRID) focus on vital areas of environmental concern, including climate and atmosphere, oceans, renewable resources, transboundary pollution and the health consequences of pollution. GEMS involves some 25 major global monitoring networks, while GRID has 12 network nodes, each with an associated database, and has activities in 142 countries. Over 30,000 scientists and technicians have been involved. The institutions in which they work are funded by Governments and international agencies.

INFOTERRA, a worldwide network with national focal points in 170 countries, assists organizations and individuals in obtaining environmental information. It processes over 38,000 queries a year.

The International Register of Potentially Toxic Chemicals (IRPTC) strives to bridge the gap between the world's chemical knowledge and those who need to use it. Some 70,000 chemicals are in use today, and IRPTC provides vital information for chemical safety decisions. Some 120 countries have appointed national correspondents to dispatch news on their latest research and laws to IRPTC and to relay information back to interested parties at home.

UNEP's Industry and Environment Office provides access to practical information and brings industry and government together for environmentally sound industrial development through technical cooperation and information transfer.

Under its regional seas programme, UNEP protects the marine environment and promotes sound, sustainable use of marine resources. Beginning with the Mediterranean Action Plan, plans are now in effect or being developed for 13 regions and over 140 countries.

UNEP is also active in the areas of the working environment, energy, technology, human settlements and environmental economics.

UNEP's series of environmental agreements is having an ever-increasing international effect. The historic Vienna Convention (1983) and Montreal Protocol (1987), negotiated under UNEP's auspices, and the London (1990) and Copenhagen (1992) Amendments to the Montreal Protocol, seek to reduce damage to the Earth's ozone layer which shields life on Earth from the sun's harmful ultra-violet radiation. The Basel Convention on the Control of Transboundary Movements of Hazardous Wastes and their Disposal (1989) reduces the danger of pollution from toxic waste. The Convention on International Trade in Endangered Species (1973) is universally recognized for its achievements in controlling the trade in wildlife products. Other major international initiatives are the preparation of the Convention on Biological Diversity (1992) and the Framework Convention on Climate Change (1992).

UNEP uses all the means at its disposal to raise public awareness and encourage community and non-governmental action to address global, regional and local problems.

To commemorate the anniversary of the opening day of the Stockholm Conference in 1972, World Environment Day is celebrated annually on 5 June.

United Nations Conference on Environment and Development

Governments took an historic step towards ensuring the future of the planet when they adopted Agenda 21, a comprehensive blueprint for action on global sustainable development, at the United Nations Conference on Environment and Development (Rio de Janeiro, Brazil, 1992). The Conference, known as the Earth Summit, was the largest gathering of world leaders up to that time, with more than 100 Heads of State or Government in attendance.

The Earth Summit, called for by the General Assembly in 1989, took steps to reverse environmental deterioration and establish the basis for a sustainable way of life into the twenty-first century.

In addition to Agenda 21, the Summit adopted the Rio Declaration on Environment and Development, which defines the rights and responsibilities of States and a set of principles to guide the sustainable management of forests worldwide.

Climate change and biodiversity. Two legally binding conventions were negotiated leading up to the Summit. Under the United Nations Framework Convention on Climate Change, industrialized countries are obliged to reduce emissions of greenhouse gases that cause global warming and related atmospheric problems. The Convention on Biological Diversity calls for halting the destruction of species, habitats and ecosystems. Both Conventions were opened for signature at the Summit. The Convention on Biological Diversity entered into force in 1993; the Convention on Climate Change in 1994. The Conference of Parties to both Conventions are currently considering protocols that will strengthen the agreements.

Agenda 21. Agenda 21 makes detailed recommendations for changing patterns of behaviour which cause ill-health in humans and stress to the environment. Areas for action include protecting the atmosphere; combating deforestation, soil loss and desertification; preventing air and water pollution; halting the depletion of fish stocks; and promoting the safe management of toxic wastes. Agenda 21 also addresses patterns of development which cause stress to the environment: poverty and external debt in developing countries; unsustainable patterns of production and consumption in industrialized countries; demographic pressures; and the structure of the international economy.

Commission on Sustainable Development. The Commission was established by the General Assembly, at the request of the Earth Summit, to monitor the implementation of Agenda 21 by Governments, businesses, NGOs and others. The Department for Policy Coordination and Sustainable Development provides substantive support for the 53-member Commission, which is a subsidiary of ECOSOC and meets annually.

Finance and technology. A key area under discussion by the Commission and its working groups is how to promote the transfer of environmentally sound technology to developing countries and provide them with the financial assistance they need to put Agenda 21 into action. One important funding mechanism is the Global Environment Facility (GEF), which makes grants to countries for projects to prevent climate change, depletion of the ozone layer, loss of biological diversity, pollution of international waters, and desertification where this is caused by climate change or loss of biodiversity. The GEF is managed by UNDP, UNEP and the World Bank. Funding is also made available under Capacity 21, a UNDP initiative which is working to strengthen human skills and institutions in developing countries so they can implement the policies called for in Agenda 21.

Desertification. At the Earth Summit, Governments requested the United Nations to begin negotiations on an international convention to combat desertification—a problem which affects over 900 million people worldwide, particularly in Africa. The Convention was completed in June 1994 and opened for signature in Paris in October. It is expected to come into force in 1996. (See also Desertification, below.)

Fish. At the request of the Summit, the United Nations Conference on straddling and highly migratory fish stocks has been meeting since 1993. At issue is the global depletion of fish and the need for sustainable management, particularly of high-seas fishing. A legal agreement to prevent conflicts over fishing rights and preserve fish stocks is expected to be finalized and opened for signature in August 1995.

Small Islands. The Summit called for the United Nations to hold a Global Conference on the Sustainable Development of Small Island Developing States. The Conference, held in Barbados in 1994, adopted a programme of action on problems affecting small islands, including economic isolation, overpopulation, degradation of land and marine environments, and possible sea-level rise caused by climate change.

Desertification

Severe recurrent droughts affected the western parts of the Sudano-Sahelian region of Africa during the late 1960s, then spread throughout the region during the early 1970s and the 1980s. The droughts had disastrous consequences, depleting vegetal species, accelerating land degradation, and destroying traditional ways of life through heavy losses of livestock and repeated crop failures.

Relief efforts began in 1972, with a $8.9 million assistance package in food and cash. In 1973, the Food and Agriculture Organization of the United Nations (FAO) established an Office for Sahelian Relief Operations, which has concentrated on providing seeds, supplying animal feed and vaccines, cooperating with other United Nations agencies in non-agricultural fields, and disseminating information on the relief effort.

The affected States in West Africa set up in 1973 the Permanent Inter-State Committee for Drought Control in the Sahel (CILSS) as a regional body to coordinate their efforts to combat drought and to alert the international community to their problems. The same year, the **United Nations Sudano-Sahelian Office (UNSO)** was established, to help those countries achieve food self-sufficiency, mitigate the effects of future droughts, and achieve development. In 1976, UNSO was transferred to UNDP. Activities are funded through the United Nations Trust Fund for Sudano-Sahelian activities, managed by UNSO.

A Plan of Action to Combat Desertification was adopted at the Conference on Desertification (Nairobi, 1977). In 1978, UNSO was given the responsibility for assisting countries to implement the Plan of Action on behalf of UNEP, and a UNDP/UNEP Joint Venture was signed.

During 1979-1993, UNDP and UNEP contributed $26.7 million to the Joint Venture. Activities focused on efforts to control desertification and the effects of drought by assisting the countries of the region to manage and protect their land resources. UNSO's work has evolved from field projects such as agroforestry and sand dune fixation, to putting in practice participatory methods of local land management, developing environmental information systems, and strategic framework processes which bring together all the local stakeholders.

UNSO has assisted the African countries in preparations for negotiating the International Convention to Combat Desertification in Those Countries Experiencing Serious Drought and/or Desertification, Particularly in Africa. The Convention, signed by 87 countries on 14 October 1994, provides the framework for all activity to combat desertification. (See also above.)

Natural resources and energy

The United Nations has long been involved in assisting countries in the management of their natural resources on a sustainable basis.

The General Assembly declared in 1952 that developing countries have "the right to determine freely the use of their natural resources" and that they must use such resources towards realizing their economic development plans in accordance with their national interests.

The importance of natural resources for economic development was further emphasized in 1970, when the Economic and Social Council established the Committee on Natural Resources. The Committee develops guidelines on policies and strategies for ECOSOC and Governments, reviews arrangements to coordinate United Nations activities in natural resources development and evaluates trends and issues concerning natural resources exploration and development, as well as prospects for selected water and mineral resources. The Committee is also concerned with the availability and sustainability of resources.

Water. During the 1970s, the Committee on Natural Resources played a central role in focusing world attention on another crisis—the status of the global stock of water resources to meet human, commercial and agricultural needs. As a result of an initiative of the Committee, the United Nations Water Conference was convened in 1977 in Mar del Plata, Argentina. The Conference adopted the Mar del Plata Action Plan to guide international efforts to manage, develop and use water resources. Giving impetus to the Action Plan, the General Assembly, in 1980, launched the International Drinking Water Supply and Sanitation Decade (1981-1990). The Decade helped some 1.3 billion people in the developing countries gain access to safe drinking water.

An International Conference on Water and the Environment (Dublin, 1992), was convened jointly by 21 United Nations agencies in preparation for the United Nations Conference on Environment and Development (see above). A major thrust of the United Nations activities in this area is geared towards sustainable development of fragile and finite water resources, which are coming under increasing stress through population growth, pollution and increasing demand for agricultural and industrial purposes.

In 1994, the Committee on Natural Resources requested the Secretary-General to prepare a report on the state of the world's freshwater resources, to be considered by a special session of the General Assembly in 1997. This was reinforced by a request from the Commission on Sustainable Development that the United Nations and its specialized agencies carry out a comprehensive assessment of freshwater resources, to identify the availability of such resources and make projections of future needs.

Energy. During the 1970s, with the rise and volatility of petroleum costs which affected the economies of all countries, particularly those of the poorer countries, and the growing awareness that known supplies of petroleum would, in the long run, be unable to meet global requirements, more attention was focused on new and renewable sources of energy.

This led the General Assembly to convene the United Nations Conference on New and Renewable Sources of Energy (Nairobi, 1981). The Conference examined alternative forms of energy, including solar energy, biomass energy, wind power, hydropower, fuelwood and charcoal, geothermal energy, ocean energy, oil shale and tar sands, peat and the use of draught animals for energy purposes. It adopted the Nairobi Programme of Action for the Development and Utilization of New and Renewable Sources of Energy, a blueprint for national and international action endorsed by the Assembly in 1981.

In this field, the Committee on New and Renewable Sources of Energy and Energy for Development acts as an advisory body to the Economic and Social Council.

Addressing another area of significance in the energy field—nuclear energy for the economic and social development of developing countries—the Assembly in 1977 set in motion arrangements for an international conference, the first global effort in this field: the United Nations Conference for the Promotion of International Cooperation in the Peaceful Uses of Nuclear Energy (Geneva, 1987). The high-level participants expressed views and exchanged experience on topics ranging from the production of electricity to the application of nuclear techniques to food and agriculture, medicine, hydrology, research and industry.

The United Nations maintains an active programme of technical cooperation in the field of natural resources and energy. The programme comprises advisory services on policies and strategies; project and programme formulation and implementation in natural resources management; and meetings, symposia and workshops, together with a publications programme.

To assist developing countries requesting short-term advisory missions, the United Nations provides the services of its technical advisers. These experts provide advice on policy, the evaluation, exploration and exploitation of indigenous resources, the transfer of technology, and the design of projects and feasibility studies.

During the last two decades, hundreds of technical cooperation and pre-investment projects in natural resources and energy involving hundreds of millions of dollars have been implemented. A roughly equivalent amount was provided by the recipient Governments in the form of national staff, facilities and local operating costs. As a result, each year some 300 field projects assist developing countries in the development of their natural resources. Such projects strengthen national capacities and stimulate further investment.

HUMAN SETTLEMENTS

United Nations Centre for Human Settlements (Habitat)

The United Nations Centre for Human Settlements (Habitat) was established in 1978, with its Headquarters in Nairobi, Kenya. It serves as a focal point for human settlements development, for action to improve shelter for the poor globally, and for coordinating human settlements activities within the United Nations system.

The Centre serves as the secretariat of the **Commission on Human Settlements**. The 58-member body assists countries and regions in solving human settlements problems and promotes greater international cooperation.

The Centre's major areas of concern include the provision

of technical cooperation to government programmes; the conducting of research; the organization of expert meetings, workshops and training seminars; the publication of technical documents; and the worldwide dissemination of information about human settlements issues and the Centre's activities.

The 1994-1995 work programme was structured under eight subprogrammes: global policies and strategies; national policies and instruments; managing human settlement development including financial and land resources; improving infrastructure and the living environment; managing disaster mitigation, reconstruction and development; housing for all; strengthening local communities; and reducing poverty and promoting equity.

In September 1994, the Centre had 219 technical cooperation projects under execution in 91 countries.

One major Centre effort, in collaboration with UNDP and the World Bank, is the Urban Management Programme to improve urban efficiency and living conditions for the poor. Its technical cooperation activities are focused on the need to improve the urban management capacity of local and central government staff in developing countries, together with research to identify solutions to problems created by rapid urbanization. In 1990, the Programme added a component on Urban Environmental Management specifically to address the environmental challenges confronting the cities and towns of developing countries.

In the same year, the Centre launched the Sustainable Cities Programme. Its principal goal is to provide municipal authorities and their partners in the public, private and popular sectors with an improved environmental planning and management capacity. By the end of 1994, this Programme had city-level activities in some 15 countries.

The Global Strategy for Shelter to the Year 2000, unanimously adopted by the General Assembly in 1988, emphasizes the enabling approach, whereby Governments provide not shelter itself but a facilitating legal, institutional and regulatory environment to encourage people to provide and improve upon their own shelter. The Strategy will continue to provide the basis of the Centre's programme of work to the year 2000.

The first Monday in October each year is World Habitat Day—a global observance coordinated by the Centre. On that day, Governments, NGOs, community groups, academic institutions and other bodies are urged to undertake activities focused on themes which address national shelter needs and which promote actions to satisfy them.

United Nations Conference on Human Settlements (Habitat II), 1996

Meeting in Istanbul, Turkey, in June 1996—20 years after the first Habitat Conference in Vancouver—the United Nations Conference on Human Settlements (Habitat II) will evaluate accomplishments since 1976, including progress in implementing the Global Strategy for Shelter to the Year 2000. In 1993, the Commission on Human Settlements recommended that the Conference should focus on sustainable human settlements in an urbanizing world, and adequate shelter for all. In the preparatory activities, the Commission appealed to Governments to establish broad-based processes for the participation of community groups, local authorities, NGOs and the private sector. Habitat II is expected to develop a global plan of action to achieve sustainable human settlements and shelter for all.

FOOD AND AGRICULTURE

The United Nations has addressed food-related issues since its earliest days, with the founding of the Food and Agriculture Organization of the United Nations (FAO) in 1945 (see FAO in Chapter 8). The World Food Conference (Rome, 1974) addressed world food problems within the broader context of development. The Conference led to the creation of the World Food Council, the International Fund for Agricultural Development (see IFAD in Chapter 8) and the Committee on World Food Security.

World Food Programme (WFP)

The World Food Programme (WFP) is a Rome-based United Nations agency working to combat hunger and poverty around the world. Established in 1963, it provides relief assistance to victims of natural disasters and wars, and supplies food aid to poor people in developing countries to build self-reliance.

The Programme has offices in 83 countries. The largest multilateral food aid organization, WFP provides 26 per cent of global food aid. In 1994, it delivered 3.3 million tonnes of food aid by ship, plane, barge, railroad and truck. WFP also arranges for the purchase and transport of a growing share of food aid provided bilaterally by individual countries.

WFP assistance during 1994 directly benefited 57 million poor people. Of this number, 32.5 million were victims of emergencies like civil war and natural disasters. WFP-assisted development projects involved 24.5 million people. WFP's total expenditure in 1994 was $1.5 billion.

WFP has become the main channel for and coordinator of food aid for refugees. In 1994, emergency relief assistance accounted for 81 per cent of expenditures, for a total of $1.1 billion, and a food aid commitment of some 2.4 million tonnes. Women and children, who suffer most in emergencies caused by war or drought, are the main beneficiaries of WFP assistance.

Because of the increase in the number of emergencies worldwide, WFP was able to allocate only 19 per cent of its resources in 1994 to development projects that would actually help free people from the need for food aid.

The hungry poor who receive WFP development assistance include landless agricultural workers, small-scale farmers and the urban poor—people below the poverty line with insufficient food and insufficient money to buy food for themselves and their families. More than half of the beneficiaries of WFP development aid obtain family rations by participating in labour-intensive food-for-work programmes to build infrastructure and create assets essential for their longer-term advancement. Most of the remaining beneficiaries receive WFP assistance through human resource development projects such as nutrition and health improvement schemes and education and training pro-grammes.

WFP is the largest supporter of development projects involving and benefiting poor women; the largest provider of grant assistance within the United Nation system to sub-Saharan Africa; the largest provider of grant assistance to environmental protection and improvement; and the largest purchaser of food and services in developing countries.

Over the past three decades, WFP has invested more than $14 billion to combat hunger, promote economic and social development and deliver relief assistance in emergencies.

(See also **Humanitarian Assistance** in Chapter 6.)

World Food Council (WFC)

The 36-member World Food Council (WFC) was established by the General Assembly in 1974 to review major policy issues affecting the world food situation and to develop an integrated approach to their solution.

Made up of government ministers, WFC is the highest-level body in the United Nations dealing exclusively with food problems. It is concerned with setting global objectives, outlining measures to attain them and mobilizing political and financial support among member countries. It normally meets once a year, but can hold special sessions.

One of the major initiatives of WFC has been the elaboration of the concept of national food strategies, aiming at high-level coordination of national food and agriculture policies in developing countries. Such strategies formulate medium- and long-term programmes to reverse negative production and consumption trends by focusing the combined efforts of Governments, matching them with support from multilateral and bilateral assistance agencies.

In the last decade, WFC has concentrated on reviewing international support to developing countries, including resource flows and technology transfers. It has developed proposals to enhance technical cooperation among developing countries through exchanges between policy strategies in Africa, Asia and Latin America. It has launched a review of the successes and failures of the Green Revolution, with a view to starting a new, indigenous Green Revolution in Africa. It has advocated the importance of protecting the nutritional levels of the poor by incorporating in adjustment programmes long-term objectives for food security and poverty alleviation. To this end, it has created an informal group of representatives of multilateral agencies, including the international financial institutions, to harmonize activities in selected adjustment policy areas.

In 1993, the functions and activities of the WFC secretariat were transferred to the Department for Policy Coordination and Sustainable Development, whose mandate includes the global management and coordination of food security and hunger alleviation issues.

Committee on World Food Security

Established in 1975, the Committee on World Food Security of the Food and Agriculture Organization of the United Nations (FAO) is the only intergovernmental body in the United Nations system responsible exclusively for monitoring, evaluating and consulting on the world food security situation. It analyses food needs, assesses the availability and transportation of basic foodstuffs, and monitors stock levels throughout the world. It also recommends short- and long-term policies to ensure adequate cereal supplies.

The work of the Committee is backed by the extensive network of monitoring systems and satellite surveillance of the FAO. The most important of these is the Global Information and Early Warning System, widely recognized as the authoritative international source of food information and early warning, particularly in vulnerable developing countries.

POPULATION AND DEVELOPMENT

The United Nations has been concerned with population questions since its earliest years. The 27-member **Commission on Population and Development** (originally known as the Population Commission), set up in 1947, was one of the first subsidiary bodies established by the Economic and Social Council. The Population Division of the now Department for Economic and Social Information and Policy Analysis has been the secretariat of the Commission since its inception.

Since its early days, the Commission has provided guidance to the United Nations population programme. Its mandate includes advising the Council and arranging studies on population issues and trends, including determinants and consequences; integrating population and development strategies; population and related development policies and programmes; provision of population assistance; arranging for studies and advising the Council not only on the size and structure of populations and the changes therein, but also on the interplay of demographic, economic and social factors, as well as on the policies designed to influence the size and structure of populations and the changes therein; as well as any other population and development questions on which United Nations organs and agencies may seek advice.

The Commission has primary responsibility for reviewing the implementation of the Programme of Action of the International Conference on Population and Development (see below).

The best known part of the United Nations population programme has been its quantitative and methodological work, particularly its authoritative estimates and projections of population size and change and the preparation of research manuals.

In the 1960s, the extraordinarily rapid growth of the world's population became an urgent concern. The rate of population growth peaked in the late 1960s, declined moderately during the 1970s and remained steady during the 1980s. The world's population more than doubled between 1950 and 1990, increasing from 2.5 billion to 5.3 billion. It is currently estimated at 5.6 billion. While the rate of growth is on the decline, absolute increments have been increasing, currently exceeding 86 million persons per year. Annual population increments are likely to remain above 86 million until the year 2015.

Such a rapidly increasing population weighs heavily on the earth's resources and environment, and severely hinders efforts towards development. The United Nations has increasingly addressed the relationship between population and development, among other things by seeking to advance women's status—the key to all efforts on population and development.

United Nations Population Fund (UNFPA)

In 1966, the General Assembly authorized the United Nations to provide technical assistance in the population field. A trust fund was established the following year, later named the United

Nations Population Fund (UNFPA). UNFPA is now the largest internationally funded provider of population assistance to developing countries. All contributions to the Fund are voluntary.

UNFPA's role is to build up, on an international basis, the capacity to respond to needs in population and family planning; to promote awareness of population factors (such as population growth, fertility, mortality, age structure, spatial distribution, migration, etc.); to assist Governments in developing population programmes and projects; and to provide financial assistance for their implementation.

About half of UNFPA funds go to the area of reproductive health, including family planning. Activities range from support for contraceptive research and production to training, infrastructure and logistics, and expansion and improvement of service delivery. Other priority programme areas include information and education activities, population data collection and analysis, research on demographic and socio-economic relationships, policy formulation and evaluation, and programmes to improve the situation of women. Special efforts are also undertaken in the areas of AIDS control and prevention, and population and the environment.

International Conference on Population and Development, 1994

The first global intergovernmental conference on population—the World Population Conference—held in 1974 at Bucharest, Romania, adopted the World Population Plan of Action, which stressed the fundamental relationship between population factors and overall economic and social development. The International Conference on Population (Mexico City, 1984) addressed issues such as migration, urbanization and ageing populations.

In connection with the periodic review and appraisal of the 1974 World Population Plan of Action, the Economic and Social Council, concerned about the magnitude and urgency of population issues, approved in 1989 the convening of an international meeting on population in 1994. Subsequently, the Council decided that the meeting would have population, sustained economic growth and sustainable development as its overall theme.

The International Conference on Population and Development (Cairo, Egypt, 1994) was attended by representatives from 179 countries and addressed by 249 speakers. Almost 11,000 people participated.

The six high-priority issues were population growth and demographic structure; population policies and programmes; population, the environment and development; population distribution and migration; population and women; and family planning, health and family well-being.

Although 23 States expressed reservations, the 20-year Programme of Action was adopted by acclamation. The Programme recognizes that the formulation and implementation of population policies is the responsibility of each country and should take into account the economic, social, environmental and cultural diversity of conditions in each country, including religious beliefs and ethical values.

The Programme of Action endorses a new strategy that emphasizes the inseparability of population and development and focuses on meeting the needs of individuals rather than demographic targets. Key to the new approach is empowering women and providing them with more choices through expanded access to education and health services and promoting skill development and employment. The Programme calls for making family planning universally available by the year 2015 or sooner, as part of a broadened approach to reproductive health and rights. It also includes goals in regard to education, especially for girls, and for the further reduction of infant, child and maternal mortality levels. For the first time, it calls on Governments to address unsafe abortion as a leading cause of maternal mortality and a "major public health concern". The Programme also addresses issues relating to population, the environment and consumption patterns; the family; internal and international migration; prevention and control of the HIV/AIDS pandemic; information, education and communication; and technology, research and development. It also estimates the resources required for comprehensive reproductive health services in developing countries through 2015, and calls for a partnership among Governments, NGOs and the private sector in implementing the Conference's recommendations.

ROLE OF WOMEN IN DEVELOPMENT

The importance of women's role in the development process and the need to intensify action to improve the status of women were recognized internationally in 1975, which was proclaimed by the General Assembly as International Women's Year. The Year focused on the triple objective of equality, development and peace.

In 1975, the World Conference of the International Women's Year was held at Mexico City, and the General Assembly subsequently proclaimed 1976-1985 as the United Nations Decade for Women. A mid-decade world conference (Copenhagen, 1980) adopted a Programme of Action for the second half of the Decade.

In 1985, the World Conference to Review and Appraise the Achievements of the United Nations Decade for Women was held at Nairobi. It adopted the Nairobi Forward-looking Strategies for the Advancement of Women to the Year 2000, a blueprint of action to further the status of women everywhere. Emerging areas of concern were addressed, among them the economic value of underpaid work by women; the need for women to play a larger role in decision-making; violence against women; data banks and statistics on women's activities; and family planning.

Implementation of the Strategies is reviewed and appraised every five years. In 1990, the Commission on the Status of Women (see Promoting the Rights of Women in Chapter 4), noted that the pace of the improvement in the status of women had slowed down considerably and that measures were necessary to close the widening gap between equality in law and in practice.

To renew interest in the advancement of women, and to revive political will at the national and international levels, the Economic and Social Council recommended in 1990 to hold a **Fourth World Conference on Women: Action for Equality, Development and Peace.** The Conference is to be held at Beijing, China, from 4 to 15 September 1995. Preparations at the national and regional levels, with strong participation by NGOs, focused on ensuring an action-oriented international conference which would concentrate on ways to overcome fundamental obstacles to the advancement of women.

This section focuses on the role of women in development. For United Nations efforts to ensure full equality and women's rights, see Promoting the Rights of Women in Chapter 4.

United Nations Development Fund for Women (UNIFEM)

The United Nations Development Fund for Women (UNIFEM) was created in 1976 as the Voluntary Fund for the United Nations Decade for Women. Based in New York and with 11 regional offices in Asia and the Pacific, Western Asia, Africa and Latin America and the Caribbean, the Fund became an autonomous organization in association with UNDP in 1985.

UNIFEM provides direct technical and financial support to women's initiatives in developing countries. It also seeks to bring women into mainstream development planning and decision-making. UNIFEM improves the quality of life for all people by helping women to achieve equality through economic and social development.

UNIFEM works primarily in three programme areas: agriculture and food security, trade and industry, and macro policy-making and national planning. It seeks to promote women's access to training, science and technology, credit, information and other tools for development. It also links grass-roots women to national and international policy-making bodies and into global debates on issues such as poverty alleviation, the environment and human rights. UNIFEM manages several hundred projects, whose funding ranges from $2,000 up to a million dollars.

Financial support for UNIFEM comes from United Nations Member States along with contributions from UNIFEM's 17 National Committees, women's organizations, foundations, corporations and individuals.

International Research and Training Institute for the Advancement of Women (INSTRAW)

The General Assembly in 1975 established the International Research and Training Institute for the Advancement of

Women (INSTRAW), on the recommendation of the 1975 World Conference of the International Women's Year. INSTRAW is an autonomous body within the United Nations system with a mandate to carry out research, training and information activities worldwide to promote women as key agents of development. The Institute works in close cooperation with the United Nations, governmental organizations, research centres and NGOs, and has developed a growing network of national focal points and correspondents.

The Institute is funded by voluntary contributions from United Nations Member States, inter- and non-governmental organizations, foundations and private sources. Its headquarters has been in Santo Domingo, Dominican Republic, since 1983.

INSTRAW responds to issues of concern to women through its research, training and information activities. The Institute is now involved in four themes: empowerment of women; women, environment and sustainable development; statistics and indicators on women; and women and communication. One of INSTRAW's programmes focuses on improving statistics and indicators to better reflect the status and role of women compared with men.

INSTRAW advocates women as major agents in development. The Institute's research results underscore women's contribution to sustainable development; that is, growth with equity and with a human dimension. Its training and communication activities are a means of empowering women and men to change gender relations for mutual and equitable benefit.

ASSISTANCE TO CHILDREN

United Nations Children's Fund (UNICEF)

The United Nations Children's Fund (UNICEF) is unique among organizations working for long-term, sustainable human development, owing to its universal mandate for the survival, protection and development of children. Created by the General Assembly in 1946 to meet emergency needs of children in post-war Europe and in China, UNICEF now cooperates with Governments to improve the lives of children everywhere.

Through its extensive field network in developing countries

and within national development objectives, UNICEF carries out with Governments, local communities and other partners, programmes in health, nutrition, education, water and sanitation, the environment, women in development and other areas of importance to children. Emphasis is placed on low-cost, community-based programmes in which people participate actively and train in such skills as health care, midwifery and teaching.

UNICEF supports programmes through efforts in information, advocacy, education for development and fund-raising throughout the world, especially in industrialized countries. In these efforts, UNICEF works with 38 National Committees and over 180 NGOs.

As the only United Nations agency devoted exclusively to the needs of children, UNICEF speaks on their behalf and promotes the universal ratification and full implementation of the Convention on the Rights of the Child. The Convention, which became international law in 1990, less than a year after it was unanimously adopted by the General Assembly, had been ratified by 169 countries as of 31 March 1995. It is the most comprehensive treaty ever to address the rights of children, and sets universally accepted standards for their protection.

As a result of efforts by UNICEF, a World Summit for Children was held at United Nations Headquarters in 1990, attended by representatives from more than 150 countries, including 71 heads of State or Government. The resulting Declaration and Plan of Action recognized the rights of the young to "first call" on their nation's resources.

UNICEF encourages and helps countries develop 10-year national programmes of action to honour their leaders' promises at the World Summit. As of February 1995, 100 countries had finalized such programmes and over 50 were preparing them. The Summit Plan of Action set goals for the year 2000 in such areas as health, nutrition, education, and water and sanitation.

UNICEF sets its priorities for children according to their vulnerability. Almost all its resources are therefore invested in the poorest developing countries, with the greatest share going to children in the high-risk early years, up to age five. Almost 13 million children in this age group die every year from causes related to infectious diseases and malnutrition, unsafe drinking water and unsanitary surroundings. The healthy development of many millions more is stifled by poverty, ill health, lack of formal education, discrimination, the trauma of military conflicts, exploitation and abuse.

In cooperation with the World Health Organization (WHO), UNICEF supports an immunization programme that every year prevents more than 3 million child deaths and untold suffering from six diseases—diphtheria, measles, pertussis (whooping cough), poliomyelitis, tetanus and tuberculosis. When the programme was launched in 1974, fewer than 5 per cent of children in the developing world were immunized against these deadly illnesses, but in 1991 both agencies announced that their goal of protecting 80 per cent of the world's children before their first birthday had been achieved. This is widely recognized as the most important public health achievement of the past decade, and represents a logistical and mobilization feat that also established channels for delivering other services to children, such as vitamin A supplements and additional vaccines against yellow fever and hepatitis B.

UNICEF works closely with WHO to control diarrhoeal dehydration, one of the biggest causes of death in the developing world. It promotes the manufacture and use of pre-packaged salt or home-made solutions. The use of oral rehydration therapy rose from 17 per cent in 1985 to 44 per cent in 1994, saving the lives of more than one million children.

Again with WHO, UNICEF launched a "baby-friendly hospital initiative" in 1992 to save breast-feeding from becoming an "endangered practice"—a trend which hospital and medical practitioners in both rich and poor countries have encouraged by separating mother and child at birth and starting the artificial feeding of newborns. The initiative aims to educate health care providers in the developing world to ensure that they reinforce a mother's first, best, cheapest and most natural option to nurture and protect her infant. It also aims to advocate breast-feeding in community health facilities and hospitals. As of August 1994, over 1,000 hospitals had become baby-friendly by implementing the "ten steps to successful breast-feeding" recommended by UNICEF and WHO.

About one million children globally are born infected with the human immunodeficiency virus (HIV). UNICEF supports AIDS education programmes and helps AIDS-affected families and communities to cope with the problem.

In cooperation with UNDP and UNFPA, UNICEF advocates the 20/20 formula—an initiative which calls on Governments of developing countries to allocate at least 20 per cent of their budget to basic social services, and donor countries to earmark a similar proportion of their official development assistance for such services.

UNICEF relies entirely on voluntary public and government contributions. More than 30 per cent of its $1,006 million income in 1994 came from the public. UNICEF supports programmes for children in 144 countries and territories.

UNICEF was awarded the Nobel Peace Prize in 1965.

(See also **The Rights of the Child** in Chapter 4, and **Humanitarian Assistance** in Chapter 5.)

YOUTH AND DEVELOPMENT

In 1965, the General Assembly adopted the Declaration on the Promotion among Youth of the Ideals of Peace, Mutual Respect and Understanding between Peoples, stressing the importance of the role of youth in today's world, especially its potential contribution to development.

In 1979, the General Assembly proclaimed 1985 International Youth Year: Participation, Development, Peace, to increase awareness of the situation, needs and aspirations of youth, with a view to engaging them in the development process.

The symbolic culmination of the Year was a series of plenary meetings of the General Assembly at its 1985 session, designated as the United Nations World Conference for the International Youth Year. The Conference adopted the guidelines for further planning and suitable follow-up in the field of youth, a global long-term strategy for youth work. Since 1985, the United Nations has been involved in promoting the implementation of the guidelines. This has entailed assisting Governments in developing integrated youth policies and programmes, strengthening channels of communication between the United

Nations and youth organizations, and reinforcing inter-agency cooperation on youth. The United Nations Youth Fund has continued to operate to support projects involving young people.

The observance of the tenth anniversary of the Year in 1995 has been the occasion for launching global activities seeking to strengthen youth-related concerns in development activities. In this connection, the General Assembly at its fiftieth session will devote up to four plenary meetings to the observance of the Year's tenth anniversary. The Assembly is expected to adopt a world youth programme of action towards the year 2000 and beyond, providing a practical guide, in a global framework, for national and regional action on a long-term basis.

AGEING AND OLDER PERSONS

The World Assembly on Ageing was convened at Vienna in 1982 in response to the ageing of populations and the consequent increase in the number and proportions of older persons. This Assembly adopted the International Plan of Action on Ageing, endorsed by the General Assembly later that year. The Plan discusses demographic ageing, a result of declining fertility and increasing longevity, and provides guidance for individuals, families, communities and countries in making the necessary socio-economic adjustments. It includes recommendations for action in such sectors as employment and income security, health and nutrition, housing, education and social welfare. It envisages older persons as a diverse and active population group with wide-ranging capabilities and, at times, particular health-care needs. It draws attention to the policy implications of the preponderance of women among the aged and to the particular needs of older refugees and migrants.

The Commission for Social Development, which reviews implementation of the Plan, has identified such priorities for action as the creation of national committees on ageing, coordinated planning and strengthening of information exchange, training, research and education programmes.

The General Assembly and the Economic and Social Council have urged Governments and NGOs to give priority to the question of ageing, and to contribute to the United Nations

Trust Fund for Ageing, which assists developing countries in activities aimed at formulating and implementing policies and programmes on ageing. The Assembly and the Council have initiated many international activities, including the establishment, in 1988, of an International Institute on Ageing, in Valletta, Malta, and in 1991, of the Banyan Fund: A World Fund for Ageing, in Torcy, France. In 1991, the Assembly adopted a set of 18 United Nations Principles for Older Persons, dealing with the themes of independence, participation, care, self-fulfilment and dignity.

On the occasion of the tenth anniversary of the adoption of the International Plan of Action on Ageing, the Assembly in 1992 devoted four plenary meetings to an international conference on ageing. The International Conference adopted the Proclamation on Ageing, laying out the main direction for implementing the Plan of Action in its second decade, and proclaimed 1999 the International Year of Older Persons. The Assembly also adopted the global targets on ageing for the year 2001 as a practical strategy on ageing.

In 1993, the General Assembly requested the Secretary-General to prepare a draft conceptual framework for the observance of the International Year of Older Persons in 1999. The conceptual framework was issued in March 1995, and will be submitted to the Assembly at the end of 1995.

DISABLED PERSONS

In 1971, the General Assembly adopted the Declaration on the Rights of Mentally Retarded Persons, which states that such individuals have the same rights as other human beings, including the right to proper medical care, economic security, rehabilitation and training, as well as the right to live with one's own family or foster parents. The Assembly's 1975 Declaration on the Rights of Disabled Persons proclaims that disabled persons have the same civil and political rights as other persons, and provides for equal treatment and services developing to the maximum the capabilities of persons with disabilities. In 1976, the General Assembly proclaimed 1981 the International Year of Disabled Persons.

The International Year was followed by the adoption in

1982 of the World Programme of Action concerning Disabled Persons, which provides a policy framework and a guiding philosophy based on the recognition of the human rights of disabled persons. Its framework of prevention, rehabilitation and equalization of opportunities for disabled persons proved to be a valid basis for progress.

The General Assembly in 1982 proclaimed the United Nations Decade of Disabled Persons (1983-1992). Two monitoring exercises during the Decade, in 1987 and in 1992, acknowledged that despite many efforts, disabled persons continued to be denied equal opportunities and in many societies remained isolated. While progress had been made in raising awareness, too little practical action had yet been taken.

In 1993, the General Assembly adopted a new set of international standards, the Standard Rules on the Equalization of Opportunities for Persons with Disabilities. The Secretary-General appointed a Special Rapporteur on disabilities to monitor implementation of the Standard Rules.

The General Assembly in 1994 endorsed a Long-term Strategy to further the implementation of the 1982 World Programme of Action. The Strategy sets as its ultimate goal "a society for all", encompassing human diversity and the development of the human potential of each person.

THE FAMILY

In the early 1980s, the General Assembly, the Economic and Social Council and the Commission for Social Development reviewed issues relating to the family. This led to a growing conviction that there was an urgent need for increased international cooperation on family issues as part of the global effort to advance social progress and development. As a result, in 1989, the General Assembly proclaimed 1994 as the International Year of the Family, with the theme "Family: resources and responsibilities in a changing world".

The International Year sought to raise awareness of the role and needs of the family among policy makers as well as the general public, and to promote action to improve its well-being. During the Year, substantive family-oriented programmes were undertaken in several countries. For instance, some countries established Government ministries devoted to the family, while others passed family-oriented legislation.

On 18 October 1994, the General Assembly convened in New York an International Conference on Families to follow up the Year. The Conference discussed directions for a draft plan of action for the 1995 General Assembly.

CRIMINAL JUSTICE

United Nations work in crime prevention and criminal justice has six goals:
♦ the prevention of crime within and among States;
♦ the control of crime both nationally and internationally;
♦ the strengthening of regional and international cooperation in crime prevention, criminal justice and the combating of transnational crime;
♦ the integration and consolidation of the efforts of Member States in preventing and combating transnational crime;
♦ more efficient and effective administration of justice, with due respect for the human rights of all those affected by crime and all those involved in the criminal justice system;
♦ the promotion of the highest standards of fairness, humanity, justice and professional conduct.

In this way, the United Nations contributes to lessen the human and material costs of crime and its impact on socio-economic development, and to promote the observance of international standards and norms in criminal justice, by furthering the dissemination and exchange of information, the training of personnel and direct aid to Governments.

To provide a forum for the presentation of policies and to stimulate progress, the General Assembly in 1950 authorized the convening every five years of a United Nations Congress on the Prevention of Crime and the Treatment of Offenders. Participants include criminologists, penologists and senior police officers, as well as experts in criminal law, human rights and rehabilitation. Nine such congresses have been held:
♦ the First Congress (Geneva, 1955) approved a set of Standard Minimum Rules for the Treatment of Prisoners, which the Economic and Social Council adopted in 1957;
♦ the Second Congress (London, 1960) dealt with measures

for preventing juvenile delinquency and considered the questions of prison labour, parole and after-care;

♦ the Third Congress (Stockholm, 1965) approved measures for crime prevention by the community and for combating recidivism;

♦ the Fourth Congress (Tokyo, 1970) stressed the need to take crime into account in development planning, particularly in view of the effects of urbanization, industrialization and the technological revolution on the human environment;

♦ the Fifth Congress (Geneva, 1975) adopted the Declaration on the Protection of All Persons From Being Subjected to Torture and Other Cruel, Inhuman and Degrading Treatment or Punishment, which the General Assembly approved later the same year (see also The Fight against Torture in Chapter 4); it also laid the basis for the Code of Conduct for Law Enforcement Officials, which was approved by the Assembly in 1979;

♦ the Sixth Congress (Caracas, 1980) dealt with such topics as crime trends and crime prevention strategies, juvenile delinquency, crime and the abuse of power, and de institutionalization of corrections. The Caracas Declaration was endorsed later in 1980 by the General Assembly.

♦ the Seventh Congress (Milan, 1985) adopted the Milan Plan of Action for strengthening international cooperation in crime prevention and criminal justice, which was subsequently approved by the General Assembly. Among other Congress documents were: a set of Guiding Principles for Crime Prevention and Criminal Justice in the Context of Development and a New International Economic Order; Basic Principles on the Independence of the Judiciary; a Model Agreement on the Transfer of Foreign Prisoners; a Declaration on the Basic Principles of Justice for Victims of Crime and Abuse of Power; and Standard Minimum Rules for the Administration of Juvenile Justice, known as the Beijing Rules, all of them adopted or endorsed by the General Assembly.

The Eighth Congress (Havana, 1990) approved new instruments and resolutions which were adopted in the same year by the General Assembly, namely, four model treaties on extradition, mutual assistance in criminal matters, the transfer of proceedings in criminal matters and the transfer of supervision of offenders conditionally sentenced or conditionally released; the United Nations Standard Minimum Rules for Non-custodial Measures (Tokyo Rules); the Basic Principles for the Treatment of Prisoners; the Guidelines for the Prevention of Juvenile Delinquency (the Riyadh Guidelines); and the Rules for the Protection of Juveniles Deprived of Their Liberty.

The Ninth Congress (Cairo, 1995) dealt with four major subjects: international cooperation and technical assistance for strengthening the role of law; action against national and transnational economic and organized crime, and the role of criminal law in the protection of the environment; improvement of police and criminal justice systems; and crime prevention strategies, in particular against urban, juvenile and violent crime. Resolutions were adopted on all four subjects, addressing problems such as the proliferation of firearms, deliberate environmental damage, attacks on minorities, violence against women, and crimes of terrorism. The Congress also reviewed practical measures aimed at combating corruption among public officials.

The **Commission on Crime Prevention and Criminal Justice**, a new functional body of ECOSOC, established in 1992 to strengthen United Nations activities in this field, is comprised of 40 members and meets annually at Vienna.

As recommended by the Commission, a World Ministerial Conference on Transnational Organized Crime was held at Naples, Italy, in 1994. Also in 1994, an International Conference on Preventing and Controlling Money Laundering and the Use of the Proceeds of Crime was held in Courmayeur, Italy. The recommendations of these meetings, as contained in the Naples Political Declaration and Global Action Plan, were approved by the General Assembly in December 1994. The Commission is charged with promoting and monitoring their implementation.

United Nations Interregional Crime and Justice Research Institute (UNICRI)

The United Nations Interregional Crime and Justice Research Institute (UNICRI) was established in 1968 to undertake and promote action-oriented research aimed at the prevention of crime and the treatment of offenders.

Located in Rome, Italy, the Institute is an autonomous body operating as the interregional research and training arm of the United Nations crime and criminal justice programme. It seeks to contribute, through research, training, technical cooperation and information dissemination, to the formulation of improved policies in crime prevention and control.

INTERNATIONAL DRUG CONTROL

The control of narcotic drugs has been of global concern ever since the first international conference on the subject was held in Shanghai in 1909. The international control system has been built up step by step, beginning in 1920 under the auspices of the League of Nations and since 1946 by the United Nations.

A series of treaties adopted under United Nations auspices require that Governments exercise control over production and distribution of narcotic drugs and psychotropic substances, combat drug abuse and illicit traffic, maintain the necessary administrative machinery, and report to international organs on their actions.

This international regime includes:
♦ the Single Convention on Narcotic Drugs (1961), which codifies earlier treaties on natural or synthetic narcotics, cannabis and cocaine;
♦ the Convention on Psychotropic Substances (1971), which covers hallucinogens, amphetamines, barbiturates, non-barbiturate sedatives and tranquillizers;
♦ the 1972 Protocol Amending the Single Convention, which highlights the need for treatment and rehabilitation of drug addicts; and
♦ the 1988 United Nations Convention against Illicit Traffic in Narcotic Drugs and Psychotropic Substances, which is designed to deprive drug traffickers of their ill-gotten financial gains and freedom of movement.

One of the innovative provisions of the 34-article Convention against Illicit Traffic is the tracing, freezing and confiscation of proceeds and property derived from drug trafficking. Courts are empowered to make available or to seize bank, financial or commercial records. Bank secrecy cannot be invoked in such cases. The Convention bars all havens to drug traffickers, particularly by providing for the extradition of drug traffickers, mutual legal assistance between States on drug-related investigations and the transfer of proceedings for criminal prosecution. Under the Convention, parties commit themselves to eliminate or reduce illicit demand for drugs.

The central objective of these treaties is to limit the supply of and demand for narcotic drugs and psychotropic substances to medical and scientific needs.

The **Commission on Narcotic Drugs**, one of the functional commissions of ECOSOC, considers all matters pertaining to the aims of the treaties and the implementation of their provisions, and makes recommendations to ECOSOC on the control of narcotic drugs and psychotropic substances. Established in 1946, the Commission is the main policy-making body for international drug control within the United Nations system. It has primary responsibility for amending the schedules annexed to the international treaties in order to bring substances under international control, delete them from control, or change the regime of control to which they are subject. The Commission reviews the global drug situation and recommends measures to strengthen international drug control, including proposals for new treaties.

The International Narcotics Control Board, which began operating in 1968, is responsible for the continuous evaluation and overall supervision of governmental implementation of drug control treaties. It reviews and confirms annual estimates of licit narcotic drug requirements submitted by Governments which limit the manufacture and trade in narcotic drugs to medical and scientific purposes, and monitors the licit movement of psychotropic substances. It may, in cases of breaches of the treaties, require Governments to adopt remedial measures, and it may bring treaty violations to the attention of the parties, ECOSOC and the Commission on Narcotic Drugs.

United Nations International
Drug Control Programme (UNDCP)

Established in 1990 to enhance the effectiveness of the United Nations structure for drug control, UNDCP became operational in 1991. With 20 field offices, UNDCP serves as the worldwide centre of expertise and information on drug abuse control, and plays a major role in monitoring developments in order to recommend action and provide technical assistance to Governments. UNDCP provides services to ECOSOC, the General Assembly and other United Nations bodies dealing with drug control matters. It serves as the focal point for promoting the observance of the United Nations Decade against Drug Abuse (1991-2000).

In particular, UNDCP:

♦ helps Member States implement the international drug control treaties; endeavours to reduce illicit demand for drugs, suppress illicit traffic, free farmers from their economic dependence on illicit narcotic crops by creating alternative sources of income and improving their living standards;

♦ works with Governments, intergovernmental and non-governmental organizations and the private sector in areas such as legal assistance, treatment and rehabilitation and social reintegration of drug addicts;

♦ coordinates the activities of specialized agencies and United Nations programmes in matters of international drug control;

♦ generates public awareness of the harmful effects of drug abuse;

♦ services meetings of the Commission on Narcotic Drugs and the International Narcotics Control Board;

♦ promotes regional and interregional cooperation.

The **Fund of the United Nations International Drug Control Programme**, established by the General Assembly in 1991, is the major source within the United Nations System for financial and technical assistance, mainly to developing countries. The Fund is supported entirely from voluntary contributions of Member States and private organizations. It provides the United Nations with the extrabudgetary resources needed to cope more effectively with new trends in abuse and to fight illicit drug trafficking.

The International Conference on Drug Abuse and Illicit Trafficking (Vienna, 1987) adopted the Comprehensive Multidisciplinary Outline of Future Activities in Drug Abuse Control, which recommends action by Governments and organizations to prevent and reduce demand for narcotic drugs and psychotropic substances, control supply, suppress illicit trafficking, and promote policies for treatment and rehabilitation. The Conference, attended by 138 States, adopted a Declaration committing participants to take vigorous international action against drug abuse and illicit trafficking. It also expressed the determination of participants to strengthen action and cooperation towards the goal of a society free of drug abuse. As recommended by the Conference, the General Assembly in 1987 proclaimed 26 June as the International Day against Drug Abuse and Illicit Trafficking.

In 1990, at a special session devoted to international drug control, the General Assembly proclaimed the United Nations Decade against Drug Abuse (1991-2000). This period is to be devoted to promoting the implementation of the Global Programme of Action adopted at that session. In a Political Declaration, the Assembly expressed the conviction of Member States that action against drug abuse and illicit trafficking should be accorded higher priority by the international community.

TRAINING AND RESEARCH

United Nations Institute for Training and Research (UNITAR)

Following a 1963 decision of the General Assembly, the United Nations Institute for Training and Research (UNITAR) was established in 1965 as an autonomous body within the framework of the United Nations.

UNITAR's mandate is to enhance, through training and research, the effectiveness of the United Nations in achieving its major objectives, particularly the maintenance of international peace and security and the promotion of economic and social development.

UNITAR, which has its headquarters in Geneva, derives its funding from voluntary contributions from Governments, intergovernmental organizations, foundations and other non-governmental sources and income generated by its Reserve Fund.

The Institute has two main functions: training and research. Recently, however, the main focus has been shifted to training.

Current research activities concentrate on research on, with and for training.

UNITAR designs and organizes some 70 training programmes per year for the benefit of some 3,000 participants in the five continents. Training is provided at various levels to persons, particularly from developing countries, for assignments with the United Nations or the specialized agencies and for assignments in their national services connected with the work of the United Nations system and institutions operating in related fields. By September 1994, more than 21,000 participants from some 180 nations had taken part in courses, seminars or workshops organized by UNITAR.

UNITAR's training programmes comprise courses on multilateral diplomacy and international cooperation, offered primarily to diplomats accredited to the United Nations. Other programmes cover economic and social development, including environmental management and environmental negotiations; dispute resolution; debt management and international finance, with special emphasis on the legal aspects; energy; and disaster control.

Each year, in cooperation with the United Nations Office of Legal Affairs, UNITAR organizes a fellowship programme in international law. A fellowship programme in international environmental law is organized jointly with UNEP. UNITAR also offers, jointly with the International Peace Academy, a fellowship programme in peace-making and preventive diplomacy, which provides advanced training in conflict analysis and mediation to international and national civil servants.

United Nations University (UNU)

The United Nations University (UNU) was established in 1973, with the approval of its Charter by the General Assembly. Located in Tokyo, UNU is as an autonomous institution within the framework of the United Nations.

As a new kind of academic institution, UNU works to promote scholarly international and scientific cooperation to help solve urgent global problems. It is different in its structure and mode of operation from a traditional teaching university. It has no students of its own, no faculty and no campus. It operates through worldwide networks of academic and research institutions, including its own research and training centres and programmes, as well as individual scholars, to address global problems.

Current priority areas of concern are universal human values and global responsibilities; new directions for the world economy; sustaining global life-support systems; advances in science and technology; population dynamics and human welfare. UNU also aims to strengthen research and training capabilities in developing countries.

The University's research and training centres and programmes (RTC/Ps) specialize in particular areas of research and training. They conduct in-house research and training, and coordinate research and training involving higher education institutions in many countries. The University has the following RTC/Ps:

♦   UNU World Institute for Development Economics Research (UNU/WIDER), Helsinki, Finland (1985);

♦   UNU Institute for New Technologies (UNU/TECH), Maastricht, The Netherlands (1990);

♦   UNU International Institute for Software Technology (UNU/IIST), Macau (1992);

♦   UNU Institute for Natural Resources in Africa (UNU/INRA), Accra, Ghana, with a Mineral Resources Unit in Lusaka, Zambia (1990).

The University has also the Programme for Biotechnology in Latin America and the Caribbean (UNU/BIOLAC), Caracas, Venezuela (1988).

United Nations Research Institute for Social Development (UNRISD)

The United Nations Research Institute for Social Development (UNRISD) is an autonomous agency that engages in multidisciplinary research on the social dimensions of contemporary problems affecting development. Its work is guided by the conviction that, for effective development policies to be formulated, an understanding of the social and political context is crucial. The Institute seeks to provide Governments, development agencies, grass-roots organizations and scholars with a better understanding of how development policies and processes of economic, social and environmental change affect different social groups. Working through an extensive network of national research centres, UNRISD aims to promote original research and strengthen research capacity in developing countries.

Current research themes are structural adjustment, illicit drugs, sustainable development, integrating gender into development policy, ethnic conflict, changes in property relations in Communist and post-Communist societies, political violence, and themes relating to the 1995 World Summit for Social Development.

The Institute, which is based at Geneva, relies wholly on voluntary contributions for financing its activities.

CHAPTER 4

HUMAN RIGHTS

In the Preamble to the United Nations Charter, the peoples of the United Nations declare their determination "to save succeeding generations from the scourge of war, reaffirm faith in fundamental human rights, and to promote social progress and better standards of life in larger freedom". Accordingly, Article 1 of the Charter proclaims that one of the purposes of the United Nations is to achieve international cooperation in promoting and encouraging respect for human rights and fundamental freedoms for all without distinction as to race, sex, language or religion.

UNIVERSAL DECLARATION OF HUMAN RIGHTS

One of the first major achievements of the United Nations in the field of human rights was the adoption of the Universal Declaration of Human Rights by the General Assembly on 10 December 1948. The Assembly proclaimed the Declaration to be "a common standard of achievement for all peoples and all nations". It called upon Member States and all peoples to promote and secure the recognition and observance of the rights and freedoms set forth in the Declaration.

Each year, the anniversary of the adoption of the Declaration, 10 December, is observed internationally as Human Rights Day.

Articles 1 and 2 of the Declaration state that "all human beings are born equal in dignity and rights" and are entitled to all the rights and freedoms set forth in the Declaration "without distinction of any kind such as race, colour, sex, language, religion, political or other opinion, national or social origin, property, birth or other status".

Articles 3 to 21 set forth the civil and political rights to which all human beings are entitled, including:

♦ the right to life, liberty and security;
♦ freedom from slavery and servitude;
♦ freedom from torture or cruel, inhuman or degrading treatment or punishment;

♦　the right to recognition as a person before the law; the right to judicial remedy; freedom from arbitrary arrest, detention or exile; the right to a fair trial and public hearing by an independent and impartial tribunal; the right to be presumed innocent until proved guilty;

♦　freedom from arbitrary interference with privacy, family, home or correspondence; freedom from attacks upon honour and reputation; the right to protection of the law against such attacks;

♦　freedom of movement; the right of asylum; the right to a nationality;

♦　the right to marry and to found a family; the right to own property;

♦　freedom of thought, conscience and religion; freedom of opinion and expression;

♦　the right to peaceful assembly and association;

♦　the right to take part in government and to equal access to public service.

Articles 22 to 27 set forth the economic, social and cultural rights to which all human beings are entitled, including:

♦　the right to social security;

♦　the right to work; the right to equal pay for equal work; the right to form and join trade unions;

♦　the right to rest and leisure;

♦　the right to a standard of living adequate for health and well-being;

♦　the right to education;

♦　the right to participate in the cultural life of the community.

The concluding Articles, 28 to 30, recognize that everyone is entitled to a social and international order in which the human rights set forth in the Declaration may be fully realized; that these rights may only be limited for the sole purpose of securing recognition and respect of the rights and freedoms of others; and that each person has duties to the community in which she or he lives.

INTERNATIONAL COVENANTS ON HUMAN RIGHTS

Following adoption of the Universal Declaration, work began on the drafting of two International Covenants on Human

Rights—one on economic, social and cultural rights and the other on civil and political rights—to put into binding legal form the rights proclaimed in the Declaration.

The International Covenant on Economic, Social and Cultural Rights, the International Covenant on Civil and Political Rights and the Optional Protocol to the latter Covenant were adopted unanimously by the General Assembly on 16 December 1966. These instruments, along with the Declaration itself and a second Optional Protocol adopted in 1989, make up what is now widely known as the International Bill of Human Rights.

Although the Covenants are based on the Universal Declaration, the rights covered are not identical. The most important right guaranteed by both Covenants and not contained in the Declaration is the right of peoples to self-determination, including the right to dispose freely of their natural wealth and resources.

The International Covenant on Economic, Social and Cultural Rights entered into force on 3 January 1976. By 31 December 1994, it had 131 States parties.

The human rights which the Covenant seeks to promote and protect are of three kinds:

♦ the right to work in just and favourable conditions;
♦ the right to social protection, to an adequate standard of living and to the highest attainable standards of physical and mental well-being;
♦ the right to education and the enjoyment of benefits of cultural freedom and scientific progress.

The Covenant provides for the realization of these rights without discrimination of any kind. States parties to the Covenant submit periodic reports to the Economic and Social Council (ECOSOC). The Committee on Economic, Social and Cultural Rights, an 18-member body of experts set up by the Council to assist it in implementing the Covenant, studies these reports and discusses them with representatives of the Governments concerned. Its comments on the Covenant aim to help States parties in their task of implementation as well as to bring to their attention deficiencies in reports and reporting procedures. The Committee may also make recommendations to the Council based on its consideration of individual reports.

The International Covenant on Civil and Political Rights and the First Optional Protocol to that Covenant both entered into force on 23 March 1976. By 31 December 1994, the Covenant had 129 States parties, and the Protocol 80.

The Covenant deals with such rights as freedom of movement, equality before the law, the right to a fair trial and presumption of innocence, freedom of thought, conscience and religion, freedom of opinion and expression, peaceful assembly, freedom of association, participation in public affairs and elections and protection of minority rights. It prohibits arbitrary deprivation of life; torture, cruel or degrading treatment or punishment; slavery and forced labour; arbitrary arrest or detention and arbitrary interference with privacy; war propaganda, and advocacy of racial or religious hatred.

The Covenant established an 18-member Human Rights Committee, which considers reports submitted by States parties on measures taken to implement the Covenant's provisions. The Committee makes recommendations to the States parties, based on its study of their reports. The Committee also makes general comments on certain provisions of the Covenant which are designed to help States parties to give effect to the Covenant. If certain requirements are met, the Committee may receive communications from one State party claiming that another State party is not carrying out its obligations under the Covenant.

The Human Rights Committee receives and considers communications from individuals who claim that their human rights, being those rights protected by the Covenant, have been violated by a State party. This function was established under the First Optional Protocol. The Committee considers in private meetings communications from individuals. Their letters and other documentation about individual cases, remain confidential. The findings of the Committee, however, are made public immediately after the session at which they were adopted and are reproduced in the Committee's annual report to the General Assembly. Several countries have changed their laws as a result of decisions taken by the Committee on individual complaints under the First Optional Protocol. In a number of cases, prisoners have been released and compensation paid to victims of human rights violations. The Committee has instituted a mechanism whereby it seeks to monitor more closely whether States parties have given effect to its decisions.

The Second Optional Protocol of the International Covenant on Civil and Political Rights Aiming at Abolition of the Death Penalty was adopted by the General Assembly on 15 December 1989. As of 31 December 1994, 26 States had agreed to be bound by the provisions of the Second Protocol, the implementation of which is supervised by the Human Rights Committee.

SPECIALIZED HUMAN RIGHTS TREATIES

The International Bill of Rights has been further supplemented by several international legal instruments dealing with particular kinds of human rights violations such as torture and racial discrimination, or focusing on particular groups of vulnerable persons such as children and migrant workers.

In addition to the two Covenants, six of the major specialized human rights treaties provide for committees of experts to oversee the implementation of their provisions. States parties to such treaties agree to submit regular reports to the applicable committee, giving details about implementation and identifying problems which have arisen. By examining these reports and any other information it may have at hand, the Committee can make recommendations to assist a State in fulfilling its legal obligations.

HUMAN RIGHTS BODIES

Set up by ECOSOC in 1946, the **Commission on Human Rights** is responsible for submitting proposals, recommendations and investigative reports on human rights issues through ECOSOC to the General Assembly. Over time, the Commission has grown to be the prevailing human rights organ of the United Nations, providing a forum for States, intergovernmental and non-governmental organizations to voice their concerns about human rights issues. Made up of 53 Member States elected for three-year terms, the Commission meets for six weeks each year in Geneva.

In recent years, the Commission has set up mechanisms to investigate human rights problems in specific countries and territories as well as on thematic situations. These mechanisms include Working Groups as well as Special Rapporteurs on specific countries and issues.

The **Sub-Commission on the Prevention of Discrimination and the Protection of Minorities** was set up by ECOSOC in 1946 to aid the Commission in its task. Composed of 26 experts from all regions of the world, the Sub-Commission makes recommendations and conducts investigations on issues dealing with the prevention of discrimination and the protection of ethnic, religious, racial and linguistic minorities.

(For **Commission on the Status of Women**, see Promoting the Rights of Women, below.)

WORLD CONFERENCE ON HUMAN RIGHTS

Twenty years after the adoption of the Universal Declaration of Human Rights, the United Nations commemorated the occasion by declaring 1968 as the International Year for Human Rights. The major event of the Year was the International Conference on Human Rights in Teheran, which adopted a programme of action and a Proclamation.

Twenty-five years after the Teheran Conference, the 1993 World Conference in Vienna marked a significant step forward in the attempt by the international community to promote and protect human rights and fundamental freedoms everywhere. The Vienna Declaration and Programme of Action, emanating from the Conference, represents the basis for common future efforts by the international community for the universal enjoyment of human rights and fundamental freedoms.

The agenda of the Conference, as set by the General Assembly in 1992, included identifying obstacles to further progress in the field of human rights and ways to overcome them; the relationship between development, democracy and the universal enjoyment of all human rights; new challenges to the full realization of human rights; and ways of strengthening international cooperation in the field of human rights, of enhancing the effectiveness of United Nations activities and mechanisms, and of securing financial and other resources for such activities.

The preparatory process reflected differences between developing and industrialized countries on various issues, such as universality of human rights versus regional particularity, the interlinkage and indivisibility of all human rights, the interdependence between the right to development and civil and political rights, the threat of terrorism to the enjoyment of civil and political rights, and the question of the implementation machinery, monitoring and prevention. It was only at the last preparatory session that some progress was visible.

The Conference was marked by an unprecedented degree of participation by Governments, United Nations agencies and bodies, national institutions and 841 non-governmental organizations (NGOs). The Vienna Declaration and Programme of Action was adopted by consensus by 171 States, and endorsed by the General Assembly in December 1993. The Assembly called for further action to fully implement the recommendations of the Conference.

The Conference's achievements include:

♦ recommending the establishment of a High Commissioner for Human Rights (see below);

♦ reinforcement of the universality of human rights;

♦ recognition for the first time, by consensus, that the right to development is an inalienable right;

♦ integration of economic, social and cultural rights as indivisible and interlinked with civil and political rights;

♦ recognition of democracy as a human right, thus opening the way to the strengthening and promotion of democracy, democratization and the rule of law;

♦ recognition that the acts, methods and practices of terrorism aim at the destruction of human rights; and

♦ reinforcement of policies and programmes to eliminate racism and racial discrimination, xenophobia and intolerance.

The Vienna Declaration and Programme of Action also focus on massive violations of human rights, especially genocide, ethnic cleansing and systematic rape; on self-determination, referring for the first time to "a government representing the whole people belonging to a territory without distinction of any kind"; on the environmental needs of present and future generations; on groups "rendered vulnerable", including migrant workers, disabled persons and refugees; and on the human rights of women and the girl child, including the establishment of new policy guidelines to bring the human rights of women into the mainstream of United Nations human rights activities.

The Declaration and Programme of Action also recognize that organizations, agencies and organs of the United Nations system, as well as regional organizations and financial and development institutions, should have an enhanced role in promoting and protecting human rights.

HIGH COMMISSIONER FOR HUMAN RIGHTS

The General Assembly in December 1993 established the post of United Nations High Commissioner for Human Rights as the United Nations official with principal responsibility for United Nations human rights activities, under the direction and authority of the Secretary-General. The first High Commissioner was appointed in February 1994.

The High Commissioner is responsible for promoting and protecting the enjoyment by all of all civil, cultural, political and social rights; promoting and protecting the realization of the right to development and enhancing support from bodies of the United Nations system for that purpose; providing, through the Centre for Human Rights and other institutions, advisory services and technical and financial assistance in the field of human rights; coordinating United Nations education and public information programmes on human rights; helping to remove the obstacles and meet the challenges of the full realization of all human rights and preventing the continuation of human rights violations throughout the world; engaging in a dialogue with Governments to secure respect for human rights; and carrying out tasks assigned to him/her by the competent bodies of the United Nations system and making recommendations to them with a view to improving the promotion and protection of all human rights.

The High Commissioner is also responsible for enhancing international cooperation for the promotion and protection of all human rights; coordinating human rights promotion and protection activities throughout the United Nations system; rationalizing, adapting, strengthening and streamlining the

United Nations machinery to improve its efficiency and effectiveness; and supervising the Centre for Human Rights.

CENTRE FOR HUMAN RIGHTS

The purpose of the Centre for Human Rights is to assist the organs of the United Nations in the promotion and protection of human rights, to carry out research at the request of the organs concerned, and to publish and disseminate information on human rights. The Centre also services several human rights bodies, including the Commission on Human Rights and the Subcommission on the Prevention of Discrimination and the Protection of Minorities.

The Centre, located in Geneva, comprises the Office of the Assistant Secretary-General for Human Rights and five branches, as well as the Office of the High Commissioner on Human Rights. The Communications Branch processes communications concerning alleged human rights violations. The Special Procedures Branch services the investigative organs set up by human rights bodies, such as Working Groups and Special Rapporteurs, and organizes field missions. The International Instruments Branch follows the implementation of human rights treaties and conventions. The Legislation and Prevention of Discrimination Branch assists in preparing international human rights instruments and prepares studies and reports requested by the Sub-Commission. The Technical and Advisory Services Branch administers the programme of advisory services and technical assistance, including the Voluntary Fund for Technical Cooperation and Advisory Services. In 1994, technical assistance was provided upon request to 37 countries. Field offices of the Centre have been established in Guatemala, Cambodia, Burundi, Croatia, Rwanda and Malawi.

PUTTING AN END TO VIOLATIONS

The United Nations strives to combat human rights violations both through the public discussion and investigation of pattern of violations and the confidential consideration of complaints from individuals and organizations.

Each year the Commission on Human Rights and its Subcommission on Prevention of Discrimination and Protection of Minorities discuss, in meetings open to the press and public, violations of human rights wherever they occur in the world. Members of these bodies and non-governmental organizations (NGOs) present information on situations of concern to them; the Governments involved often submit replies. In light of the examination of such situations, fact-finding groups or experts may be designated, on-the-spot visits may be organized, discussions with Governments pursued, assistance provided and violations condemned.

If a particular "country" situation is deemed sufficiently serious, the Commission may order an investigation by either a group of independent experts (Working Group) or an individual (Special Rapporteur). Based on information received from these experts, the Commission then calls upon the Government concerned to bring about needed changes. It may also appoint experts to assess, in cooperation with the Government concerned, the assistance needed to help restore full enjoyment of human rights. Circumstances will often require an investigation to continue for many years. For example, the question of violations of human rights in the territories occupied by Israel, including Palestine, has been considered by the Commission since 1968.

As of March 1995, there were country-specific Special Rapporteurs of the Commission for Afghanistan, Burundi, Cuba, Equatorial Guinea, Iran, Iraq, Myanmar (formerly Burma), the occupied Arab territories including Palestine, Rwanda, Sudan, the former Yugoslavia and Zaire.

The Commission also studies human rights as a global phenomenon by investigating "thematic" human rights issues and violations which are not specific to a particular country. Examples are the Working Group on Enforced and Involuntary Disappearances and the Working Group on Arbitrary Detention.

Special Rapporteurs have been named to investigate reports of summary or arbitrary executions and to look into reports of torture. Other human rights issues examined by Special Rapporteurs include religious intolerance; freedom of expression; violence against women; child prostitution, child pornography and adoptions for commercial purposes. The Rapporteurs receive reports from individuals and organizations and, where appropriate, deal with the Governments concerned to clarify allegations and bring human rights violations to an end.

Complaints of human rights violations

Complaints under the specialized treaties. The Convention on the Elimination of All Forms of Racial Discrimination, the Convention against Torture and the Convention on the Rights of Migrant Workers all contain provisions whereby States may authorize the United Nations to receive complaints from their citizens about violations of the rights covered in that instrument.

When a convention-monitoring committee receives a complaint about a State party, provided the State party has declared itself willing to let people under its jurisdiction complain to the United Nations, it seeks clarification from the Government concerned. It must determine that the case is not under consideration in any other international forum, and that all domestic legal remedies have been exhausted. Once those conditions are satisfied, the committee renders an opinion based on the information presented by the plaintiff and by the State, and sends it to both parties.

Complaints under the 1503 procedure. Each year, the United Nations receives hundreds of thousands of letters and reports of human rights violations which fall outside the treaty-based complaint mechanisms outlined above. The procedure developed to deal with these complaints, since it is governed mainly by ECOSOC resolution 1503 (XLVIII), is commonly known as the 1503 procedure.

Letters and reports containing allegations of human rights violations which cannot be dealt with by one of the specialized committees are summarized in confidential documents, which are sent to members of the Commission on Human Rights and of its Subcommission. Copies of the letters are sent to the Member State, which has an opportunity to send a response to the United Nations.

Individual complaints and government responses are discussed first in the Subcommission. If it concludes that they appear to be "a consistent pattern of gross and reliably attested violation of human rights", it refers the complaint to the

Commission, which may then investigate further. Complaints are discussed in closed meetings and remain confidential until the Commission decides to submit a report to ECOSOC. In these closed meetings, the Commission considers complaints concerning many countries from all regions of the world.

Preventing extrajudicial executions and disappearances

The Commission on Human Rights has established special procedures to investigate both summary executions and disappearances.

The Working Group on Enforced or Involuntary Disappearances, which meets three times a year, receives reports from Governments, intergovernmental organizations and NGOs, as well as from individuals, their families or their representatives. It examines the reports and forwards them to the Governments concerned with a request for the fullest possible information on the fate and whereabouts of the missing person. Any information obtained is then sent to the relatives of the missing person. Specific recommendations, as well as general recommendations concerning the causes of disappearances and measures to alleviate them, may then be made to the Government and transmitted to the Commission. The Working Group has established an "urgent action procedure" which allows it to act quickly in emergency situations.

In 1982, the Commission on Human Rights appointed a Special Rapporteur to investigate summary or arbitrary executions—killings carried out by order of a Government or with its complicity which are in violation of international human rights norms or of the laws which govern wars and armed conflicts. The Special Rapporteur is empowered to respond to information received, particularly when the information indicates that an arbitrary or summary execution is imminent. In such case, he may send urgent messages to the Government concerned asking for its compliance with international standards and protection of the lives of persons allegedly at risk of being executed. In other situations, he will communicate allegations of summary or arbitrary executions to the Government concerned, requesting additional information. He may also visit countries at the invitation of Governments. His report is discussed publicly in the Commission on Human Rights.

Preventing arbitrary detention

In 1991 the Commission established a Working Group on Arbitrary Detention to investigate cases of arbitrary detention inconsistent with international standards. The Working Group receives information from a wide variety of sources, including Governments, intergovernmental organizations and NGOs, concerned individuals, their families or their representatives. The Working Group transmits this information to the relevant Governments, who are asked to reply within nine months. After this time has elapsed and based on all information at its disposal, the Working Group takes a decision on the detention and its alleged arbitrariness in the context of international standards and the obligations of the country concerned.

The fight against torture

In 1975, the General Assembly adopted the Declaration on the Protection of All Persons from Being Subjected to Torture and Other Cruel, Inhuman or Degrading Treatment or Punishment, which states that such acts are an offence to human dignity and a violation of human rights and fundamental freedoms. In 1982, it adopted Principles of Medical Ethics relating to the role of health personnel, particularly doctors, in protecting prisoners and detainees against torture and other cruel punishment.

In 1984, the General Assembly adopted the Convention against Torture and Other Cruel, Inhuman and Degrading Treatment or Punishment. By 31 December 1994, there were 86 States parties to the Convention, which obliges States to make torture a crime and prosecute and punish those guilty of it. The Convention states that neither higher orders nor exceptional circumstances can justify torture. It provides for the trial of torturers in the courts of States parties, no matter where the torture took place, and allows for an international inquiry if there is reliable information that torture is being practised in a State party.

The Convention established a 10-member Committee Against Torture, which receives reports from States parties on measures taken to prevent torture. The Committee considers such reports, makes general comments on them and informs other States parties and the General Assembly of its activities.

The United Nations Voluntary Fund for Victims of Torture provides humanitarian, legal and financial aid to torture victims and their relatives. Most of the grants made through the Fund finance therapy and rehabilitation projects.

In 1985, the Commission on Human Rights appointed a Special Rapporteur on torture, who receives information in individual cases of torture and has the capacity to act quickly in urgent cases. He also engages in fact-finding to establish the situation in a country, and makes recommendations to the Commission on the problem of torture in general.

Advisory services and technical assistance

Since 1955, the Centre for Human Rights has administered a programme of advisory services and technical assistance which aims to foster a climate conducive to respect for human rights. The programme encompasses a wide range of activities from the training of public officials and law enforcement personnel to the establishment of national human rights institutions such as offices of the ombudsman, national commissions and documentation centres. Governments are provided with expert assistance in a number of crucial areas, including election procedure, drafting of constitutions and legislation, and the development of effective and accessible legal systems.

ELIMINATING RACIAL DISCRIMINATION

In 1963, the General Assembly adopted the United Nations Declaration on the Elimination of All Forms of Racial Discrimination. The Declaration affirms the fundamental equality of all persons and confirms that discrimination between human beings on the grounds of race, colour or ethnic origin is an offence to human dignity, a denial of the principles of the United Nations Charter, a violation of the human rights proclaimed in the Universal Declaration and an obstacle to friendly and peaceful relations among nations and peoples.

Two years later, the General Assembly adopted the International Convention on the Elimination of All Forms of Racial

Discrimination. The Convention entered into force on 4 January 1969 and by 31 December 1994, 142 States were party to it. States parties undertake to pursue a policy of eliminating racial discrimination and promoting understanding among races.

The Committee on the Elimination of Racial Discrimination, an 18-member body of experts set up by the Convention, reviews reports submitted by States parties on the measures they have adopted to implement the Convention, discusses the reports with government representatives and makes general recommendations. It may also consider complaints submitted by individuals or groups alleging that the Convention has been violated, provided that the State concerned has made a declaration under the Convention recognizing the competence of the Committee to receive such complaints.

The General Assembly in 1993 proclaimed the Third Decade to Combat Racism and Racial Discrimination (1993-2003), and called on all States to take measures to combat new forms of racism, especially through laws, administrative measures, education and information. It declared that all forms of racism and racial discrimination, including those resulting from official doctrines of racial superiority, such as ethnic cleansing, are among the most serious violations of human rights in the contemporary world and must be combated by all available means.

The first Decade for Action to Combat Racism and Racial Discrimination was proclaimed in 1973, and the Second Decade in 1983. Two World Conferences to Combat Racism and Racial Discrimination were held in Geneva in 1978 and 1983.

PROMOTING THE RIGHTS OF WOMEN

The United Nations Charter is the first international instrument to mention the equal rights of men and women in specific terms. It proclaims the determination of the peoples of the United Nations "to reaffirm faith in fundamental human rights, in the dignity and worth of the human person, in the equal rights of men and women". This principle is elaborated in the Universal Declaration, which proclaims that "all human beings are born free and equal in dignity and rights" and that "everyone is entitled to all the rights and freedoms set forth (therein) without distinction of any kind", including distinction based on sex.

When designing the human rights machinery of the United Nations, a special body to deal with women's issues—the **Commission on the Status of Women**—was established in 1946 by the Economic and Social Council. The 45-member Commission examines women's progress towards equality throughout the world, prepares recommendations on promoting women's rights in political, economic, social and educational fields, and addresses problems requiring immediate attention in the field of women's rights. It also drafts treaties and other instruments aimed at improving the status of women in law and in practice.

The activities of the Commission have evolved from defining rights to exploring factors that have prevented women from enjoying them. Thus emphasis has shifted to underlying social and cultural causes of discrimination. In 1993, for example, a Declaration on the Elimination of Violence against Women, elaborated by the Commission, was adopted by the General Assembly. The Declaration includes a clear definition of violence as being physical, sexual and psychological violence occurring in the family or the community and perpetrated or condoned by the State. It identifies measures to address the factors conducive to such violence and to the victimization of women and spells out the rights to be protected as well as the action to be taken by States and international organizations.

Convention on the Elimination of All Forms of Discrimination against Women

The first concern of the Commission on the Status of Women was to establish a firm base in international law of the norms of equality. The Convention on the Political Rights of Women, adopted by the General Assembly in 1952, was the first United Nations instrument in which States parties undertook legal obligations involving the principle of equal rights between women and men. The Convention on the Nationality of Married Women, adopted by the General Assembly in 1952, was a response to the lack of equal rights between men and women in terms of family law. The Convention on Consent to Marriage, Minimum Age for Marriage and Registration of

Marriages, adopted in 1962, was intended to ensure by national legislation equal rights for both spouses.

The culmination of the work of the Commission in terms of human rights law is the Convention on the Elimination of All Forms of Discrimination against Women. Adopted by the Assembly in 1979, the Convention was rapidly ratified and is now the main instrument for women's human rights. The six-part, 30-article Convention covers measures to be taken by States to eliminate discrimination against women in many areas, including political and public life, nationality, education, employment, health, marriage and family life. It defines women's rights in the context of the international human rights regime and reflects the evolution from the recognition of women's rights by law to their exercise in practice. As of 31 December 1994, the Convention had 138 States parties.

The Committee on the Elimination of Discrimination against Women, made up of 23 experts, is the body established under the Convention to monitor its implementation. States parties report periodically to the Committee on measures they have taken to give effect to the provisions of the Convention.

(See also Role of Women in Development in Chapter 3.)

THE RIGHTS OF THE CHILD

The Declaration of the Rights of the Child, adopted by the General Assembly in 1959, affirms the right of children to special protection, opportunities and facilities for a healthy, normal development. These and other rights have been transformed into binding legal obligations through the adoption by the Assembly in 1989 of the Convention on the Rights of the Child. By 31 December 1994, the Convention had 168 States parties. A Committee on the Rights of the Child, established under the Convention, meets regularly to monitor the progress made by States parties in fulfilling their obligations. The Committee can make suggestions and recommendations to Governments and to the General Assembly on ways in which the objectives of the Convention may be met.

(On **Rights of disabled persons,** see Disabled Persons in Chapter 3).

OTHER HUMAN RIGHTS QUESTIONS

Human rights and development

In 1986, the General Assembly adopted the Declaration on the Right to Development, proclaiming that right to be an inalienable human right by virtue of which each person and all peoples are entitled to participate in, contribute to and enjoy economic, social, cultural and political development in which all human rights and fundamental freedoms can be realized. The question of the realization of the right to development continues to be considered by the Commission on Human Rights. The Committee on Economic, Social and Cultural Rights has also addressed the issue. On the proposal of the Committee, a Global Consultation on the Realization of the Right to Development as a Human Right was held in Geneva in 1990.

Protecting minorities

The Declaration on the Rights of Persons Belonging to National or Ethnic, Religious and Linguistic Minorities, adopted by the General Assembly in 1992, proclaims the right of minorities to enjoy their own culture; to profess and practice their own religion; to use their own language; to establish and maintain contacts with other members of their group; and to leave any country, including their own, and to return to their country. The Declaration calls for action by States to promote and protect the human rights and fundamental freedoms of persons belonging to minorities, especially in the areas of teaching, education, culture and information.

Protecting indigenous people

The term "indigenous people" is used to refer to the descendants of those who inhabited a country or geographical region at a time when peoples of a different culture or ethnic origin arrived and subsequently became dominant through conquest, occupation, settlement or other means. Today, there are millions of indigenous people inhabiting large but usually marginal areas of the planet. In 1982, the Subcommission established a Working Group on Indigenous Populations which drafted a Universal Declaration on the Rights of Indigenous Peoples for adoption by the General Assembly. The draft was approved by the Subcommission in 1994. In 1990, the General Assembly proclaimed 1993 as the International Year of the World's Indigenous People. The aim was to strengthen international cooperation for solving problems faced by indigenous communities in the areas of human rights, the environment, development, education and health. At the conclusion of the Year, the Assembly proclaimed an International Decade of the World's Indigenous People (1994-2004). A Voluntary Fund is to be established to finance projects and programmes during the Decade.

Protecting migrant workers

In 1990, the General Assembly adopted the Convention on the Protection of the Rights of All Migrant Workers and the Members of their Families, which sets standards for the laws and judicial and administrative procedures of States. Governments which become parties to the Convention undertake to apply its provisions, and to ensure that migrant workers whose rights have been violated may seek judicial remedy. As of 30 September 1994, the Convention had not yet acquired the necessary number of ratifications (20) to enter into force. Once this number is reached, a Committee on the Protection of the Rights of All Migrant Workers and the Members of their Families will be established to review implementation. The Committee will receive regular reports from States parties indicating problems encountered in implementing the Convention and information on migration flows.

QUESTION OF APARTHEID

Apartheid (an Afrikaans word meaning separateness) was a system of institutionalized racial segregation and discrimination imposed by the South African Government as official policy from 1948 until early 1990.

Under apartheid, the South African population was divided into separate groups according to colour—Black (African), White (European), Coloured and Indian. Black South Africans—some 73 per cent of the population—were denied fundamental rights and liberties. They were not allowed to participate in political life and were subject to repressive laws and regulations.

Segregation was enforced and regulated by a myriad of laws, chief among which was the Population Registration Act (1950), which defined racial categories, compiled a register of the population and issued "identity cards". Segregation was further entrenched by dividing the country into a White (European) area and African reserves, and by segregating people in the White area into so-called "group areas". Within the White urban areas, the Group Areas Act (1950) was used to divide the non-White population into different residential areas (Coloured, Indian, Black), while the African population was further divided on an "ethnic" basis within the townships set aside for them.

Ten reserves, called "bantustans" (or so-called "home-lands"), were assigned to Africans, one for each of the "national units" of the African population as defined by the Government. These were scattered in 81 separate and non-contiguous pieces of land. Although Africans outnumber Whites by more than 4 to 1, these reserves constituted only 13 per cent of the land in South Africa and contained some of the most arid and infertile areas in the country.

International efforts for eliminating apartheid

The racial policies of the Government of South Africa were a major concern of the United Nations for more than 47 years. The question was first raised in the United Nations in 1946, when India complained that the South African Government had enacted legislation discriminating against South Africans of Indian origin. The wider question of racial conflict arising from the apartheid policies was placed on the Assembly's agenda in 1952.

During the 1950s, the General Assembly repeatedly appealed to the South African Government to abandon apartheid in the light of the principles of the Charter. However, South Africa refused to heed the appeals of the Assembly, viewing the United Nations decisions as illegal and unacceptable and as violating the principle of non-interference in its internal affairs.

In 1960, following the Sharpeville incident of 21 March in

which 69 anti-apartheid demonstrators were killed, the Security Council called on South Africa to abandon its apartheid policy.

From 1966, 21 March has been observed as the International Day for the Elimination of Racial Discrimination, commemorating the Sharpeville incident.

In 1962, the General Assembly established the United Nations Special Committee against Apartheid to keep the racial policies of South Africa under review. The Special Committee quickly became the focal point in the efforts of the international community to promote a comprehensive programme of action against apartheid, and to encourage support and assistance to the people of South Africa and to their liberation movements.

From 1961, the General Assembly asked States to consider taking a broad range of actions. It called on States to end diplomatic relations with South Africa; close ports to all South African flag vessels; prohibit ships from entering South African ports; boycott all trade with South Africa; refuse landing and passage facilities to all aircraft belonging to the Government and companies registered under South African laws; and institute a voluntary embargo on the supply of oil and strategic raw materials to South Africa. From 1962 to 1988, the General Assembly repeatedly urged the Security Council to impose mandatory sanctions against South Africa.

The Security Council instituted a voluntary arms embargo in 1963, and made the arms embargo mandatory on 4 November 1977. The measure was taken under Chapter VII of the Charter, which provides for enforcement action with respect to threats to international peace and security.

In another censure of South Africa, the General Assembly did not accept its credentials to the Assembly's regular sessions from 1970 through 1974. In 1974, the Assembly President noted the consistency with which the Assembly had refused to accept the credentials of the South African delegation and said it was "tantamount to saying in explicit terms that the General Assembly refuses to allow the delegation of South Africa to participate in its work". After that, South Africa did not participate in the proceedings of the Assembly.

Also in 1974, the Assembly recommended that the regime

be excluded from participation in all international organizations and conferences held under United Nations auspices so long as it continued to practise apartheid. However, a proposal made to the Security Council in 1974 for the expulsion of South Africa from the Organization did not receive the necessary majority of Council members.

The United Nations also adopted a wide range of measures aimed at providing political, moral and material support for the South African liberation movements recognized by the Organization of African Unity (OAU)—the African National Congress of South Africa (ANC) and the Pan Africanist Congress of Azania (PAC).

Both the General Assembly (1971) and the Security Council (1972) recognized the "legitimacy of the struggle of the oppressed people of South Africa" in pursuance of their human and political rights. The Assembly subsequently declared that the people had an inalienable right to use all available means, including armed struggle.

From 1974, the Assembly invited representatives of the ANC and PAC to participate as observers in debates on the question of South Africa.

The General Assembly appealed on several occasions for the liberation of political prisoners. It condemned executions of freedom fighters and the torture and killing of detainees and demanded prisoner-of-war treatment for freedom fighters. The Security Council appealed several times for the commutation of death sentences passed after political trials. In 1976, the Assembly proclaimed 11 October as the Day of Solidarity with South African Political Prisoners.

To draw attention to South Africa's discriminatory policy in sports, the General Assembly called on individual sportsmen and sportswomen to boycott South Africa (1971), adopted the International Declaration against Apartheid in Sports (1977) and adopted the International Convention against Apartheid in Sports (1985).

In 1973, the General Assembly adopted the International Convention on the Suppression and Punishment of the Crime of Apartheid. In 1976, following the uprising in Soweto and other areas on 16 June, the Assembly proclaimed that date as

International Day of Solidarity with the Struggling People of South Africa, and 9 August as the International Day of Solidarity with the Struggle of Women in South Africa.

Also in 1976, the General Assembly approved a Programme of Action against Apartheid for implementation by Governments, intergovernmental organizations, trade unions, churches, anti-apartheid and solidarity movements and other NGOs. In 1977, the Assembly proclaimed the year beginning 21 March 1978 as International Anti-Apartheid Year, and declared 1982 as the International Year of Mobilization of Sanctions against South Africa.

International and regional conferences and seminars, convened under United Nations auspices to explore ways to eliminate apartheid, were held in all parts of the world.

Dismantling apartheid

Beginning in 1989, a series of developments, both within and outside South Africa, set the scene for a process which held the promise for the elimination of apartheid through negotiations. Improvements in the international climate facilitating the peaceful resolution of conflicts were manifested in southern Africa by agreements that led to the independence of Namibia. Within South Africa, renewed demands by anti-apartheid organizations for a negotiated end to apartheid and a new constitutional order led to a change of thinking within the country's ruling National Party towards a new policy which acknowledged the failure of apartheid and the need for constitutional change.

Steps taken towards the dismantling of apartheid by the South African Government from 1990 included the lifting of the ban on ANC, PAC, the South African Communist Party and other political organizations; the release of political leaders like Mr. Nelson Mandela, imprisoned for over 27 years; the granting of immunity for political offences to South Africans both inside and outside the country; and an agreement with the United Nations High Commissioner for Refugees which allowed the return of exiles and refugees.

The Government also repealed major legal structures and apartheid legislation and entered into a National Peace Accord with major political parties and organizations aimed at promoting peace and reconciliation in violence-stricken communities and the country as a whole. A Commission of Inquiry Regarding the Prevention of Violence and Intimidation (Goldstone Commission) was set up to facilitate the implementation of the Accord.

To support this process, the General Assembly at a special session on apartheid in December 1989, adopted the Declaration on Apartheid and its Destructive Consequences in Southern Africa. The Declaration encouraged the people of South Africa to join together to negotiate an end to the apartheid system and agree on measures to transform their country into a non-racial democracy.

In December 1991, the Government entered into negotiations with the parties concerned to reach agreement on constitutional principles, political participation, the role of the international community, transitional arrangements, and the time-frame for implementing decisions leading to the adoption of a new Constitution and the holding of free, democratic and non-racial elections.

The United Nations continued to support the transition. Both the General Assembly and the Security Council welcomed the political process that led to the convening of multi-party talks. The Assembly and the Council expressed concern at the escalation of political violence, and urged the parties to make efforts to end the violence and reach agreement on transitional arrangements.

Two Security Council resolutions in July and August 1992 emphasized the involvement by the international community in facilitating the transition. In response to these resolutions, the Secretary-General dispatched a Special Representative to visit South Africa and to make recommendations on measures to end the violence; he also dispatched two special envoys to carry out fact-finding missions. The Security Council deployed in September a **United Nations Observer Mission in South Africa (UNOMSA)**.

The objective of UNOMSA was to strengthen the structures of the National Peace Accord and help end the violence. The Mission coordinated its work with the National Peace Committee, the National Peace Secretariat and the Goldstone

Commission, as well as with observer teams of the OAU, the European Union and the Commonwealth Secretariat. UNOMSA personnel observed demonstrations, marches and other forms of mass action, noting the conduct of all parties. They also established contacts at all levels with governmental structures, political parties and organizations, civic associations and other community-based groups.

The General Assembly in December 1992 called upon the international community to support the process under way in South Africa and to review restrictive measures as warranted by positive developments. In view of the progress made, the Assembly called for the resumption of academic, scientific, cultural and sports links with democratic, anti-apartheid organizations and individuals.

By September 1993, significant progress had been achieved at the Multi-Party Negotiating Forum, and agreement was reached on constitutional issues and transitional arrangements such as the holding of free and democratic elections to a non-racial Constituent Assembly, the formation of a Transitional Executive Council and the establishment of an independent electoral commission.

On 24 September, ANC President Nelson Mandela addressed the Special Committee against Apartheid at United Nations Headquarters. He called on the international community to lift all economic sanctions against South Africa in response to the historic advances achieved towards democracy and to add impetus to the process under way. The General Assembly in October unanimously called for the lifting of economic sanctions.

The Security Council welcomed in November the completion of the multi-party negotiations and the conclusion of agreements on an interim Constitution and electoral bill. In December, the Council approved the appointment of a new Secretary-General's Special Representative for South Africa, who visited the country to assess the needs of the United Nations in carrying out its mandate of assisting in the electoral process.

The elections were held from 26 to 29 April 1994. They were observed by 2,527 UNOMSA personnel deployed throughout the country. The elections were won by the ANC with 62.6 per cent of the vote, followed by the ruling National Party (20.4 per cent), the Inkatha Freedom Party (10.5 per cent) and four other parties. On 9 May, the parliament proclaimed Mr. Nelson Mandela President of South Africa. He was inaugurated on 10 May as President of the Government of National Unity.

South Africa's first non-racial, democratic Constitution entered into force, ending 46 years of apartheid. On 25 May, the Security Council lifted the arms embargo and other restrictions against South Africa. And on 23 June, after 24 years, South Africa took its place once again in the General Assembly.

CHAPTER 5

HUMANITARIAN ASSISTANCE AND ASSISTANCE TO REFUGEES

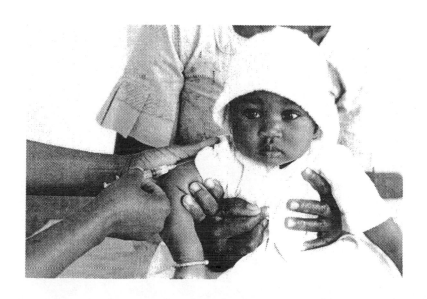

Millions of children, women and men have suffered in the explosion of ethnic, religious and civil conflicts since the end of the cold war. In 1994, conflict and genocidal acts in Rwanda and continuing emergencies elsewhere—particularly in Africa, western Asia, the former Yugoslavia and some areas of the former Soviet Union—further strained a system already stretched in its efforts to provide international humanitarian assistance.

Natural disasters also affect a growing number of people, particularly in developing countries. The global death toll from natural disasters has risen almost tenfold since the 1960s, with developing countries accounting for 90 per cent of the total. This indicates the degree to which poverty, population pressures and environmental degradation magnify the scale of destruction. Economic losses from natural disasters worldwide increased threefold from the 1960s to the 1980s, and rose 40 per cent—from an estimated $44 billion to $62 billion—between 1991 and 1992.

Improving the speed and effectiveness of international humanitarian assistance, and strengthening national capacities to prevent and cope with emergency situations are among the main responsibilities of the United Nations. Effective international assistance in response to major humanitarian emergencies requires planning, coordination, logistics, diplomacy and fund-raising. The United Nations plays a major role in all these fields, coordinated through the Department of Humanitarian Affairs (DHA).

The United Nations is active as a provider of humanitarian assistance, primarily through its six operational agencies, and as a catalyst for action by Governments, intergovernmental humanitarian organizations and non-governmental organizations (NGOs).

Humanitarian diplomacy by the United Nations is often critical in securing access to populations suffering the effects of conflicts. Violations of humanitarian principles by warring parties and threats to the security of relief workers are, however, a growing concern.

Between June 1992 and June 1995, the United Nations launched 52 consolidated appeals to finance programmes aimed at helping an estimated 180 million people in some 30 countries. Total funding sought amounted to some $11.4 billion, of which $7.3 billion was received.

Humanitarian action by the United Nations system goes beyond relief, to involve long-term rehabilitation and development. The goal is to ensure that emergency relief contributes to future development. Sustainable economic and social development remains the best protection against disaster—both natural and that resulting from human action.

Helping countries incorporate disaster prevention and preparedness into their overall development plans is one of the ways the United Nations tries to assist. To raise awareness of the need for prevention and preparedness, the General Assembly has declared the period 1990-2000 to be the International Decade for Natural Disaster Reduction. One objective of the Decade is to encourage improvements in the ability of countries to reduce their vulnerability to disasters. The Decade also strives to increase international cooperation aimed at reducing loss of life, economic damage and social disruption caused by natural disasters, particularly in developing countries. A global mid-decade conference (Yokohama, Japan, 1994), brought together scientists, technicians and policy makers to develop a strategy for disaster prevention, preparedness and mitigation.

DEPARTMENT OF HUMANITARIAN AFFAIRS (DHA)

The United Nations Department of Humanitarian Affairs (DHA) coordinates the response of the United Nations system to major humanitarian emergencies, both natural and man-made, and promotes action to improve disaster prevention and preparedness. DHA works closely with United Nations operational agencies, Governments, regional organizations, NGOs and intergovernmental humanitarian organizations. An arrangement between DHA and the United Nations Environment Programme (UNEP) now covers environmental aspects of emergencies.

Established by the Secretary-General in 1992, following a 1991 request by the General Assembly, DHA incorporates the former Office of the United Nations Disaster Relief Coordinator (UNDRO), which focused mainly on natural disasters, and the Secretariat of the Decade. DHA's role is to provide leadership in order to ensure a rapid response by the United Nations system to natural disasters, technological disasters such as the 1986 explosion at the Chernobyl nuclear power plant in Ukraine and major humanitarian crises, many of which result from conflicts within or between States.

The Under-Secretary-General for Humanitarian Affairs, who also serves as United Nations Emergency Relief Coordinator, is the United Nations system's principal policy advisor, coordinator and advocate on issues pertaining to humanitarian emergencies. Working with the heads of the system's operational agencies and major NGOs, as well as with Governments and intergovernmental humanitarian organizations, the Coordinator advises the Secretary-General on emergencies and recommends action to be taken.

The Emergency Relief Coordinator chairs the Inter-Agency Standing Committee (IASC) whose members are the heads of United Nations operational agencies engaged in humanitarian relief—the United Nations Development Programme (UNDP), the United Nations Children's Fund (UNICEF), the Office of the United Nations High Commissioner for Refugees (UNHCR), the World Food Programme (WFP), the Food and Agriculture Organization of the United Nations (FAO) and the World Health Organization (WHO). Major humanitarian organizations such as the International Organization for Migration and the International Committee of the Red Cross also participate. The International Federation of Red Cross and Red Crescent Societies and other NGOs are also invited to participate.

The IASC formulates system-wide responses to specific emergencies, determines priorities and aims at supporting activities to strengthen relief capacities within countries. It also addresses several other aspects of emergencies, such as assistance to the world's estimated 26 million internally displaced persons (persons displaced by disasters or by humanitarian crises within the borders of their own countries), action to deal with landmines—estimated at some 100 million worldwide—and demobilization of former combatants.

DHA coordinates field missions by the United Nations operational agencies to assess needs; issues inter-agency appeals for funding humanitarian assistance; organizes donor meetings and follow-up arrangements; monitors the status of contributions in response to the appeals; and issues reports to keep donors and others apprised of developments.

Virtually all United Nations humanitarian relief is funded by voluntary contributions. During 1994 alone, DHA launched consolidated inter-agency appeals which raised more than $2.7 billion to assist 27 million people in some 20 countries, in addition to appeals already in effect.

DHA administers a $50 million Central Emergency Revolving Fund which facilitates rapid humanitarian action in emergency situations until funds are made available by the donor community. By the end of May 1995, humanitarian agencies had borrowed from the fund on 38 occasions, drawing some $116 million since it became operational in 1992. Some $100 million had been paid back into the fund by that time.

In areas affected by humanitarian emergencies, coordination is critical in organizing a timely and coherent system-wide response while avoiding overlap, duplication and wasted resources, and in identifying shortfalls in resources. In the event of an emergency in a developing country, the Resident Coordinator (normally the UNDP Resident Representative) or a specially appointed Humanitarian Coordinator reports directly to the Emergency Relief Coordinator and coordinates the United Nations system's response at the country level, working with Governments, NGOs and other humanitarian agencies as well.

In addition, United Nations Disaster Management Teams, consisting of country-level representatives of the United Nations agencies under the leadership of the Resident Coordinator, have been established in many disaster-prone developing countries. These teams make arrangements to coordinate relief activities in anticipation of an emergency.

DHA operates a 24-hour duty system for immediate response and dissemination of information on disasters. To permit rapid response to emergencies, particularly natural disasters, DHA has established, with the participation of donor

Governments, a United Nations Disaster Assessment and Co-ordination Team which can be deployed immediately to an affected country to help local and national authorities determine relief requirements and carry out coordination. DHA may also call upon civil and military emergency teams and expertise in response to natural disasters. The Department operates a warehouse of relief items in Pisa, Italy, which can serve as a hub for airlifts of relief goods.

In collaboration with other international bodies and NGOs, DHA has helped launch programmes aimed at improving disaster preparedness in more than 70 countries. The Department's early warning system for natural disasters is being expanded to include information about other emergency situations. A Disaster Management Training Programme run jointly by DHA and UNDP has provided training to some 1,500 people from more than 40 countries. DHA has also developed a Central Register of Disaster Management Capacities, which includes registers of emergency stockpiles run by humanitarian organizations, of disaster management expertise and of military and civil defence assets available for international disaster relief assistance.

In calling for improved coordination of humanitarian assistance in 1991, the General Assembly stressed the need to address the root causes of emergencies and to ensure early warning, prevention and preparedness, effective humanitarian relief as well as the transition to rehabilitation and development. Humanitarian relief needs to be provided in ways which support rehabilitation, recovery and long-term development.

OPERATIONAL AGENCIES

The **Food and Agriculture Organization of the United Nations (FAO)** is often called on to help farmers re-establish production following floods, outbreaks of livestock disease and similar emergencies. FAO's disaster relief assistance is coordinated by its Office for Special Relief Operations. Between 1977 and October 1994, the Office undertook 444 projects at a total cost of $240.9 million.

The FAO Global Information and Early Warning System issues monthly reports on the world food situation. Special alerts identify, for Governments and relief organizations, countries threatened by food shortages. (See also FAO in Chapter 8.)

The **United Nations Children's Fund (UNICEF)**, while primarily concerned with helping to build lasting services for children and mothers in developing countries, also moves swiftly to meet their immediate needs in emergencies.

Working closely with DHA, other United Nations agencies and many NGOs, UNICEF emergency interventions focus on the provision of health care, nutrition, water supply and sanitation, basic education and the psychosocial rehabilitation of traumatized children. In pioneering the concept of safe passage for humanitarian relief to meet the needs of children during armed conflict, UNICEF has created "days of tranquillity" and "corridors of peace" in Africa, Asia, Europe and the Middle East. UNICEF has also become increasingly involved in programmes for unaccompanied children separated from their families and in the effort to ban the use of land-mines.

UNICEF's Emergency Programme Fund is one of the most important means of responding rapidly to emergencies and allocating funds pending the receipt of donor contributions. (See also Assistance to Children in Chapter 3.)

When emergencies and natural disasters occur, the **United Nations Development Programme (UNDP)** Resident Representatives play a vital role in managing relief and rehabilitation efforts, in cooperation with the Emergency Relief Coordinator. Often Governments call on UNDP to help design rehabilitation programmes and to direct donor aid.

UNDP assists in ensuring that recovery activities are integrated with relief operations. Humanitarian aid and development support are thus linked, bringing the earliest possible resumption of sustainable development to a troubled area.

UNDP rehabilitation projects aim to alleviate poverty, often the root of civil strife. To ensure that the resources provided will have the greatest possible impact, each project is implemented in consultation with local and national government officials, as well as with the UNDP field office in the country. This community-based approach has helped provide urgent but lasting relief for hundreds of thousands of victims of war or civil upheaval in countries such as Afghanistan, Cambodia, El Salvador and Sudan. Today, many conflict-scarred communities have improved their living standards thanks to training programmes, credit schemes and infrastructure projects. (See also UNDP in Chapter 3.)

United Nations High Commissioner for Refugees (UNHCR) (See Assistance to Refugees, below.)

The **World Food Programme (WFP)** is one of the key United Nations players in mounting emergency relief operations for victims of natural disasters and food shortages caused by war, civil strife and ethnic or religious violence.

Its responsibilities include supplying relief assistance; coordinating emergency supplies from all sources through the unique services it has to offer in transportation and logistics; providing its expertise and experience to donors; and administering the International Emergency Food Reserve, its food reserve for emergency needs around the world.

WFP works closely with DHA, other United Nations agencies, governmental organizations and NGOs. It handles needs assessments, mobilizes contributions from donors, transports and manages distribution of food aid on a country-wide basis. New working arrangements between WFP and UNHCR, which came into effect in 1992, resulted in WFP handling most of the food provided to refugees.

An increasing number of WFP development projects foster the transition from relief to development. In some cases, emergency and relief operations have strengthened the communities' capacity to carry out development activities. (See also Food and Agriculture in Chapter 3.)

Within the United Nations system, the **World Health Organization (WHO)** Division of Emergency and Humanitarian Action (EHA) coordinates the international response to emergencies and natural disasters in the area of health. WHO's vast technical network is utilized to provide expert advice to member States on epidemiological surveillance, control of communicable diseases, public health information and health emergency training. EHA's emergency relief activities include the provision of emergency drugs and supplies, fielding of technical emergency assessment missions and technical support. In emergency preparedness, EHA's main objective is to strengthen the national capacity of member States to reduce the adverse health consequences of emergencies and disasters.

In 1994, WHO was involved in relief operations in many countries, providing technical expertise and emergency medical supplies. Following outbreaks of cholera, meningitis or malaria in Africa, Europe and Latin America, WHO was called upon to help mobilize international assistance for control and prevention activities. In 1995, after the outbreak of Ebola haemorrhagic fever in Zaire, WHO was instrumental in establishing an international Scientific and Technical Committee which successfully controlled the epidemic. (See also WHO in Chapter 8.)

ASSISTANCE TO REFUGEES

The **Office of the United Nations High Commissioner for Refugees (UNHCR)**, established in 1951, carries out two main functions: to provide international protection to refugees and to seek durable solutions to their problems. Since its establishment, UNHCR has helped more than 30 million refugees to start a new life by finding durable solutions to their problems. To effectively respond to today's refugee problem, the High Commissioner has adopted a three-pronged strategy of prevention, emergency response and solutions.

In early 1995, there were 27 million refugees and other people of concern to UNHCR. This figure included 14.5 million refugees, as well as other related groups such as returnees and displaced people who have not crossed an international border.

The High Commissioner is guided by strictly humanitarian considerations in dealing with refugees and other people of concern to the Office. According to the Statute of the Office, a refugee is a person who, owing to a well-founded fear of persecution for reasons of race, religion, nationality or political opinion, is outside the country of his or her nationality and is unable or, owing to such fear, unwilling to avail himself or herself of the protection of that country. An essential element of the refugee's international legal status is the widely accepted principle of *non-refoulement*, which prohibits the expulsion or forcible return of a person to a country where he or she may have reason to fear persecution.

Persons of concern to UNHCR are those defined as refugees under the Statute; returnees, in accordance with General Assembly resolution 40/118 of 1985; and displaced persons whom UNHCR is called upon to assist by the United Nations.

While the original definition of refugee still forms the core of UNHCR's mandate, additional criteria have been progressively introduced. In many situations today, UNHCR provides protection and assistance to refugees fleeing persecution, conflict and widespread human rights violations.

Displaced persons, now some 26 million worldwide, often have needs very similar to those of refugees. The General Assembly and the Secretary-General have increasingly called on UNHCR to protect or assist particular groups of internally displaced persons. For example, in early 1995 UNHCR was providing humanitarian relief to internally displaced persons in Azerbaijan, Bosnia and Herzegovina, the Chechnya region of the Russian Federation, Georgia, Rwanda, Somalia, Sri Lanka and Tajikistan.

To provide international protection to refugees, UNHCR seeks to promote the adoption and implementation of international standards for the treatment of refugees, notably protection of refugees' rights in countries of asylum and protection against enforced return to the country of origin. In seeking durable solutions to refugees' problems, the Office attempts to facilitate the voluntary repatriation of refugees and reintegration into their country of origin or, where this is not feasible, to facilitate their integration in the country of asylum or their resettlement in a third country.

The legal status of refugees is defined in two international treaties, the 1951 Convention relating to the Status of Refugees and its 1967 Protocol, which define the rights and duties of refugees. As of 1 May 1995, 128 States were parties to one or both instruments. Another important legal instrument is the Convention Governing the Specific Aspects of Refugee Problems in Africa, adopted by the Organization of African Unity in 1969, to which 41 States were party at 1 May 1995.

Some of the basic administrative costs of UNHCR are covered by the regular United Nations budget, as it is a subsidiary organ of the General Assembly. But it depends entirely on voluntary contributions for its programmes of protection and assistance.

UNHCR assistance activities are grouped under two broad categories, namely General Programmes (including an Emergency Fund) and Special Programmes. In 1994, UNHCR spent around $415 million under General Programmes and $776 million under Special Programmes (which include those funded through appeals by the Secretary-General).

UNHCR works with other bodies of the United Nations system, with intergovernmental organizations and with NGOs. NGOs not only provide substantial aid from their own resources, but often also act as UNHCR's operational partners in carrying out specific projects. They are also important in advocating refugee causes. Over 200 NGOs cooperate in UNHCR's relief and legal assistance programmes.

UNHCR was awarded the Nobel Peace Prize in 1954 and in 1981.

(On Palestine refugees, see United Nations Relief and Works Agency for Palestine Refugees in the Near East (UNRWA) in Chapter 2).

Refugees worldwide. In Africa, millions of people have been uprooted from their homes because of civil and ethnic conflict, human rights abuses, drought and the famine and suffering that accompany these events. By early 1995, Africa hosted some 6.8 million refugees—close to half of the world's refugee population—including over 2 million Rwandese. Many more people have become internally displaced. In 1994, an estimated 16 million people in Africa were internally displaced, a dramatic increase from the estimated 4 million in 1980.

Refugee and asylum issues were a major concern for European States in the early 1990s, as the conflict which flared in the former Yugoslavia in late 1991 produced the largest refugee flows in Europe since the Second World War. In November 1991, UNHCR received a mandate from the Secretary-General to act as the lead United Nations agency in providing protection and assistance to those affected by the conflict, then estimated at about 500,000 people. By May 1995, the number of people in need of assistance had risen to 3.5 million.

In contrast to the major emergencies which arose in Europe and in parts of Africa and Asia during the early 1990s, there were positive developments in the solution of refugee problems in various countries. For example, more than 2 million voluntary repatriations were recorded worldwide in 1994, mostly in Africa and Asia. The repatriation in Mozambique was the largest such operation ever undertaken by UNHCR in Africa. By April 1995, 1.6 million Mozambican refugees in six neighbouring countries had returned home.

To ensure that refugees and internally displaced persons can rebuild their lives when they return home, UNHCR works with a range of other agencies to facilitate reintegration. Successful reintegration requires emergency assistance for those affected, supported by development programmes for the areas which have been devastated, to ensure that there will be income-earning opportunities for the returnees.

To this end, UNHCR implements "quick impact projects" in returnee communities and works with development agencies. In the search for durable solutions to the refugee problem, the links between peace, stability, security, respect for human rights and sustainable development are now clearly recognized.

CHAPTER 6

DECOLONIZATION

More than 80 nations whose peoples were formerly under colonial rule have joined the United Nations as sovereign independent States since the world Organization was founded in 1945. The United Nations has played a crucial role in that historic change by encouraging the aspirations of dependent peoples and by setting goals and standards to accelerate their attainment of independence.

The decolonization efforts of the United Nations derive from the Charter principle of "equal rights and self-determination of peoples", as well as from three specific chapters in the Charter—XI, XII and XIII—devoted to the interests of dependent peoples. Since 1960, the United Nations has also been guided by the General Assembly's Declaration on the Granting of Independence to Colonial Countries and Peoples (resolution 1514(XV) of 14 December 1960), also known as the Declaration on decolonization, by which Member States proclaimed the necessity of bringing colonialism to a speedy end.

Despite the great progress made against colonialism, almost 2 million people still live under colonial rule, and the United Nations continues its efforts to help achieve self-determination or independence in the remaining Non-Self-Governing Territories.

INTERNATIONAL TRUSTEESHIP SYSTEM

Under Chapter XII of the Charter, the United Nations established the International Trusteeship System for the supervision of Trust Territories placed under it by individual agreements with the States administering them. The System applied to: (i) Territories then held under Mandates established by the League of Nations after the First World War; (ii) Territories detached from enemy States as a result of the Second World War; and (iii) Territories voluntarily placed under the System by States responsible for their administration. The basic objective of the System was to promote the political, economic and social advancement of the Trust Territories and their progressive development towards self-government or independence.

The Trusteeship Council was established under Chapter XIII of the Charter to supervise the administration of Trust Territories and to ensure that Governments responsible for their administration took adequate steps to prepare them for the achievement of the Charter goals.

In the early years of the United Nations, 11 Territories were placed under the Trusteeship System. By 1975, all except the Trust Territory of the Pacific Islands, a strategic Trust Territory administered by the United States under an agreement approved by the Security Council, had either attained independence or were united with a neighbouring State to form an independent country.

The Trust Territory of the Pacific Islands originally comprised three archipelagos with a total of 2,100 islands. In 1975, one of the archipelagos, the Northern Mariana Islands, voted to become a Commonwealth of the United States upon termination of the trusteeship and was administratively separated from the balance of the Territory. Subsequently, the remaining islands became three separate self-governing entities with their own constitutions: the Marshall Islands, the Federated States of Micronesia and Palau. In 1983, the Marshall Islands and the Federated States of Micronesia, in exercise of their right to self-determination, chose free association with the United States as their political status, leading the Security Council in 1990 to terminate the Trusteeship Agreement for the two entities except Palau. Finally, following a 1993 plebiscite in which the people of Palau had chosen free association with the United States, the Security Council in 1994 terminated the United Nations Trusteeship Agreement for Palau (see Trusteeship Council in Chapter 1). The Trusteeship System has no territories left on its agenda and has thus completed its historic task.

By 1994, the following Territories had exercised the right to self-determination:

TRUST TERRITORIES WHICH HAVE EXERCISED
THE RIGHT TO SELF-DETERMINATION

Togoland under British administration	United with the Gold Coast (Colony and Protectorate), a Non-Self-Governing Territory administered by the United Kingdom, in 1957 to form Ghana
Somaliland under Italian administration	United with British Somaliland Protectorate in 1960 to form Somalia
Togoland under French administration	Became independent as Togo in 1960
Cameroons under French administration	Became independent as Cameroon in 1960
Cameroons under British administration	The northern part of the Trust Territory joined the Federation of Nigeria on 1 June 1961 and the southern part joined the Republic of Cameroon on 1 October 1961
Tanganyika under British administration	Became independent in 1961 (in 1964, Tanganyika and the former Protectorate of Zanzibar, which had become independent in 1963, united as a single State under the name of the United Republic of Tanzania)
Ruanda-Urundi under Belgian administration	Voted to divide into the two sovereign States of Rwanda and Burundi in 1962
Western Samoa under New Zealand administration	Became independent as Samoa in 1962
Nauru, administered by Australia on behalf of Australia, New Zealand and the United Kingdom	Became independent in 1968
New Guinea, administered by Australia	United with the Non-Self-Governing Territory of Papua, also administered by Australia, to become the independent State of Papua New Guinea in 1975
Trust Territory of the Pacific Islands	
(a) Federated States of Micronesia	Became fully self-governing in free Association with the United States in 1990
(b) Republic of the Marshall Islands	Became fully self-governing in free Association with the United States in 1990
(c) Commonwealth of the Northern Mariana Islands	Became fully self-governing as a Commonwealth of the United States in 1990
(d) Palau	Became fully self-governing in free Association with the United States in 1994

NON-SELF-GOVERNING TERRITORIES

The Charter of the United Nations also addresses the issue of other Non-Self-Governing Territories not brought into the Trusteeship System.

The Declaration regarding Non-Self-Governing Territories (Chapter XI of the Charter) provides that Members of the United Nations which administer Territories whose peoples have not attained a full measure of self-government recognize the principle that the interests of the inhabitants of those Territories are paramount, and accept as a sacred trust the obligation to promote to the utmost the well-being of the inhabitants.

To this end, administering Powers, in addition to ensuring the political, economic, social and educational advancement of the peoples, as well as their just treatment, undertake to develop self-government, to take due account of the political aspirations of the peoples, and to assist them in the development of their free political institutions. Administering Powers are obliged to transmit regularly to the Secretary-General statistical and other information on the economic, social and educational conditions in their respective Territories.

In 1946, eight Member States—Australia, Belgium, Denmark, France, the Netherlands, New Zealand, the United Kingdom and the United States—enumerated the Territories under their administration which they considered to be non-self-governing. In all, 72 Territories were enumerated, of which eight became independent before 1959. Transmission of information by the administering Power was discontinued for 21 others for various reasons. In some cases such as Puerto Rico, Greenland, Alaska and Hawaii, the General Assembly accepted the cessation of information, while in others, the decision was taken unilaterally by the administering Power.

In 1963, the Assembly approved a revised list of Territories to which the 1960 Declaration on the Granting of Independence to Colonial Countries and Peoples applied. This list of 64 Territories included the two remaining Trust Territories (Nauru and the Trust Territory of the Pacific Islands); all the Non-Self-Governing Territories for which information was transmitted under Article 73e of the Charter, including four administered by Spain; Namibia (then referred to as South West

Africa); and those Non-Self-Governing Territories about which no information had been transmitted, but which the Assembly had deemed to be Non-Self-Governing Territories, namely the Territories under Portuguese administration and Southern Rhodesia (now Zimbabwe). In 1965, the list was further expanded to include French Somaliland, now Djibouti, and Oman, while in 1972 the Comoro Islands were also included. New Caledonia was added in 1986.

From 1960 to 1990, 53 Territories attained self-government. As of 1994, there were 17 Non-Self-Governing Territories.

TERRITORIES TO WHICH THE DECLARATION ON DECOLONIZATION CONTINUES TO APPLY (AS AT 31 DECEMBER 1994)

Territory	Administering Authority
Africa:	
Western Sahara	Spain[1]
Asia and the Pacific:	
American Samoa	United States
East Timor	Portugal[2]
Guam	United States
New Caledonia[3]	France
Pitcairn	United Kingdom
Tokelau	New Zealand
Atlantic Ocean, Caribbean and Mediterranean:	
Anguilla	United Kingdom
Bermuda	United Kingdom
British Virgin Islands	United Kingdom
Cayman Islands	United Kingdom
Falkland Islands (Malvinas)	United Kingdom
Gibraltar	United Kingdom
Montserrat	United Kingdom
St. Helena	United Kingdom
Turks and Caicos Islands	United Kingdom
United States Virgin Islands	United States

[1] On 26 February 1976, Spain informed the Secretary-General that as of that date it had terminated its presence in the Territory of the Sahara and deemed it necessary to place on record that Spain considered itself thenceforth exempt from any responsibility of an international nature in connection with the administration of the Territory, in view of the cessation of its participation in the temporary

administration established for the Territory. In 1990, the General Assembly reaffirmed that the question of Western Sahara was a question of decolonization which remained to be completed by the people of Western Sahara.

[2] On 20 April 1977, Portugal informed the Secretary-General that effective exercise of its sovereignty over the Territory had ceased in August 1975 and that the only information that could be transmitted would concern the first months of 1975. In subsequent years, Portugal informed the Secretary-General that conditions prevailing in East Timor continued to prevent it from assuming its responsibilities for the administration of the Territory.

[3] On 2 December 1986, the General Assembly determined that New Caledonia was a Non-Self-Governing Territory.

DECLARATION ON THE GRANTING OF INDEPENDENCE TO COLONIAL COUNTRIES AND PEOPLES

The urgent demands of dependent peoples to be free of colonial domination, and the international community's perception that Charter principles were being too slowly applied, led to the General Assembly's proclamation on 14 December 1960 of the Declaration on the Granting of Independence to Colonial Countries and Peoples (resolution 1514(XV)).

The Declaration states that the subjection of peoples to alien subjugation, domination and exploitation constitutes a denial of fundamental human rights, is contrary to the Charter, and is an impediment to the promotion of world peace and cooperation, and that "immediate steps shall be taken, in Trust and Non-Self-Governing Territories or all other Territories which have not yet attained independence, to transfer all powers to the peoples of those Territories, without any conditions or reservations, in accordance with their freely expressed will and desire, without any distinction as to race, creed or colour in order to enable them to enjoy complete independence and freedom".

In 1961, the Assembly established a 17-member Special Committee—enlarged to 24 members in 1962—to examine the application of the Declaration, and to make suggestions and recommendations on the progress and extent of its implementation. Commonly referred to as the Special Committee of 24 on decolonization, its full title is the Special Committee on the Situation with regard to the Implementation of the Declaration on the Granting of Independence to Colonial Countries and Peoples.

The General Assembly has also adopted resolutions to mark milestone anniversaries of the Declaration. In 1988, the General Assembly, recalling that 1990 would mark the thirtieth anniversary of the Declaration, declared 1990-2000 as the International Decade for the Eradication of Colonialism, and requested the Secretary-General to submit a report enabling the Assembly to consider and adopt an action plan aimed at ushering in the twenty-first century a world free from colonialism.

In 1990, the Assembly expressed its conviction that the thirtieth anniversary should provide an opportunity for Member States to rededicate themselves to the principles and objectives enunciated in the Declaration and for concerted efforts to remove the last vestiges of colonialism in all regions of the world. It also urged the administering Powers to ensure that the activities of foreign economic interests did not run counter to the interest of the inhabitants of the Territories; requested Member States to ensure that the permanent sovereignty of the colonial Territories over their natural resources was respected; and reiterated that, as regards smaller Territories, factors such as size, location, size of population and limited natural resources should not delay the speedy exercise of the people of colonial Territories of their right to self-determination and independence.

In three decades since the Declaration on decolonization was adopted in 1960, some 60 former colonial Territories, inhabited by more than 80 million people, have attained independence and joined the United Nations as sovereign Members.

In its consideration of the Non-Self-Governing Territories, the General Assembly has each year reaffirmed that the continuation of colonialism in all its forms and manifestations is incompatible with the Charter, the Universal Declaration of Human Rights and the Declaration on decolonization.

The Assembly has called upon the administering Powers to take all necessary steps to enable the dependent peoples of the Territories to exercise fully and without delay their inalienable right to self-determination and independence. It has also called upon the administering Powers to withdraw immediately and unconditionally their military bases and installations from colonial Territories and to refrain from establishing new ones, and it has condemned the continuing activities of foreign economic and other interests which are impeding the implementation of the Declaration.

With regard to the smaller Territories, the Assembly has repeatedly affirmed that questions of territorial size, geographical location, size of population and limited natural resources should in no way delay the implementation of the Declaration.

The Assembly has urged the specialized agencies and other organizations of the United Nations system to extend all necessary moral and material assistance to peoples of colonial Territories and to their national liberation movements. It has also invited all States to make, or continue to make, offers of study and training facilities for inhabitants of Non-Self-Governing Territories, including scholarships and travel funds.

In respect of certain territories, such as East Timor, the Falkland Islands (Malvinas) and Western Sahara, the Assembly has entrusted the Secretary-General with specific tasks in assisting in and facilitating the process of decolonization, in accordance with the United Nations Charter and the objectives of the Declaration.

TRUST AND NON-SELF-GOVERNING TERRITORIES THAT HAVE ACHIEVED INDEPENDENCE SINCE THE ADOPTION OF GENERAL ASSEMBLY RESOLUTION 1514(XV) ON 14 DECEMBER 1960

State or other entity	Date of admission to the United Nations
Africa	
Algeria	8 October 1962
Angola	1 December 1976
Botswana	17 October 1966
Burundi	18 September 1962
Cape Verde	16 September 1975
Comoros	12 November 1975
Djibouti	20 September 1977
Equatorial Guinea	12 November 1968
Gambia	21 September 1965
Guinea-Bissau	17 September 1974
Kenya	16 December 1963

State or other entity	Date of admission to the United Nations
Lesotho	17 October 1966
Malawi	1 December 1964
Mauritius	24 April 1968
Mozambique	16 September 1975
Namibia	23 April 1990
Rwanda	18 September 1962
Sao Tome and Principe	26 September 1975
Seychelles	21 September 1976
Sierra Leone	27 September 1961
Swaziland	24 September 1968
Uganda	25 October 1962
United Republic of Tanzania[1]	14 December 1961
Zambia	1 December 1964
Zimbabwe	18 April 1980
Asia	
Brunei Darussalam	21 September 1984
Democratic Yemen	14 December 1967
Oman	7 October 1971
Singapore	21 September 1965
Caribbean	
Antigua and Barbuda	11 November 1981
Bahamas	18 September 1973
Barbados	9 December 1966
Belize	25 September 1981
Dominica	18 December 1978
Grenada	17 December 1974
Guyana	20 September 1966
Jamaica	18 September 1962
Saint Christopher and Nevis	23 September 1983
Saint Lucia	18 September 1979
Saint Vincent and the Grenadines	16 September 1980
Suriname[2]	4 December 1975
Trinidad and Tobago	18 September 1962
Europe	
Malta	1 December 1964
Pacific	
Federated States of Micronesia	17 September 1991
Fiji	13 October 1970
Kiribati[3]	—
Marshall Islands	17 September 1991
Nauru[3]	—
Papua New Guinea	10 October 1975

State or other entity	Date of admission to the United Nations
Republic of Palau	15 December 1994
Samoa	15 December 1976
Solomon Islands	19 September 1978
Tuvalu[3]	–
Vanuatu	15 September 1981

[1] The former Trust Territory of Tanganyika, which became independent in December 1961, and the former Protectorate of Zanzibar, which achieved independence in December 1963, united into a single State in April 1974.

[2] By resolution 945(X), the General Assembly accepted the cessation of the transmission of information regarding Suriname following constitutional changes in the relationship between the Netherlands, Suriname and the Netherlands Antilles which were embodied in the Charter of the Kingdom of the Netherlands.

[3] Kiribati, Nauru and Tuvalu, which became independent on 12 July 1979, 31 January 1968 and 1 October 1978, respectively, have not applied for United Nations membership.

NAMIBIA

Namibia—formerly known as South West Africa—was the only one of the seven African Territories once held under the League of Nations Mandate System that was not placed under the Trusteeship System. The General Assembly recommended in 1946 that South Africa do so, but South Africa refused. Instead, South Africa informed the United Nations in 1949 that it would no longer transmit information on the Territory, on the grounds that the Mandate had lapsed with the demise of the League.

In 1950, the International Court of Justice held that South Africa continued to have international obligations towards the Territory, and that the United Nations should exercise the supervisory functions of the League of Nations in the administration of the Territory. South Africa refused to accept the Court's opinion, and continued to oppose any form of United Nations supervision over the Territory.

In 1966, the Assembly declared that South Africa had failed to fulfil its obligations under the Mandate. It terminated that Mandate, and placed the Territory under the direct responsibility of the United Nations. In 1967, the Assembly established the United Nations Council for South West Africa to administer the Territory until independence. It thus became the only

Territory for which the United Nations, rather than a Member State, assumed direct responsibility. In 1968, the Council was renamed the United Nations Council for Namibia, when the Assembly proclaimed that, in accordance with the wishes of its people, the Territory would be thenceforth known as Namibia.

Later that year, in the face of South Africa's refusal to accept the Assembly's decision and cooperate with the Council for Namibia, the Assembly recommended that the Security Council take measures to enable the Council to carry out its mandate.

In its first resolution on the question, the Security Council, in 1969, recognized the termination of the Mandate, described the continued presence of South Africa as illegal, and called on South Africa to withdraw its administration immediately. In 1970, the Security Council declared for the first time that all acts taken by South Africa concerning Namibia after the termination of the Mandate were "illegal and invalid".

This view was upheld in 1971 by the International Court of Justice. The Court stated that South Africa's presence was illegal, and that South Africa was under obligation to withdraw its administration. South Africa, however, continued to refuse to comply with the United Nations resolutions, and continued its illegal administration of Namibia, including the imposition of apartheid laws, the "bantustanization" of the Territory, and the exploitation of its resources.

The Council for Namibia enacted in 1974 a Decree for the Protection of the Natural Resources of Namibia, under which no person or entity could search for, take or distribute any natural resources found in Namibia without the Council's permission. Any person or entity contravening the Decree could be held liable for damages by the future government of an independent Namibia.

Also in 1974, the Council established the Institute for Namibia, located in Lusaka, Zambia. The Institute, which operated until after independence, provided Namibians with education and training equipping them to administer a free Namibia.

In 1976 the Security Council for the first time demanded that South Africa accept elections for the Territory under United Nations supervision and control.

In the same year, the General Assembly condemned South

Africa for organizing so-called constitutional talks at Windhoek, Namibia's capital, and decided that any independence talks must be between South Africa and the South West Africa People's Organization (SWAPO), which the Assembly recognized as the sole representative of the Namibian people.

The Assembly also launched a comprehensive assistance programme in support of Namibia's nationhood, involving assistance by United Nations organizations and specialized agencies.

At a special session on Namibia in 1978, the Assembly expressed support for the armed liberation struggle of the Namibian people, and stated that any settlement must be arrived at with the agreement of SWAPO and within the framework of United Nations resolutions.

The United Nations plan for Namibian independence

In 1978, Canada, France, the Federal Republic of Germany, the United Kingdom and the United States submitted to the Security Council a proposal for settling the question of Namibia. According to the proposal, elections for a Constituent Assembly would be held under United Nations auspices. Every stage of the electoral process would be conducted to the satisfaction of a Special Representative of the Secretary-General for Namibia. A United Nations Transition Assistance Group (UNTAG) would be at the disposal of the Special Representative to help him supervise the political process and to ensure that all parties observed all provisions of an agreed solution.

The Security Council requested the Secretary-General to appoint a Special Representative for Namibia and to submit recommendations for implementing the settlement proposal. By resolution 435 (1978), the Council endorsed the United Nations plan for Namibia and decided to establish UNTAG.

In 1980, South Africa accepted the plan proposed by the five Powers and in 1981 participated in a pre-implementation meeting at Geneva. However, South Africa did not agree to proceed towards a cease-fire, one of the conditions set by the United Nations for implementing resolution 435. Negotiations were again stalled when South Africa attached new conditions which the United Nations did not accept, in particular one which linked the independence of Namibia with the withdrawal of Cuban troops from Angola.

In the following years, the Secretary-General and his Special Representative travelled extensively throughout southern Africa, discussing problems, clarifying positions, exploring new concepts and exchanging views with all parties. Various countries promoted talks on the issue—among them the five Western sponsors of the 1978 proposal and Zambia. Gradually the unresolved matters yielded to the give and take of negotiations.

The Secretary-General reported in 1987 that all outstanding issues relevant to the United Nations plan, including the choice of an electoral system, had been resolved. Only the condition linking independence to troop withdrawal remained an obstacle.

After eight months of intense negotiations, a tripartite agreement among Angola, Cuba and South Africa, mediated by the United States, was signed at United Nations Headquarters on 22 December 1988. The agreement committed the signatory States to a series of measures to achieve peace in the region, and opened the way to the United Nations independence plan. Under the agreement, South Africa undertook to cooperate with the Secretary-General to ensure Namibia's independence through free and fair elections.

At the same time, Angola and Cuba signed an agreement on the withdrawal of Cuban troops from Angola. In accordance with this agreement, a United Nations observer mission was dispatched to Angola to verify the withdrawal of Cuban troops. (see Angola in Chapter 2).

The operation that led to Namibia's independence was one of the most complex ever undertaken by the United Nations. The starting date for the implementation of the independence plan was 1 April 1989.

UNTAG was made up of people of 124 nationalities. An international staff of some 900 civilians observed the whole electoral process, conducted by the Namibian authorities. UNTAG's 1,500 police officers ensured a smooth electoral process and monitored the local police. Its 4,300 military staff monitored the cease-fire between SWAPO and South African forces, and the withdrawal and demobilization of all military forces.

Namibia was divided into 23 electoral districts, and registration centres were set up all over the country. Some 2,200 rural registration points were covered by 110 mobile registration teams.

Registration of voters began on 3 July 1989. When the process ended on 23 September, 701,483 Namibians had registered, and more than 34,000 had been helped to repatriate by the United Nations High Commissioner for Refugees—of some 41,000 registered with that agency.

The elections, held from 7 to 11 November 1989 to choose the 72 delegates to the Constituent Assembly, saw a voter turnout of 97 per cent. UNTAG monitored the balloting and the counting of votes. On 14 November, the Secretary-General's Special Representative for Namibia, Martti Ahtisaari, declared that the elections had been free and fair. SWAPO obtained 41 Assembly seats, the Democratic Turnhalle Alliance 21 seats, and five smaller parties shared the remaining 10.

By 22 November 1989, South Africa's remaining troops had left Namibia. The Constituent Assembly met for the first time on 21 November to draft a new Constitution, which was unanimously approved on 9 February 1990. On 16 February the Assembly elected SWAPO leader Sam Nujoma as President of the Republic for a five-year term.

Namibia became independent on 21 March 1990. On that day, at the National Stadium in Windhoek, the United Nations Secretary-General administered the oath of office to Namibia's first President. On 23 April 1990, Namibia became the United Nations' 160th Member.

WESTERN SAHARA

Western Sahara, a Territory on the north-west coast of Africa bordered by Morocco, Mauritania and Algeria, was administered by Spain until 1976. Both Morocco and Mauritania affirmed their claim to the Territory, a claim opposed by the Popular Front for the Liberation of Saguia el-Hamra and Río de Oro (Frente POLISARIO).

The United Nations has considered the situation in the Territory since 1963. Over the years, the General Assembly reaffirmed the right of the people of Western Sahara to self-determination, and called on the administering Power to take steps to ensure the realization of that right.

In response to a request by the General Assembly for an advisory opinion, the International Court of Justice concluded in 1975 that the materials and information presented to it did not establish any tie of territorial sovereignty between Western Sahara and Morocco or Mauritania.

Also in 1975, Spain, Morocco and Mauritania agreed upon a Declaration of Principles by which Spain confirmed its resolve to decolonize the Territory by 28 February 1976. Under that agreement, Spain would institute a temporary administration in which Morocco and Mauritania would participate, in collaboration with the Jema'a, a local assembly expressing the views of the Saharan population.

Spain completed its withdrawal on 26 February 1976, stating that, although it did not consider that the people of Western Sahara had exercised their right to self-determination, it considered itself released from international responsibility towards the Territory.

On 27 February, the Secretary-General received a message, through Morocco, from the President of the Jema'a informing him that the Jema'a had approved the "reintegration" of the Territory with Morocco and Mauritania. In March, the Frente POLISARIO proclaimed the "Saharan Arab Democratic Republic" and stated that it would engage in an armed struggle to achieve the right of self-determination of the people of the Territory. In April, Mauritania and Morocco announced an agreement whereby the northern two thirds of the Territory would be integrated with Morocco and the southern part with Mauritania. The Frente POLISARIO and Algeria opposed the arrangement, maintaining that the Jema'a had not been democratically elected.

Following a change of Government, Mauritania in 1979 signed a peace agreement in Algiers with the Frente POLISARIO by which it renounced all claims to Western Sahara. Morocco declared the accord null and void, and Moroccan troops took over the Mauritanian sector of Western Sahara. The Frente POLISARIO stepped up its attacks on Moroccan forces, and fighting in the Territory was reported in the following years.

Besides the United Nations, the Organization of African

Unity (OAU) became involved in seeking a peaceful settlement. In 1979, the OAU called for a referendum so that the people of the Territory might exercise their right to self-determination. It established a committee to work out the modalities for a referendum in cooperation with the United Nations.

At the 1981 summit of the OAU, the King of Morocco announced that he was prepared to agree to a cease-fire and to a referendum under international supervision. Welcoming the announcement, the summit called for a cease-fire and a referendum to be held in cooperation with the United Nations. Also in 1981, the General Assembly appealed to Morocco and the Frente POLISARIO to begin negotiation on a cease-fire. However, Morocco made it clear that it was not prepared to negotiate directly with the Frente POLISARIO.

In 1982, after 26 OAU member States had recognized the "Saharawi Arab Democratic Republic (SADR)", it was admitted to the OAU Council of Ministers. Morocco withdrew from the OAU when the Frente POLISARIO was seated at the 1984 OAU summit.

In 1983 and 1984, the General Assembly reaffirmed that the question of Western Sahara was a decolonization issue. The people of the Territory had yet to exercise their right to self-determination and independence. It requested both sides to negotiate a cease-fire so as to create the conditions for a referendum.

In 1985, the Secretary-General and the OAU Chairman began a joint good offices mission. In 1988, they proposed a settlement providing for a cease-fire and a referendum to choose between independence and integration with Morocco. Morocco and the Frente POLISARIO accepted the settlement proposal.

In 1990, the Security Council approved the settlement proposal and the Secretary-General's plan for implementing it. The plan provided for a transitional period, during which a Special Representative of the Secretary-General would have sole responsibility for all matters relating to the referendum, assisted by the **United Nations Mission for the Referendum in Western Sahara (MINURSO)**. The transitional period would begin with the coming into effect of a cease-fire and end with the proclamation of the results of the referendum.

All Western Saharans aged 18 and over counted in the

1974 Spanish census would have the right to vote, whether present in the Territory or living outside as refugees or for other reasons. An Identification Commission would update the 1974 census to provide a basis for issuing lists of voters. A census on refugees living outside the Territory would be taken, with assistance from UNHCR.

The Security Council established MINURSO on 29 April 1991. On 24 May, in accordance with the plan, the Secretary-General proposed that the cease-fire should enter into effect on 6 September, a date both parties accepted.

But it soon became clear that the tasks to be achieved before the cease-fire could not be completed by 6 September. It also became clear that, despite the parties' acceptance of the plan, substantial disagreements remained. One party was therefore unable to agree that the transitional period should begin on 6 September.

Meanwhile, fighting broke out in the Territory, interrupting an informal cease-fire that had been into effect for over two years. In these circumstances, the Secretary-General decided that the formal cease-fire should come into effect on 6 September as initially agreed, and that the transitional period would begin as soon as the outstanding tasks had been completed. The Security Council supported his proposal that observers be deployed to verify the cease-fire and the end of hostilities. Thus 228 MINURSO military observers were dispatched to the Territory.

According to the settlement plan, the referendum was to take place in 1992, but it was not possible to conform with the original timetable. While both parties reiterated their confidence in the United Nations and their commitment to the plan, they continued to have different views on key elements of the plan, in particular the criteria for eligibility of voters in the referendum.

The Secretary-General had set out criteria for voter eligibility in a 19 December 1991 report to the Security Council. While considering them unduly restrictive, they were accepted by Morocco. The Frente POLISARIO maintained that, in the initial agreement, the two parties had agreed that the list of Saharans counted in the 1974 Spanish census would be the exclusive basis of the electorate. In its view, the criteria of 19 December 1991 would unduly expand the electorate beyond the 1974 census list and were thus incompatible with the settlement plan.

In 1993, following consultations with the Special Representative, both sides confirmed their desire to proceed with the registration of voters. It was decided to establish the Identification Commission, and in April the Secretary-General appointed the Chairman of the Commission.

During a visit to the area in May-June 1993, the Secretary-General presented a compromise solution on the interpretation and application of the criteria for voter eligibility. According to the compromise, the potential electorate would encompass members of all Saharan tribal groups ("subfractions"), but only those which were represented in the 1974 census, regardless of the number of individuals from these subfractions who were counted in the census. All applicants for participation in the referendum would have to meet this requirement before claiming eligibility to vote under any of the criteria of 19 December 1991.

During this and later consultations, both parties reaffirmed their commitment to the peace plan, and their determination to move towards a referendum. In spite of its reservations, Morocco then accepted the compromise proposal. The Frente POLISARIO, when finally accepting all of the eligibility criteria of 19 December 1991, expressed substantial reservations on the proposal.

In July 1993, preliminary talks between the parties were held in Laayoune, the capital of Western Sahara, attended by the Special Representative as an observer. In the meantime, the Chairman of the Identification Commission had travelled to the region to prepare the process of identification and registration of voters. The Commission began work on establishing with both parties the procedures for identification and registration.

The Special Representative visited the area in January 1994. In February, he stated that the basic problem facing the Frente POLISARIO was that, since the criteria set forth by the previous Secretary-General in 1991 enlarged the electorate beyond the persons included in the 1974 census, there was a danger that applying such criteria might result in an inclusion of persons who were not Saharans from the Territory.

In March, the Security Council asked the Identification Commission to proceed with the identification and registration of potential voters, on the basis of the compromise proposal. The process of identifying and registering potential voters was launched in August 1994. In November, the Secretary-General visited the region for consultation with both parties.

In January 1995, the Security Council expanded MINURSO to ensure the timely completion of the identification process. The process continued at seven identification centres, and by mid-March over 21,000 persons had been identified.

CHAPTER 7

International Law

A central task of the United Nations is the adjustment or settlement of international disputes by peaceful means in conformity with the principles of justice and international law, as called for in Article 1 of the United Nations Charter. Among the methods of peaceful settlement, the Charter specifies, in Article 33, arbitration and judicial settlement.

Under Article 13, one of the General Assembly's functions is "encouraging the progressive development of international law and its codification". This function has been accomplished by the Assembly and other bodies, among other things, through the preparation of a large number of international conventions. Over the past five decades, the United Nations has secured the conclusion of more than 456 multilateral agreements covering virtually every area of State interaction and human endeavour. In new areas of global concern, such as the environment, outer space, migrant labour, drug trafficking and terrorism, its work has been pioneering.

JUDICIAL SETTLEMENT OF DISPUTES

The primary organ of the United Nations for the settlement of disputes is the **International Court of Justice** (see also Chapter 1). Since its founding, in 1946, States have submitted over 72 cases to it, and 22 advisory opinions have been requested by international organizations. Nearly all cases have been dealt with by the full Court, but since 1981 four have been referred to special chambers at the request of the parties. Eleven contentious cases are pending. The cases submitted cover a wide range of topics.

Some have involved questions of territorial rights. In 1953, in a case between France and the United Kingdom, the Court found that certain Channel islets were under British sovereignty. In another case (1959), the Court upheld the claims of Belgium to an enclave situated near its frontier with the Netherlands. In 1960, the Court found that India had not acted contrary to the obligations imposed on it by the existence of

Portugal's right of passage between enclaves. In 1986, a chamber of the Court delimited part of the frontier between Burkina Faso and Mali. Another territorial dispute was jointly referred to the Court by the Libyan Arab Jamahiriya and Chad in 1990. Other cases have involved the law of the sea. In 1949, the Court found Albania responsible for damage caused by mines in its territorial waters to British warships exercising the right of innocent passage. In a fisheries dispute between the United Kingdom and Norway, the Court held in 1951 that the method employed by Norway in delimiting its territorial waters was not contrary to international law. In 1969, in a case between Denmark, the Netherlands and the Federal Republic of Germany, the Court indicated the principles and rules of international law applicable to the delimitation of the areas of the North Sea continental shelf appertaining to each of them. In 1974, the Court found that Iceland was not entitled unilaterally to exclude the fishing vessels of the United Kingdom and the Federal Republic of Germany from areas between fishery limits agreed in 1961 and the 50-mile limit proclaimed by Iceland in 1972.

In 1982, at the request of Tunisia and Libya, and in 1985, in a case referred to it by Libya and Malta, the Court indicated the principles and rules of international law applicable to the delimitation of the areas of the Mediterranean continental shelf appertaining to each of them respectively. In 1984, a Chamber of the Court determined the course of the maritime boundary dividing the continental shelf and fisheries zones of Canada and the United States in the Gulf of Maine area. In 1993, the full Court determined the course of the maritime boundary in the area between Greenland and the Island of Jan Mayen dividing the continental shelf and fisheries zones of Denmark and Norway. One more case, between Guinea-Bissau and Senegal, is pending on the subject of maritime boundaries. In 1995, Spain brought a case against Canada concerning the Canadian Coastal Fisheries Protection Act and its application.

In 1992, a Chamber of the Court gave its decision in a dispute between El Salvador and Honduras involving questions of both land and maritime frontier delimitation. Two other cases pending, one between Qatar and Bahrain and one between

Cameroon and Nigeria, also involve questions of both territorial and maritime frontier delimitation.

Other cases have involved questions of diplomatic protection in such matters as rights of asylum in Latin America (Colombia v. Peru, 1950) and the rights of United States nationals in Morocco (France v. United States, 1951) and a question of nationals (Liechtenstein v. Guatemala, 1955). In 1970, the Court held that Belgium had no legal capacity to protect the interests of Belgian shareholders in a Canadian company which had been the subject of certain measures in Spain. In 1989, a Chamber of the Court rejected a claim for compensation put forward by the United States against Italy in respect of the requisition of a company in Sicily owned by United States corporations.

A pending case concerning the *Gabcikovo Nagymaros Project*, which was brought by Hungary and the Slovak Republic in 1994, involves issues of environmental protection. That case is before the full Court. However, since 1993, States may submit their disputes in this field to a Chamber of the Court for Environmental Matters.

In cases concerning the discharge of duties of the Mandatory Power for the Territory of South West Africa (Namibia), the Court found in 1966 that Ethiopia and Liberia had not established any legal interests in the claim they had brought against South Africa. Four of the advisory opinions given by the Court have also concerned Namibia. Three of these were requested by the General Assembly. In the first (1950), the Court expressed the opinion that South Africa continued to have international obligations under the Mandate despite the dissolution of the League of Nations. The fourth opinion, requested by the Security Council, was given in 1971 when the Court stated that the continued presence of South Africa in Namibia was illegal and that South Africa was under obligation to withdraw its administration and put an end to its occupation of the Territory. Another contentious case, withdrawn in 1993 following an agreement between the parties (Nauru and Australia), concerned a Territory once under Mandate—the island of Nauru. In 1991, Portugal, the former colonial power in East Timor, instituted proceedings against Australia in a dispute concerning "certain activities of Australia with respect to East Timor".

Certain advisory opinions requested by the General Assembly have concerned relations between the United Nations and its Members. One was given in 1949 on a question put after the assassination of the United Nations mediator in Palestine: the Court found that the United Nations had the capacity to maintain a claim against a State for injuries to an agent of the Organization. In 1988, the Court expressed the opinion that, by virtue of the United Nations Headquarters Agreement, the United States was under obligation to submit to arbitration a dispute with the United Nations concerning an order to close the office of the Palestine Liberation Organization observer mission in New York. Another advisory case concerned the refusal of certain States to contribute to the expenses of peace-keeping operations in the Middle East and the Congo. The Court held in 1962 that the expenses in question should be borne by all Member States in accordance with the Charter. The last advisory opinion, rendered by the Court in 1989, concerned a request submitted by the Economic and Social Council on the applicability to a former rapporteur of a subcommission of certain provisions of the Convention on the Privileges and Immunities of the United Nations.

Five advisory opinions have reviewed aspects of judgements of the Administrative Tribunals of the United Nations or the International Labour Organization. Two requests for an advisory opinion are at present pending: one, made by the World Health Organization, concerns the legality of the use by a State of nuclear weapons in armed conflict; and one, made by the General Assembly, concerns the legality of the threat or use of nuclear weapons.

Some recent cases have been referred to the Court against the background of political upheaval or regional conflicts. In 1980, in a case brought by the United States concerning the seizure of its Embassy in Teheran and the detention of its diplomatic and consular staff, the Court held that Iran must release the hostages, hand back the Embassy and make reparation. However, before the Court could fix the amount of reparation, the case was withdrawn following agreement reached between the two States. In 1989, Iran asked the Court to condemn the shooting down of an Iranian airliner by the USS *Vincennes* and to find the United States responsible to pay Iran compensation. The case is still pending.

In 1984, Nicaragua alleged that the United States was using military force against it and intervening in its internal affairs. The United States denied that the Court had jurisdiction. However, after written and oral proceedings, the Court found that it had jurisdiction and that Nicaragua's application was admissible. The United States refused to recognize either this ruling or the subsequent 1986 Judgment in which the Court determined that the United States had acted in breach of its obligations towards Nicaragua, must desist from the actions in question, and should make reparation. The request by Nicaragua that the Court determine the form and amount of reparation was withdrawn in 1991.

In 1986, Nicaragua brought proceedings against Costa Rica and Honduras, alleging their responsibility in connection with armed activities in border areas. These two cases were also withdrawn following an agreement between the parties.

In 1992, Libya brought a case against the United Kingdom and the United States concerning the interpretation or application of the 1971 Montreal Convention for the Suppression of Unlawful Acts against the Safety of Civil Aviation, arising out of the crash of Pan American flight 103 at Lockerbie, Scotland, on 21 December 1988.

In 1993, Bosnia and Herzegovina brought a case against Yugoslavia (Serbia and Montenegro) concerning the application of the Convention on the Prevention and Punishment of the Crime of Genocide. In April and in September 1993, the Court, in Orders issued on requests for provisional measures of protection, called upon the parties to prevent further commission of the crime of genocide and further aggravation or extension of the dispute.

DEVELOPMENT AND CODIFICATION
OF INTERNATIONAL LAW

The **International Law Commission** was established by the General Assembly in 1947 to promote the progressive development of international law and its codification. The Commission, which meets annually, is composed of 34 members who are elected by the General Assembly for five-year terms and who serve in their individual capacity, not as representatives of their Governments.

Most of the Commission's work involves the preparation of drafts on topics of international law. Some topics are chosen by the Commission and others referred to it by the General Assembly or the Economic and Social Council. When the Commission completes draft articles on a particular topic, the General Assembly usually convenes an international conference of plenipotentiaries to incorporate the draft articles into a convention which is then opened to States to become parties.

Thus, for example:

♦ in 1958, a United Nations conference adopted four conventions on the law of the sea. They were: the Convention on the High Seas; the Convention on the Territorial Sea and Contiguous Zone; the Convention on Fishing and Conservation of the Living Resources of the High Seas; and the Convention on the Continental Shelf; in 1961, a conference adopted the Convention on the Reduction of Statelessness;

♦ two conferences, held in Vienna in 1961 and 1963, respectively, adopted the Vienna Convention on Diplomatic Relations and the Vienna Convention on Consular Relations;

♦ a conference which met in Vienna in 1968, and again in 1969, adopted a Convention on the Law of Treaties;

♦ draft articles, prepared by the Commission, on Special Missions and on the Prevention and Punishment of Crimes against Internationally Protected Persons, including Diplomatic Agents, were considered directly by the General Assembly, which adopted Conventions on both subjects in 1969 and 1973, respectively;

♦ in 1975, an international conference adopted the Vienna Convention on the Representation of States in Their Relations with Organizations of a Universal Character;

♦ another conference convened by the General Assembly, which met in Vienna in 1977 and again in 1978, completed and adopted the Vienna Convention on Succession of States in Respect of Treaties;

- in 1983, a United Nations Conference on Succession of States in Respect of State Property, Archives and Debts adopted, at Vienna, a Convention on the topic;
- in accordance with a 1984 Assembly decision, a United Nations conference met in Vienna in 1986 and adopted the Vienna Convention on the Law of Treaties between States and International Organizations or between International Organizations.

Regarding the draft articles on most-favoured-nation clauses (relating to trade practices) adopted by the Commission in 1978, the General Assembly noted the valuable work done in this area and decided to bring the draft articles to the attention of Member States and interested intergovernmental organizations for their consideration.

The Commission adopted, in 1989 and 1991, respectively, draft articles on the status of the diplomatic courier and the diplomatic bag not accompanied by diplomatic courier, draft articles on jurisdictional immunities of States and their property, the law of the non-navigational uses of international watercourses and a draft statute for an international criminal court. The action to be taken on these drafts is under consideration by the General Assembly.

The current work of the Commission includes the codification and progressive development of the law of State responsibility; international liability for injurious consequences arising out of acts not prohibited by international law; and the draft Code of Crimes against the Peace and Security of Mankind (on which the Commission adopted on first reading a set of draft articles in 1991). In 1994, the Commission included in its programme of work the law and practice relating to reservations to treaties, and State succession and its impact on the nationality of natural and legal persons.

INTERNATIONAL TRADE LAW

In response to the need for the United Nations to play an active role in removing or reducing legal obstacles to the flow of international trade, the General Assembly, in 1966, established the **United Nations Commission on International Trade Law (UNCITRAL)** to promote the progressive harmonization and unification of the law of international trade. The 36-nation Commission, whose members represent the various geographical regions and the principal economic and legal systems of the world, reports annually to the General Assembly and also submits its report to the United Nations Conference on Trade and Development (UNCTAD).

The Commission's functions include coordination of the work of international organizations active in the field of international trade law, promotion of wider participation in international conventions, and the preparation of new conventions and other instruments relating to international trade law. The Commission also offers training and assistance in international trade law by way of national or regional seminars, symposia or briefing missions. Technical assistance also includes advice to States preparing trade legislation based on the Commission's texts.

The Commission's attention has been mainly directed to the study and preparation of uniform rules in international sale of goods, international payments including a legal guide on electronic fund transfers, international commercial arbitration, international legislation on shipping, countertrade and procurement.

The Convention on the Limitation Period in the International Sale of Goods, the first to be prepared by the Commission, was adopted in 1974 by a United Nations conference of plenipotentiaries convened by the General Assembly; a 1980 Protocol amended the Convention. A similar international conference adopted the United Nations Convention on the Carriage of Goods by Sea (known as the "Hamburg Rules") in 1978. A third international conference, held in 1980, adopted the United Nations Convention on Contracts for the International Sale of Goods, while the United Nations Convention on the Liability of Operators of Transport Terminals in International Trade was adopted at an international conference in Vienna in 1991. The General Assembly adopted the United Nations Convention on International Bills of Exchange and International Promissory Notes in 1988. The Commission adopted the UNCITRAL Model Law on International Commercial Arbitration (1985), the UNCITRAL Model Law on International Credit Transfers (1992) and the UNCITRAL Model

Law on Procurement of Goods, Construction and Services (1994). The UNCITRAL Arbitration Rules (1976) and the UNCITRAL Conciliation Rules (1980) are additional uniform rules prepared by the Commission. In 1987, the Commission published the UNCITRAL Legal Guide on Drawing Up International Contracts for the Construction of Industrial Works, and, in 1992, the UNCITRAL Legal Guide on International Countertrade Transactions.

Projects under way include a draft convention on independent guarantees and stand-by letters of credit, a draft model law on electronic data interchange, draft practice notes on planning arbitral proceedings, as well as work on cross-border insolvency, on legal aspects of receivables financing, and on build-operate-transfer (BOT) projects.

LAW OF THE SEA

The First United Nations Conference on the Law of the Sea (Geneva, 1958) resulted in the adoption of four conventions—on the high seas, on the territorial sea and the contiguous zone, on the continental shelf, and on fishing and conservation of the living resources of the high seas—that were based on drafts prepared by the International Law Commission (see above). The Second United Nations Conference on the Law of the Sea (1960) made an unsuccessful effort to reach agreement on the breadth of the territorial sea and on the question of fishing zones.

The General Assembly in 1968 established the Committee on the Peaceful Uses of the Sea-Bed and the Ocean Floor beyond the Limits of National Jurisdiction. In 1969, the Committee began work on a statement of legal principles to govern the uses of the seabed and its resources. The following year, the Assembly unanimously adopted the Committee's Declaration of Principles which stated that "the seabed and ocean floor, and the subsoil thereof, beyond the limits of national jurisdiction ... as well as the resources of the area are the common heritage of mankind", to be reserved for peaceful purposes, not subject to national appropriation and not to be explored or exploited except in accordance with an international regime to be established. The Assembly also decided to convene a new Conference on the Law of the Sea to prepare a single, comprehensive treaty.

The Third United Nations Conference on the Law of the Sea opened with a brief organizational session in 1973. At its second session (Caracas, Venezuela, 1974), it endorsed the Sea-Bed Committee's recommendation that it work on a new law of the sea treaty as a "package deal", with no one article or section to be approved before all the others were in place. This reflected not only the interdependence of all the issues involved but also the need to reach a delicate balance of compromises if the final document was to prove viable.

The first informal text was prepared in 1975 as a basis for negotiation. Over the next seven years, in Conference committees and in special negotiating and working groups, the text underwent several major revisions.

The final text of the new Convention was approved by the Conference at United Nations Headquarters on 30 April 1982, by a vote of 130 in favour to 4 against, with 17 abstentions. When it was opened for signature at Montego Bay, Jamaica, on 10 December 1982, the United Nations Convention on the Law of the Sea was signed by 117 States and two other entities—the largest number of signatures ever affixed to a treaty on its first day. By the end of the period of signature, 9 December 1984, the Convention had been signed by 159 States and several other entities such as the European Economic Community. The Convention entered into force on 16 November 1994, one year after the deposit of the sixtieth instrument of ratification or accession. By 2 May 1995, it had 75 States parties.

The Convention covers almost all ocean space and its uses—navigation and overflight, resource exploration and exploitation, conservation and pollution, fishing and shipping. Its 320 articles and nine annexes constitute a guide for behaviour by States in the world's oceans, defining maritime zones, laying down rules for drawing sea boundaries, assigning legal rights, duties and responsibilities to States, and providing machinery for the settlement of disputes.

Some of the key features of the Convention are:

♦ coastal States would exercise sovereignty over their territorial sea up to 12 nautical miles in breadth, but foreign vessels would be allowed peaceful "innocent passage" through those waters;

♦   ships and aircraft of all countries would be allowed "transit passage" through straits used for international navigation; States alongside the straits would be able to regulate navigation and other aspects of passage;

♦   archipelagic States—those States made up of a group or groups of closely related islands and interconnecting waters—would have sovereignty over a sea area enclosed by straight lines drawn between the outermost points of the islands; all other States would enjoy the right of passage through designated sea lanes;

♦   coastal States would have sovereign rights in a 200-nautical-mile exclusive economic zone (EEZ) with respect to natural resources and certain economic activities, and would also exercise jurisdiction over marine science research and environmental protection; all other States would have freedom of navigation and overflight in the zone, as well as freedom to lay submarine cables and pipelines; land-locked and geographically disadvantaged States would have the opportunity to participate in exploiting part of the zone's fisheries on an equitable basis when the coastal State could not harvest them all itself; highly migratory species of fish and marine mammals would be accorded special protection;

♦   coastal States would have sovereign rights over the continental shelf (the national area of the seabed) for exploring and exploiting it; the shelf would extend at least 200 nautical miles from the shore, and more under specified circumstances; coastal States would share with the international community part of the revenue they would derive from exploiting resources from any part of their shelf beyond 200 miles; a Commission on the Limits of the Continental Shelf would make recommendations to States on the shelf's outer boundaries when it extends beyond 200 miles;

♦   all States would enjoy the traditional freedoms of navigation, overflight, scientific research and fishing on the high seas; they would be obliged to adopt, or cooperate with other States in adopting, measures to manage and conserve living resources;

♦   States bordering enclosed or semi-enclosed seas would be expected to cooperate in managing living resources and on environmental and research policies and activities;

♦   land-locked States would have the right of access to and from the sea and would enjoy freedom of transit through the territory of transit States;

♦   States would be bound to prevent and control marine pollution and would be liable for damage caused by violation of their international obligations to combat such pollution;

♦   all marine scientific research in the EEZ and on the continental shelf would be subject to the consent of the coastal State, but they would in most cases be obliged to grant consent to other States when the research was to be conducted for peaceful purposes and fulfilled specified criteria;

♦   States would be bound to promote the development and transfer of marine technology "on fair and reasonable terms and conditions";

♦   States would be obliged to settle by peaceful means their disputes concerning the interpretation or application of the Convention; disputes could be submitted to an International Tribunal for the Law of the Sea to be established under the Convention, to the International Court of Justice, or to arbitration. Conciliation would also be available and, in certain circumstances, submission to it would be compulsory. The Tribunal would have exclusive jurisdiction over deep seabed mining disputes.

Deep seabed mining

For many years, following the adoption of the Convention in 1982, the provisions of Part XI, dealing with deep seabed mining, were viewed as an obstacle to the universal acceptance of the Convention. That was particularly true in view of the fact that the main opposition to those provisions came from the industrialized countries.

Under the Convention, all exploring and exploiting activities in the international seabed Area would be under the control of the International Sea-Bed Authority; the Authority would be authorized to conduct its own mining operations through its operating arm, the Enterprise, and also to contract with private and State ventures to give them mining rights in the Area, so that they could operate in parallel with the Authority. The first generation of seabed prospectors, dubbed "pioneer investors", would have guarantees of production once mining was authorized.

Objections to the Convention's provisions dealt mainly with the detailed procedures for production authorization from the deep seabed; cumbersome financial rules of contracts; decision-making in the Council of the Seabed Authority; and mandatory transfer of technology.

To overcome these objections, the Secretary-General undertook informal consultations with all parties, lasting nearly four years. As a result, the General Assembly adopted in 1994 the Agreement Relating to the Implementation of Part XI of the United Nations Convention on the Law of the Sea. The Agreement removes the obstacles that had stood in the way of universal acceptance by substituting general provisions for the detailed procedures contained in the Convention and by leaving it to the Authority to determine at a future date the exact nature of the rules it will adopt with respect to the authorization of deep seabed mining operations. The Agreement also removes the obligation for mandatory transfer of technology and ensures the representation of certain countries, or groups of countries, in the Council while giving those countries certain powers over decision-making.

The International Sea-Bed Authority has been established in Kingston, Jamaica.

Impact of the Convention

Even before its entry into force, the Convention had provided States with an indispensable foundation for their conduct in all aspects of ocean space, its uses and resources. States have consistently, through national and international legislation and through related decision-making, asserted the authority of the Convention as the pre-eminent international legal instrument on all matters within its purview. Thus far, its major impact has been on the establishment by 128 coastal States of a territorial sea not exceeding 12 nautical miles, and by 112 coastal States of exclusive economic zones or exclusive fishery zones not exceeding 200 nautical miles, all in conformity with the Convention.

Another area positively affected is the passage of ships in the territorial sea or through straits used for international navigation. The Convention's provisions relating to this matter have been incorporated into the legislation of many coastal States.

INTERNATIONAL TRIBUNALS

Following mass violations of international humanitarian law in the former Yugoslavia and in Rwanda (see Chapter 2), the Security Council established two international courts to bring persons responsible for such violations to justice before an international jurisdiction. The International Criminal Tribunal for the Former Yugoslavia and the International Tribunal for Rwanda were established in May 1993 and November 1994, respectively. Both Tribunals were created under Chapter VII of the Charter, which deals with enforcement measures. The Tribunal on the former Yugoslavia formulated its first indictments in early 1995.

INTERNATIONAL TERRORISM

Concerned by the increase of acts of terrorism, the General Assembly in 1972 established a 35-member Ad Hoc Committee on International Terrorism. In 1977 it asked the Committee to study the underlying causes of terrorism and recommend ways to combat it.

In 1979, the Assembly stressed the importance of international cooperation for dealing with acts of international terrorism. Adopting the report of the Committee, it condemned all acts of international terrorism that endangered or took human lives or jeopardized fundamental freedoms, as well as the continuation of repressive and terrorist acts committed by colonial, racist and alien regimes which denied peoples their legitimate right to self-determination and independence. The Assembly urged all States to eliminate the underlying causes of international terrorism.

In 1994, the General Assembly adopted a Declaration on Measures to Eliminate International Terrorism, which condemned all acts and practices of terrorism as criminal and unjustifiable, wherever and by whomever they were committed.

States were urged to take measures at the national and international levels to eliminate international terrorism.

International conventions on terrorism are: the Convention on Offences and Certain Other Acts Committed on Board Aircraft (Tokyo, 1963); the Convention for the Suppression of Unlawful Seizure of Aircraft (The Hague, 1970); the Convention for the Suppression of Unlawful Acts against the Safety of Civil Aviation (Montreal, 1971); the Convention on the Prevention and Punishment of Crimes against Internationally Protected Persons, including Diplomatic Agents (New York, 1973); the Convention on the Physical Protection of Nuclear Material (Vienna, 1980); the Protocol for the Suppression of Unlawful Acts of Violence at Airports Serving International Civil Aviation (Montreal, 1988); the Convention for the Suppression of Unlawful Acts against the Safety of Maritime Navigation (Rome, 1988); the Protocol for the Suppression of Unlawful Acts against the Safety of Fixed Platforms located on the Continental Shelf (Rome, 1988); and the Convention on the Marking of Plastic Explosives for the Purpose of Detection (Montreal, 1991).

Convention against Hostage-Taking. In 1976, aware of the need to devise measures to prevent, prosecute and punish acts of hostage-taking, the General Assembly established a committee to draft an international convention.

The Convention against the Taking of Hostages was adopted by the Assembly in 1979. Parties to the Convention agree to make the taking of hostages punishable by appropriate penalties. They also agree to prohibit certain activities within their territories, to exchange information, and to enable any criminal or extradition proceedings to take place. If a State party does not extradite an alleged offender, it is obliged to submit the case to its own authorities for prosecution. As of 30 September 1994, the Convention had 75 States parties.

Convention on the Safety of United Nations Personnel. The General Assembly, concerned by the increasing number of attacks against United Nations personnel which caused injury and even death, established in 1993 a committee to draft an international convention. The Convention on the Safety of United Nations and Associated Personnel was adopted by the Assembly and opened for signature and ratification in 1994.

AMENDMENTS TO THE UNITED NATIONS CHARTER

The United Nations Charter may be amended by a vote of two thirds of the Members of the General Assembly and ratification by two thirds of the Members of the United Nations, including the five permanent members of the Security Council. So far, four Charter Articles have been amended, one of them twice:

♦ in 1965, the membership of the Security Council was increased from 11 to 15 (Article 23) and the number of affirmative votes needed for a decision was increased from seven to nine, including the concurring vote of the five perma-nent members for all matters of substance rather than procedure (Article 27);

♦ in 1965, the membership of the Economic and Social Council was increased from 18 to 27, and in 1973, was further increased to 54 (Article 61);

♦ in 1968, the number of votes required in the Security Council to convene a General Conference to review the Charter was increased from seven to nine (Article 109).

OTHER LEGAL QUESTIONS

The General Assembly has adopted conventions and legal instruments on various other questions. The Declaration on the Enhancement of the Effectiveness of the Principle of Refraining from the Threat or Use of Force in International Relations was adopted by the Assembly in 1987; the Body of Principles for the Protection of All Persons under Any Form of Detention or Imprisonment was adopted in 1988; and the International Convention against the Recruitment, Use, Financing and Train-ing of Mercenaries was adopted and opened for signature and ratification in 1989.

In addition, the General Assembly has adopted a number of legal instruments on the recommendation of the 47-member Special Committee on the Charter of the United Nations and on the Strengthening of the Role of the Organization, estab-lished by the Assembly in 1974.

In 1988, on the recommendation of the Special Committee, the Assembly adopted the Declaration on the Prevention and Removal of Disputes and Situations which May Threaten International Peace and Security and on the Role of the United Nations in this Field.

In 1990, the Special Committee completed a draft concerning the rationalization of United Nations procedures, which was adopted by the General Assembly as an annex to its rules of procedure.

In 1991, the Special Committee completed the draft Declaration on Fact-Finding by the United Nations in the Field of Maintenance of International Peace and Security, and the General Assembly approved the Declaration.

In 1994, the Special Committee completed the draft Declaration on the Enhancement of Cooperation between the United Nations and Regional Arrangements or Agencies in the Maintenance of International Peace and Security, which was approved by the Assembly in the same year.

OFFICE OF LEGAL AFFAIRS

The United Nations Office of Legal Affairs was established to provide legal advice to the Secretary-General and to act on his behalf in legal matters. It serves as a unified central legal service for the Secretariat and other United Nations organs and advises them on questions of international and national, public, private and administrative law. Among other things, it deals with questions concerning privileges and immunities and the legal status of the United Nations; prepares drafts of international conventions, agreements, rules of procedures of United Nations organs and conferences and other legal texts; discharges the Secretary-General's responsibilities regarding the registration and publication of treaties as well as those as the depositary of multilateral conventions; and provides secretariat services for the Sixth Committee of the General Assembly, the International Law Commission, the Commission on International Trade Law, the United Nations Administrative Tribunal and other committees or conferences dealing with legal matters.

The head of the Office—the Legal Counsel—deals with legal questions referred to him/her by the Secretary-General and other United Nations organs; certifies legal instruments issued on behalf of the United Nations; represents the United Nations or the Secretary-General at meetings and conferences on legal matters; and advises the Secretary-General on matters of law.

CHAPTER 8

INTERGOVERNMENTAL AGENCIES RELATED TO THE UNITED NATIONS

The intergovernmental agencies related to the United Nations by special agreements are separate, autonomous organizations which work with the United Nations and each other through the coordinating machinery of the Economic and Social Council.

Fourteen of the agencies are known as "specialized agencies", a term used in the United Nations Charter. They report annually to the Economic and Social Council. They are the following:

- International Labour Organization (ILO)
- Food and Agriculture Organization of the United Nations (FAO)
- United Nations Educational, Scientific and Cultural Organization (UNESCO)
- World Health Organization (WHO)
- World Bank:
  International Bank for Reconstruction and Development (IBRD)
  International Development Association (IDA)
  International Finance Corporation (IFC)
  Multilateral Investment Guarantee Agency (MIGA)
- International Monetary Fund (IMF)
- International Civil Aviation Organization (ICAO)
- Universal Postal Union (UPU)
- International Telecommunication Union (ITU)
- World Meteorological Organization (WMO)
- International Maritime Organization (IMO)
- World Intellectual Property Organization (WIPO)
- International Fund for Agricultural Development (IFAD)
- United Nations Industrial Development Organization (UNIDO)

Although not a specialized agency, the International Atomic Energy Agency (IAEA) is an autonomous intergovernmental organization under the aegis of the United Nations. It reports annually to the General Assembly and, as appropriate, to the Security Council and the Economic and Social Council.

The World Trade Organization (WTO), established on 1 January 1995, is the intergovernmental organization overseeing international trade. Cooperative arrangements between the United Nations and WTO are under discussion.

The Administrative Committee on Coordination, composed of the Secretary-General and the executive heads of the specialized agencies and the IAEA, supervises the implementation of the agreements between the United Nations and the specialized agencies and ensures that their activities are fully coordinated.

INTERNATIONAL LABOUR ORGANIZATION

The International Labour Organization (ILO) was established in 1919, under the Treaty of Versailles, as an autonomous institution associated with the League of Nations. An agreement establishing the relationship between the ILO and the United Nations was approved in 1946, and ILO became the first specialized agency associated with the United Nations.

Aims and activities

ILO works to promote social justice for working people everywhere. It formulates international policies and programmes to help improve working and living conditions; creates international labour standards to serve as guidelines for national authorities in putting these policies into action; carries out an extensive programme of technical cooperation to help Governments in making these policies effective in practice; and engages in training, education and research to help advance these efforts.

ILO is unique among world organizations in that workers' and employers' representatives have an equal voice with those of Governments in formulating its policies. The International Labour Conference is composed of delegates from each member country—two from the government and one each representing workers and employers. One of its most important functions is the adoption of conventions and recommendations which set international labour standards in such areas as freedom of association, wages, hours and conditions of work, workmen's compensation, social insurance, vacation with pay, industrial safety, employment services, and labour inspection.

For member States that ratify them, ILO conventions create binding obligations to put their provisions into effect, while recommendations provide guidance for national policy, legislation and practice. Since ILO was founded, more than 350 conventions and recommendations have been adopted. ILO monitors the application of conventions by ratifying States and has a special procedure for investigating complaints of infringements of trade union rights.

Through the organization's programme of technical cooperation, ILO experts assist member countries in such fields as vocational training, management techniques, manpower planning, employment policies, occupational safety and health, social security systems, cooperatives and small-scale handicraft industries.

Opportunities for study and training are offered at ILO's International Institute for Labour Studies in Geneva and the International Training Centre in Turin, Italy.

On its fiftieth anniversary in 1969, ILO was awarded the Nobel Peace Prize.

Administration

Between the annual sessions of the International Labour Conference, in which all members are represented, the work of ILO is guided by the Governing Body, comprising 28 government members and 14 worker and 14 employer members.

Director-General: Michel Hansenne.

Headquarters: 4, route des Morillons, CH-1211 Geneva 22, Switzerland. Tel: (41) (22) 799 61 11; Cable: INTERLAB GENEVA; Telex: 41 56 47; Fax: (41) (22) 798 86 85.

FOOD AND AGRICULTURE ORGANIZATION OF THE UNITED NATIONS

The Food and Agriculture Organization of the United Nations (FAO) was founded at a conference in Quebec City on 16 October 1945. Since 1981, that date has been observed annually as World Food Day.

Aims and activities

The aims of FAO are to raise levels of nutrition and standards of living; to improve the production, processing, marketing and distribution of all food and agricultural products from farms, forests and fisheries; to promote rural development and improve the living conditions of rural populations; and, by these means, to eliminate hunger.

One of FAO's priority objectives is to encourage sustainable agriculture and rural development, a long-term strategy for the conservation and management of natural resources. It seeks to meet the needs of present and future generations through programmes that do not degrade the environment and are technically appropriate, economically viable and socially acceptable. FAO's other priority is food security, that is, ensuring availability of adequate food supplies; maximizing stability in the flow of supplies; and securing access to food by the poor.

The People's Participation Programme promotes the involvement of rural people and disadvantaged groups in decision-making and in the design and implementation of policies and activities affecting their lives. The aim is to strengthen rural people's organizations and encourage collaboration between them, Governments and development agencies.

In carrying out these aims, FAO promotes investment in agriculture, better soil and water management, improved yields of crops and livestock, the transfer of technology and the development of agricultural research in developing countries. It promotes the conservation of natural resources, particularly plant genetic resources, and the rational use of fertilizers and pesticides; combats animal diseases; promotes the development of marine and inland fisheries including aquaculture and of new and renewable sources of energy, in particular rural energy; and encourages the sustainable management of forests. Technical assistance is provided in all these fields and in others such as nutrition, agricultural engineering, agrarian reform, development communications, remote sensing for natural resources, and the prevention of food losses.

Special FAO programmes help countries prepare for emergency food situations and provide relief when necessary. Its Global Information and Early Warning System provides current information on the world food situation and identifies countries threatened by shortages, to guide planners and potential donors. Its Food Security Assistance Scheme is designed to assist developing countries set up national food reserves.

Other programmes aim at improving seed production and distribution in developing countries and assisting countries in the supply and use of fertilizers. There are also programmes to control animal diseases, such as trypanosomiasis, a disease severely limiting survival of livestock in Africa.

FAO acts as the lead agency for rural development in the United Nations system. It also collects, analyses and disseminates information on the above areas, provides policy and planning advice to Governments and acts as an international forum for debate on food and agriculture issues. With the United Nations, FAO sponsors the World Food Programme (see Food and Agriculture in Chapter 3).

Administration

The Conference of FAO, composed of all 169 member nations, Puerto Rico (associate member) and the European Community (member organization), meets every other year to determine the policy and approve the budget and work programme. The Council, consisting of 49 member nations elected by the Conference, serves as FAO's governing body between sessions of the Conference.

Director-General: Jacques Diouf.

Headquarters: Viale delle Terme di Caracalla, 00100 Rome, Italy.
Tel: (39) (6) 52251; Cable: FOODAGRI ROME;
Telex: 610181 FAO I; Fax: (39) (6) 5225 3152;
E-Mail: telex-room @ fao.org.

UNITED NATIONS EDUCATIONAL, SCIENTIFIC AND CULTURAL ORGANIZATION

The constitution of the United Nations Educational, Scientific and Cultural Organization (UNESCO) was prepared by a conference convened in London in 1945. UNESCO came into being in 1946.

Aims and activities

UNESCO's primary objective is to contribute to peace and security in the world by promoting collaboration among nations through education, science, culture and communication.

To realize this objective, UNESCO seeks to foster a culture of peace and human and sustainable development. It promotes education for all; fosters environmental research through international scientific programmes; encourages national cultural values and the preservation of cultural heritage so as to derive the maximum advantage from modernization without the loss of cultural identity and diversity; promotes the free flow of information, press freedom and the development of pluralistic media; supports the strengthening of the communication capacities of developing countries; and promotes the social sciences as instruments for the realization of human rights, justice and peace.

In education, its major activity, UNESCO's priorities are to achieve basic education for all adapted to today's needs, and to develop higher education. It also helps train teachers, educational planners and administrators and encourages local building and equipping of schools.

In the natural sciences, UNESCO's programmes include Man and the Biosphere; the programme of the Intergovernmental Oceanographic Commission; and the International Hydrological and International Geological Correlation programmes. In addition, through education and training programmes, UNESCO helps to correct the imbalance in scientific and technological manpower, 90 per cent of which is concentrated in the industrialized countries.

In the social and human sciences, UNESCO focuses on teaching and promoting human rights and democracy, combating all forms of discrimination, improving the status of women, and encouraging action to solve the problems faced by youth, such as education for the prevention of AIDS.

UNESCO's cultural activities are concentrated chiefly on safeguarding cultural heritage. The World Heritage List includes 400 sites, both cultural and natural, in 100 countries. Cultural activities also concentrate on promoting the cultural dimension of development, encouraging creation and creativity, preserving cultural identities and oral traditions, as well as promoting books and reading.

In communication, UNESCO surveys needs and assists developing countries, through its International Programme for the Development of Communication, to set up infrastructures in that field. It is multiplying efforts to promote the free flow of ideas by word and image among nations and within each nation, and to advance the principles of the freedom of the press and the independence, pluralism and diversity of the media.

UNESCO cooperates with more than 600 non-governmental organizations and foundations, as well as international and regional networks.

Administration

The General Conference of UNESCO, composed of representatives of the 183 member States, meets biennially to decide the policy, programme and budget of the organization. The Executive Board, consisting of 51 members elected by the General Conference, meets twice a year and is responsible for supervising the programme adopted by the Conference.

Director-General: Federico Mayor.

Headquarters: 7 place de Fontenoy, 75352 Paris 07 SP, France.
Tel: (33) (1) 45 68 10 00; Cable: UNESCO PARIS;
Telex: 270602F, 204461F; Press: PRESSUN 204379 F;
Fax: (33) (1) 45 67 16 90.

WORLD HEALTH ORGANIZATION

The World Health Organization (WHO) came into being on 7 April 1948, when 26 United Nations Member States had ratified its constitution. The date is observed annually as World Health Day.

Aims and activities

WHO's Constitution sets the ultimate objective of the Organization and its member countries as the attainment by all peoples of the highest possible level of health. It also states that the enjoyment of the highest standard of health is one of the fundamental rights of every human being. In 1977, the World

Health Assembly expressed this as "Health for All by the Year 2000", committing Governments and WHO to the attainment by all people of the world of a level of health that would permit them to lead socially and economically productive lives. The two main functions of WHO are technical cooperation with countries, and directing and coordinating international health work. They are complementary and include: advocacy for health, stimulating specific health action and disseminating information; developing norms and standards, plans and policies; developing models for monitoring, assessing and evaluating programmes and projects; training; research promotion; direct technical consultation and resource mobilization. WHO has always determined how best to carry out these functions in the light of changing needs, obstacles and opportunities.

Administration

The governing body of WHO is the World Health Assembly, on which all 190 WHO member States are represented. It meets annually to review the organization's work and decide on policy, programme and budget. The Executive Board has 32 members, designated by as many countries; it acts as the executive arm of the Assembly.

Director-General: Dr. Hiroshi Nakajima.

Headquarters: 20, avenue Appia, 1211 Geneva 27, Switzerland.
Tel: (41) (22) 791 21 11; Cable: UNISANTE GENEVE;
Telex: 845 415 416 (OMS CH); Fax: (41) (22) 791 07 46.

WORLD BANK

The World Bank is a group of four institutions: the International Bank for Reconstruction and Development (IBRD), established in 1945; the International Finance Corporation (IFC), established in 1956; the International Development Association (IDA), established in 1960; and the Multilateral Investment Guarantee Agency (MIGA), established in 1988.

The common objective of all four institutions is to reduce poverty and improve people's living standards by promoting sustainable economic growth and development.

INTERNATIONAL BANK FOR RECONSTRUCTION AND DEVELOPMENT

Aims and activities

The International Bank for Reconstruction and Development (IBRD) was established when 28 countries had signed the Articles of Agreement that had been drawn up at a United Nations monetary and financial conference of 44 Governments, held in 1944 at Bretton Woods, New Hampshire (United States). It was established to assist in the reconstruction and development of territories of its members by facilitating the investment of capital for productive purposes; to promote private foreign investment and, when private capital is not readily available on reasonable terms, to supplement private investment by providing finance for productive purposes; and to promote the long-range balanced growth of international trade and the maintenance of equilibrium in balances of payments by encouraging international investment for the development of productive resources of members.

The Bank's charter spells out the basic rules that govern its operations: it must lend only for productive purposes (such as agriculture and rural development, energy, education, health, family planning and nutrition, roads and railways, telecommunications, ports and power facilities) and must pay due regard to the prospects for repayment; each loan must be guaranteed by the Government concerned and, except in special circumstances, must be for specific projects; the Bank must assure itself that the necessary funds are unavailable from other sources on reasonable terms; the use of loans cannot be restricted to purchases in any particular member country or countries; and the Bank's decisions to lend must be based only on economic considerations. Since 1980, the Bank has made loans supporting programmes of specific policy changes and institutional reforms.

The Bank, whose capital is subscribed by its member countries, finances its lending operations primarily from its own borrowings in world markets, as well as from retained earnings and the flow of repayments on its loans. Loans may be made to member countries, to their political subdivisions or to private business enterprises in their territories. In addition to granting loans, the Bank provides a wide range of technical assistance services.

Administration

All powers of the Bank are vested in the Board of Governors, composed of one Governor and one alternate appointed by each of the 178 member countries. The Board normally meets once a year. There are 24 Executive Directors—five appointed by members having the largest number of shares and 19 elected by Governors of the remaining members. The Board of Governors delegates to the Executive Directors authority to exercise all powers of the Bank, except those reserved to the Board by the Articles of Agreement. The President of the Bank is selected by the Board of Governors, of which he is *ex officio* Chairman.

INTERNATIONAL DEVELOPMENT ASSOCIATION

Aims and activities

The need for lending to many poor countries on much easier terms than the Bank alone could give became apparent in the 1950s, and the International Development Association (IDA) was therefore established in 1960 as an affiliate of the Bank.

The bulk of IDA's resources comes from three sources: transfers from the Bank's net earnings; capital subscribed in convertible currencies by the members of IDA; and contributions from IDA's richer members.

To borrow from IDA, a country must meet four criteria: it must be very poor (the "poverty ceiling" was about $800 per capita annual income in 1992 dollars); it must have sufficient economic, financial and political stability to warrant long-term development lending; it must have an unusually difficult balance-of-payments problem and little prospect of earning enough foreign exchange to justify borrowing all it needs on conventional terms; and its policies must reflect a genuine commitment to development.

IDA "credits", as they are called to distinguish them from Bank "loans", are for a period of 35-40 years, without interest, except for a small charge to cover administrative costs. Repayment of principal does not begin until after a 10-year grace period.

Administration

The World Bank is responsible for the administration of IDA, and the Bank's Board of Governors, Executive Directors and President serve *ex officio* in IDA.

INTERNATIONAL FINANCE CORPORATION

Aims and activities

The International Finance Corporation (IFC), while closely associated with the Bank, is a separate legal entity and its funds are distinct from those of the Bank. IFC's aims are: to assist in financing private enterprise which could contribute to development by making investments, without guarantee of repayment by the member Government concerned; to bring together investment opportunities, domestic and foreign capital, and experienced management; and to stimulate the flow of private capital, domestic and foreign, into productive investment in member countries.

IFC plays an important role in mobilizing additional capital for companies in developing countries from private sources, through co-financing, loan syndications, securities underwriting, and guarantees. IFC also provides technical assistance and advice to businesses and Governments; it has offered considerable assistance to Governments in areas such as capital market development and privatization.

Administration

The Board of Governors, in which all powers of IFC are vested, consists of the Governors and alternates of the World Bank who represent countries which are also members of IFC. The Board of Directors, composed *ex officio* of the Executive Directors of the World Bank who represent countries which are also members of IFC, supervises the general operations of IFC. The President of the World Bank serves *ex officio* as Chairman of the Board of Directors of IFC.

MULTILATERAL INVESTMENT GUARANTEE AGENCY

The Multilateral Investment Guarantee Agency (MIGA) was formally constituted in 1988. As of June 1994, 121 countries had become members and an additional 26 were in the process of joining, having already signed the MIGA Convention. MIGA's basic purpose is to facilitate the flow of private investment for productive purposes to developing member countries by offering long-term political risk insurance (that is, coverage against the risks of expropriation, currency transfer and war and civil disturbance) to investors and by providing advisory and consultative services.

President of the World Bank: James D. Wolfensohn.

Headquarters: 1818 H Street, N.W., Washington, D.C. 20433, United States. Tel: (1) (202) 477 1234; Cable: INTBAFRAD WASHINGTON; Fax: (1) (202) 477 6391.

INTERNATIONAL MONETARY FUND

The International Monetary Fund (IMF) was founded in 1945. Its purposes, as stated in Article I of its Articles of Agreement, are:

♦ to promote international cooperation by providing the machinery for consultation and collaboration on international monetary issues;

♦ to facilitate the balanced growth of international trade, and contribute thereby to high levels of employment and real income, and the development of productive capacity;

♦ to promote exchange stability and orderly exchange arrangements, and facilitate the avoidance of competitive exchange depreciation;

♦ to foster a multilateral system of payments and transfers for current transaction and seek the elimination of foreign exchange restrictions which hamper the growth of world trade;

♦ to make the general resources of the Fund temporarily available to members, under adequate safeguards, to permit them to correct maladjustments in their balance of payments without resorting to measures destructive of national or international prosperity;

♦ to shorten the duration and magnitude of payments imbalances.

Functions

Participants at the Bretton Woods Conference (see International Bank for Reconstruction and Development) assigned three main functions to the Fund. Firstly, it is to administer a code of conduct regarding exchange rate policies and restrictions on payments for current account transactions. Secondly, it is to provide members with financial resources to enable them to observe the code of conduct while they are correcting or avoiding payments imbalances. Thirdly, it is to provide a forum in which members can consult with one another and collaborate on international monetary matters.

Use of IMF resources

The Fund makes financial resources available temporarily to members with payments problems, under a range of policies and facilities. In lending to its members, the Fund is guided by two principles. Firstly, the pool of currencies at the Fund's disposal exists for the entire membership and, therefore, a member borrowing currency is expected to return it as soon as its payments problems have been solved, so as not to limit other members' access. Secondly, before the Fund releases any money from the pool, the member must demonstrate how it intends to solve its payments problems, so that it can repay the Fund within the repayment period, which is normally three to five years (but can be up to ten years under certain facilities).

Administration

Each of the Fund's 179 member countries is represented on the Board of Governors, the Fund's highest authority, which meets annually. The daily business of the Fund is conducted by an Executive Board of 24 Executive Directors, chaired by the Managing Director, who is also the chief of the Fund's staff.

Managing Director: Michel Camdessus.

Headquarters: 700 19th Street, N.W., Washington, D.C. 20431, United States.
Tel: (1) (202) 623 7000; Cable: INTERFUND WASHINGTON;
Telex: 248331 IMF UR; Fax: (1) (202) 623 4661.

INTERNATIONAL CIVIL AVIATION ORGANIZATION

The International Civil Aviation Organization (ICAO) was created on 7 December 1944 with the signing of the Convention on International Civil Aviation at the end of the Chicago Conference. The organization was provisional until 4 April 1947, when the twenty-sixth State ratified the Convention. Starting in 1994, 7 December is celebrated worldwide as International Civil Aviation Day.

Aims and activities

ICAO's objectives are to: ensure the safe and orderly growth of international civil aviation; encourage the design and operation of aircraft for peaceful purposes; support the development of airways, airports and air navigation facilities for civil aviation; and meet the needs of the international public for safe, regular, efficient and economical air transport. In support of those objectives, ICAO has adopted international standards and recommended practices which specify the design and performance of aircraft and much of their equipment. Those standards also govern: the performance of airline pilots, flight crews, air traffic controllers, and ground and maintenance crews; the carriage of dangerous goods by commercial aircraft; security requirements and procedures at international airports; and the interdiction of illicit drug transportation by air.

ICAO formulates visual and instrument flight rules, as well as the aeronautical charts used for international navigation. Aircraft telecommunications systems—radio frequencies and security procedures—are also ICAO's responsibility.

ICAO works to facilitate the movement of aircraft, passengers, crews, baggage, cargo and mail across international boundaries by reducing procedural formalities involving customs, immigration and public health. It also meets requests from developing countries for help in establishing or improving air transport systems and training for aviation personnel.

Administration

ICAO has an Assembly, comprising delegates from all 183 Contracting States, and a Council of representatives of 33 nations elected by the Assembly. The Assembly meets at least once every three years, decides ICAO policy and examines any matters not specifically referred to the Council.

The Council is the executive body of ICAO and carries out Assembly directives. It administers ICAO's finances, adopts standards for international air navigation, and may act, on the request of member States, as a tribunal for the settlement of any dispute relating to international civil aviation. It may also initiate and carry out investigations related to civil aviation.

President of the Council: Dr. Assad Kotaite.

Secretary General: Dr. Philippe Rochat.

Headquarters: 1000 Sherbrooke Street West, Montreal, PQ, H3A 2R2, Canada. Tel: (1) (514) 285 8219; Cable: ICAO MONTREAL; Telex: 05 24513; Fax: (1) (514) 288 4772.

UNIVERSAL POSTAL UNION

The Universal Postal Union (UPU) was established in 1874 by the Berne Treaty, which was approved by 22 nations at Berne, Switzerland, and came into force on 1 July 1875. UPU became a specialized agency of the United Nations under an agreement which became effective in 1948.

Aims and activities

UPU forms a single postal territory of countries for the reciprocal exchange of letter-post items. Its objectives are to secure the organization and improvement of the postal services; to take part in postal technical assistance sought by the member countries of the Union; and to promote international collaboration in postal matters. Every member State of the UPU agrees to transmit the mail of all other members by the best means used for its own mail.

UPU fixes the indicative rates, the maximum and minimum weight and size limits and the conditions of acceptance of letter-post items, which include priority and non-priority items, letters and aerogrammes, postcards, printed matter, literature in raised relief for the blind, and small packets. It also prescribes the methods for calculating and collecting transit charges (for letter-post items passing through the territories of one or more countries) and terminal dues (for imbalance of mails). In addition, it establishes regulations for registered and air mail and for objects of transport which require special precautions, such as infectious and radioactive substances.

UPU's technical cooperation projects include planning, organization, management, operations, training and financial services. The aid provided, primarily to developing countries, consists in recruiting and sending experts, consultants or volunteers, granting vocational training or training fellowships, and supplying equipment and training or demonstration aids. Assistance is provided to member countries in preparing postal development studies for submission to donors and financial institutions in view of financing long-term development projects.

Administration

The Universal Postal Congress, composed of representatives of all member countries, is the supreme authority of UPU. It meets every five years; its main function is to revise the basic Acts of the UPU. It also lays down the general programme of UPU activities, and sets the budget for the following five-year period. The twenty-first Congress took place in Seoul in 1994 and the twenty-second Congress is scheduled to take place in Beijing in 1999.

The Council of Administration, composed of 41 members elected by the Congress with due regard for equitable geographical distribution, meets annually to ensure the continuity of the work of the Union between congresses.

The Postal Operations Council for Postal Studies, composed of 40 members elected by the Congress, shall be entrusted with operational, commercial, technical and economic questions concerning the postal service.

Director-General: Thomas E. Leavey.

Headquarters: Weltpoststrasse 4, 3000 Berne 15, Switzerland.
Tel: (41) (31) 350 31 11; Cable: UPU BERNE;
Telex: 912 761 UPU CH; Fax: (41) (31) 350 31 10.

INTERNATIONAL TELECOMMUNICATION UNION

The International Telecommunication Union (ITU) was founded at Paris in 1865 as the International Telegraph Union. Its name was changed to the International Telecommunication Union in 1934, following the adoption of the International Telecommunication Convention at Madrid in 1932. ITU became the United Nations specialized agency for telecommunications in 1947, as a result of an agreement concluded with the United Nations.

Aims and activities

Within ITU, the public and private sectors cooperate for the development of telecommunications and the harmonization of national telecommunication policies. ITU adopts international regulations and treaties governing all terrestrial and space uses of the frequency spectrum as well as the use of the geostationary satellite orbit within which countries adopt their national legislation. ITU also develops standards to facilitate the interconnection of telecommunication systems on a worldwide scale regardless of the type of technology used. Spearheading telecommunications development on a world scale, ITU fosters the development of telecommunications in developing countries by establishing medium-term development policies and strategies in consultation with other partners, and by providing specialized technical assistance in the areas of telecommunication policies, the choice and transfer of technologies, management, financing of investment projects and mobilization of resources, the installation and maintenance of networks, the management of human resources as well as research and development. As of 31 January 1995, ITU was composed of 184 member States and 363 members (scientific and industrial companies; public and private operators and broadcasters; and regional/international organizations).

Administration

The supreme organ of ITU is the Plenipotentiary Conference which meets every four years to adopt ITU's fundamental policies and to decide on its organization and activities. The

Administrative Council, composed of 46 members of ITU (representing 25 per cent of ITU's membership) elected by the Plenipotentiary Conference, meets annually to consider broad telecommunication policy issues to ensure that ITU's policies and strategies respond to the constantly changing telecommunication environment. The Council is responsible for ensuring the coordination of the four permanent organs at ITU headquarters: the General Secretariat, the Radiocommunication Sector, the Telecommunication Standardization Sector and the Telecommunications Development Sector. World conferences on international telecommunications meet according to needs, to establish the general principles which relate to the provision and operation of international telecommunications services offered to the public as well as the underlying international telecommunication transport means used to provide such services; they also set the rules applicable to administrations and operators in respect of international telecommunications.

Secretary-General: Dr. Pekka Tarjanne.

Headquarters: Place des Nations, CH-1211 Geneva 20, Switzerland.
Tel: (41) (22) 730 5111; Fax: (41) (22) 733 7256;
E-Mail: X.400 (C=CH; ADMD=ARCOM; PRMD=ITU; S=ITUMAIL)
Internet: itumail at itu.ch

WORLD METEOROLOGICAL ORGANIZATION

The World Meteorological Organization (WMO) was founded in 1951, but the Convention on the Organization had been in effect since March 1950. The predecessor of WMO, the International Meteorological Organization, a non-governmental organization, was founded in 1873. As at 31 May 1995, WMO had 178 member States and Territories.

Aims and activities

The Convention defines the purposes of WMO as being: to facilitate worldwide cooperation in establishing networks of stations for meteorological observations, as well as hydrological and other geophysical observations related to meteorology, and to promote the establishment and maintenance of centres charged with providing meteorological and related services; to promote the establishment and maintenance of systems for the rapid exchange of weather information; to promote the standardization of meteorological and related observations and to ensure the uniform publication of observations and statistics; to further the application of meteorology to aviation, shipping, water problems, agriculture and other activities; to promote activities in operational hydrology and to further cooperation between Meteorological and Hydrological services; and to encourage research and training in meteorology and related fields and to coordinate the international aspects of such training.

The work of WMO is carried out through eight major programmes. The World Weather Programme, which is the basic programme of WMO, has three major components: the Global Data Processing System, the Global Observation System and the Global Telecommunications System. Special activities of the Programme include: Data Management; System Support, including the Operational Information Service; Instruments and Methods of Observation Programme; WMO Satellite Activities; the Tropical Cyclone Programme; and the WMO Antarctic Activities.

The World Climate Programme provides the inter-agency interdisciplinary framework to address the full range of climate and climate change issues, including research into the economic and social consequences of climate and climate change. It assists in developing capabilities to warn Governments and the public of possible future variations and changes in climate, either natural or man-made, which may significantly affect humankind. The Programme also supports the work of the Intergovernmental Panel on Climate Change, the Global Climate Observing System, the implementation of the Framework Convention on Climate Change and the negotiations on the Convention on Desertification and Drought.

The World Climate Research Programme, undertaken jointly by WMO, the International Oceanographic Commission and the International Council of Scientific Unions, is an international scientific programme which aims to develop an improved understanding of climate and predictions of global and regional climate changes.

The Atmospheric Research and Environment Programme

contributes to the advancement of atmospheric science and assists WMO members in providing better meteorological services by fostering research in meteorology and related environmental fields. Disaster mitigation activities benefit particularly from the results of research in short- medium- and long-range predictions and from improved quality of weather forecasts in the tropical regions, especially for tropical cyclones.

The Applications of Meteorology Programme assists and coordinates the provision and application of meteorological data, forecasts and other information to weather-sensitive industries and activities. These include applications in agricultural meteorology, aeronautical meteorology (safety of air transport), marine meteorology (safety at sea) and public weather services.

The Hydrology and Water Resources Programme ensures the assessment and forecasting of the quantity and quality of water resources, in order to meet the needs of all sectors of society, to mitigate water-related hazards and to maintain or enhance the condition of the global environment. In this context, the Programme ensures the establishment of hydrogeological forecasting systems for flood protection as well as to combat drought and desertification through water-resource management.

The Education and Training Programme is designed to support the scientific and technical programmes of WMO, as well as to assist in the development of personnel in the national Meteorological and Hydrological Services of member countries.

The Technical Cooperation Programme advises and assists in the strengthening of the national Meteorological and Hydrological Services of developing countries, through the transfer of knowledge, technology and methodology, to improve the effectiveness of these Services.

Administration

The supreme organ of WMO is the World Meteorological Congress, attended by all WMO members, which is held every four years to determine general policies. The executive organ is the Executive Council, whose 36 members include the presidents of the six regional associations as *ex officio* members. The Council meets at least once a year to supervise the implementation of the decisions taken by the Congress and to make recommendations on any matter affecting international meteorology.

The six Regional Associations are for Africa, Asia, South America, North and Central America, the South-West Pacific and Europe. There are also eight technical commissions which develop international standards for methods, procedures, techniques and practices in meteorology and operational hydrology. These are the commissions for basic systems, atmospheric sciences, instruments and methods of observations, aeronautical meteorology, agricultural meteorology, marine meteorology, hydrology and climatology. The Secretariat, headed by the Secretary-General, is responsible for general administration.

Secretary-General: G.O.P. Obasi.

Headquarters: 41, Avenue Giuseppe-Motta, CH-1211 Geneva 20, Switzerland. Tel: (41) (22) 730 8111; Cable: METEOMOND GENEVA; Telex: 414199 OMM CH; Fax: (41) (22) 734 2326;

INTERNATIONAL MARITIME ORGANIZATION

The convention establishing the International Maritime Organization (IMO) (formerly called the Inter-Governmental Maritime Consultative Organization) was drafted in 1948 at a United Nations maritime conference at Geneva. The Convention came into force on 17 March 1958, when it was ratified by 21 States, including seven with at least 1 million gross tons of shipping each.

Aims and activities

IMO provides machinery for cooperation and the exchange of information among Governments on technical matters affecting shipping engaged in international trade. It encourages the adoption of the highest practicable standards in matters concerning maritime safety, navigational efficiency, and the prevention and control of marine pollution from ships.

IMO provides a forum for member Governments and interested organizations to exchange information and endeavour to solve problems connected with technical, legal and other questions concerning shipping and the prevention of marine pollution by ships. As a result of such discussions, IMO has drafted a number of conventions and recommendations which Governments have adopted. Among them are international conventions for the safety of life at sea, the prevention of marine pollution by ships, the training and certification of seafarers, the prevention of collisions at sea, several instruments dealing with liability and compensation, and many others.

In addition to conventions and treaties, IMO has adopted several hundred recommendations dealing with subjects such as the maritime transport of dangerous goods, maritime signals, safety for fishermen and fishing vessels, and the safety of nuclear merchant ships. While not legally binding, these recommendations constitute codes or recommended practices and provide guidance to Governments framing national regulations. IMO has also established the World Maritime University in Malmö, Sweden, which provides advanced training for administrators, educators and others involved in shipping at the senior level.

Administration

The Assembly, consisting of all 152 member States, is the supreme governing organ of IMO. It meets every two years to approve a biennial work programme and budget, and to adopt recommendations on regulations concerning maritime safety, prevention of marine pollution and other matters.

A 32-member Council, elected by the Assembly for two-year terms, is the governing body between the Assembly's biennial sessions. An amendment to the IMO Convention, which has yet to come into force, will raise the number of Council members to 40.

There are four principal committees—on maritime safety, legal matters, marine environment protection and technical cooperation—which submit reports or recommendations to the Assembly through the Council. A Committee on Facilitation will become the fifth principal committee when the amendment to the IMO Convention on this matter enters into force.

Secretary-General: William A. O'Neil.

Headquarters: 4 Albert Embankment, London SE1 7SR, United Kingdom. Tel: (44) (171) 735 7611; Cable: INTERMAR LONDON SE; Telex: 23588; Fax: (44) (171) 587 3210.

WORLD INTELLECTUAL PROPERTY ORGANIZATION

The World Intellectual Property Organization (WIPO) had its origins in the 1883 Paris Convention for the Protection of Industrial Property and the 1886 Berne Convention for the Protection of Literary and Artistic Works. The Convention establishing WIPO was signed in 1967 and entered into force in 1970. WIPO became a specialized agency of the United Nations in 1974, and as of 1 June 1995, had 155 member States.

Aims and activities

The main objectives of WIPO are to maintain and increase respect for intellectual property throughout the world, in order to favour industrial and cultural development by stimulating creative activity and facilitating the transfer of technology and the dissemination of literary and artistic works. Intellectual property comprises two main branches: industrial property (patents and other rights in technological inventions, rights in trade marks, industrial designs, appellations of origin, etc.) and copyright and neighbouring rights (in literary, musical and artistic works, films, performances of performing artists, phonograms, etc.).

To aid in the protection of intellectual property, WIPO promotes the wider acceptance of existing treaties and their revision, encourages the conclusion of new treaties and assists in the development of national legislation. It also gives legal technical assistance to developing countries; gathers and disseminates information; and maintains services for international registration or other administrative cooperation among the member States of the "Unions" which WIPO administers and which are founded on treaties, conventions and agreements dating back to 1883.

Administration

WIPO has a Conference of all member States and a General Assembly, composed of those member States which are also members of the Paris or Berne Unions. The governing bodies of WIPO and the Unions administered by WIPO normally meet in joint session to adopt their programmes and budgets and to discuss and decide policy. The Secretariat of WIPO—the International Bureau—is headed by the Director-General.

Director-General: Dr. Arpad Bogsch.

Headquarters: 34, chemin des Colombettes, 1211 Geneva 20, Switzerland.
Tel: (41) (22) 730 91 11; Cable: OMPI GENEVA;
Telex: 412912 OMPI CH; Fax: (41) (22) 733 54 28.

INTERNATIONAL FUND FOR AGRICULTURAL DEVELOPMENT

The idea for an International Fund for Agricultural Development (IFAD) arose at the 1974 World Food Conference. An agreement to establish the Fund was adopted on 13 June 1976, and opened for signature on 20 December, once initial pledges of $1 billion had been received. The agreement took effect in 1977.

Aims and activities

IFAD's main purpose is to mobilize resources for improved food production and better nutrition among low-income groups in developing countries. At least 20 per cent of the people in Africa, Asia and Latin America suffer the effects of chronic hunger and malnutrition, and the Fund focuses its attention on the needs of the poorest rural communities, in particular small farmers, the landless, fishermen, livestock herders, and poor rural women. The Fund pays special attention to grass-roots development and innovative approaches which build on local participation and the preservation of the natural resource base.

IFAD lends money, most of which is on highly concessional or low interest terms, and is concerned not only with raising agricultural production but with improving local prospects for employment, nutrition and income distribution. The Fund works with many Cooperating Institutions, including the World Bank, regional development banks, other regional financial agencies and United Nations agencies. Many of these institutions co-finance IFAD projects.

For every dollar contributed by IFAD in support of its projects, it has mobilized over three dollars from other external donors. By 30 April 1995, IFAD had invested $4,215.1 million in loans for 402 projects in 104 developing countries. The total cost of these projects, including the contribution of beneficiary countries, exceeded $14.2 billion and on completion they should benefit about 150 million people. The projects were expected to generate additional food production of over 40 million metric tons in wheat equivalent.

Administration

The Fund's operations are directed by a Governing Council, in which all 158 member States are represented. There are three categories of member States: developed countries (OECD), key contributor developing countries (OPEC) and other mainly recipient developing countries. However, IFAD's Governing Council in January 1995 approved amendments to the Agree ment Establishing IFAD. This would abolish the three category system of member groups, introducing a new voting system. Member countries would have two types of vote—their original membership votes and votes based on the size of contributions. These amendments will enter into force upon the completion of the Fourth Replenishment of the Fund's resources.

Operations are overseen by the Executive Board, with 18 Members and 17 alternates. The Board is chaired by the President of the Fund.

President: Fawzi H. Al-Sultan.

Headquarters: 107 Via del Serafico, 00142 Rome, Italy.
Tel: (39) (6) 54591; Cable: IFAD ROME; Telex: 620330;
Fax: (39) (6) 504 3463.

UNITED NATIONS INDUSTRIAL DEVELOPMENT ORGANIZATION

The United Nations Industrial Development Organization (UNIDO) was established by the General Assembly in 1966. It became the sixteenth specialized agency of the United Nations in 1985, with the mandate to promote industrial development and cooperation, and to act as the central coordinating body for industrial activities within the United Nations system.

Aims and activities

UNIDO is the United Nations agency specializing in promoting and accelerating industrialization in developing countries. It assists both Governments and the public and private sectors through technical cooperation, policy advice, investment promotion and technical support. It provides services to developing countries and to countries in transition to a market economy wishing to strengthen their industrial base.

Through partnership with development financial institutions, governmental and non-governmental agencies, public and private industry, and industrial associations, UNIDO makes technology and expertise more readily available to developing countries.

The agency also promotes industrial investments. Through industrial investment programmes for four developing regions and a global investment promotion network, UNIDO mobilizes investment resources for developing countries by assisting sponsors of industrial development projects and their foreign or local partners to cooperate in business ventures. Investment Promotion Service offices are in Athens, Milan, Paris, Seoul, Tokyo, Warsaw, Washington D.C. and Zurich. Centres for International Industrial Cooperation are in Beijing and Moscow.

Technical cooperation projects have benefitted some 180 countries and regions over the last 20 years. In 1993-1994, the agency delivered technical assistance worth some $215 million and promoted investment projects worth $1.1 billion.

UNIDO fosters cooperation between industrialized and developing countries by providing a forum for consultations and negotiations. Investment forums, technology markets and industrial cooperation meetings promote foreign investment and transfer of technology to developing countries. UNIDO also makes readily available industrial, business and technological information through its electronic networks, databases and publications.

Administration

The principal organs of UNIDO are: the General Conference, which determines the guiding principles, approves the budget and adopts conventions and agreements; the 53-member Industrial Development Board, which reviews Conference-approved programmes and makes recommendations; and the 27-member Programme and Budget Committee.

Director-General: Mauricio de María y Campos.

Headquarters: Vienna International Centre, P.O. Box 300, A-1400 Vienna, Austria
Tel: (43) (1) 21131; Cable: UNIDO VIENNA;
Telex: 135612; Fax: (43) (1) 232156.

INTERNATIONAL ATOMIC ENERGY AGENCY

The Statute of the International Atomic Energy Agency (IAEA) was approved in 1956 at an international conference held at United Nations Headquarters, and the Agency came into exist- ence in Vienna in 1957. Also in 1957, the General Assembly approved an agreement concerning IAEA's relationship with the United Nations.

Aims and activities

In accordance with its Statute, IAEA's two main objectives are to accelerate and enlarge the contribution of atomic energy to peace, health and prosperity throughout the world, and to ensure that assistance provided by it, or at its request or under its super- vision or control, is not used to further any military purpose

IAEA fosters and guides the development of peaceful uses of atomic energy, establishes standards for nuclear safety and environmental protection, aids member countries through tech- nical cooperation, and fosters the exchange of scientific and technical information.

One of the Agency's main functions is to apply safeguards to ensure that nuclear materials and equipment intended for peaceful use are not diverted to military purposes. The IAEA safeguards system is primarily based on nuclear material ac- countancy, verified on the spot by IAEA inspectors. Various types of safeguards agreements can be concluded with IAEA. Those in connection with the Treaty on the Non-Proliferation of Nuclear Weapons (NPT), the Treaty for the Prohibition of Nuclear Weapons in Latin America (Treaty of Tlatelolco) and the Treaty on the South Pacific Nuclear-Free-Zone (Treaty of Rarotonga) (see Disarmament in Chapter 2) require non-nuclear-weapon States to submit their entire nuclear-fuel-cycle activities to IAEA safeguards. Other agreement types cover safeguards at single facilities.

As of 31 December 1994, there were 199 safeguards agreements in force with 118 States (and with Taiwan, China). In 1994, safeguards agreements pursuant to the NPT entered into force with Armenia and Zambia.

Argentina and Brazil established a Common System of Accounting and Control of Nuclear Material (SCCC) and a Brazilian-Argentine Agency for Accounting and Control of Nuclear Materials (ABACC) whose objective is to implement the SCCC. A comprehensive safeguards agreement was negotiated between Argentina and Brazil, the ABACC and IAEA, covering all nuclear materials in all nuclear activities carried out in the two States, under their jurisdiction or under their control. This agreement entered into force in 1994.

During 1994, safeguards were applied in 49 States under agreements pursuant to NPT or to NPT and the Treaty of Tlatelolco, in one State under an agreement pursuant to the Treaty of Tlatelolco and in eight States under other agreements. Safeguards activities pursuant to NPT in Iraq continued to be subsumed by activities pursuant to Security Council resolution 687. (IAEA also applies safeguards to nuclear installations in Taiwan, China.)

Since May 1994, IAEA inspectors have been monitoring the agreed freeze of the graphite moderated reactor programme in the Democratic People's Republic of Korea. (See Korean Peninsula in Chapter 2.)

In South Africa, the world welcomed the first instance of a State abandoning its nuclear weapon capacity. This gave rise to new verification tasks for IAEA. As a result of visits by IAEA staff and other experts to the country, IAEA concluded in 1993 that the nuclear material used for the weapons was under safeguards and that there was no indication that there remained any components of the programme that had not been either rendered useless or converted to commercial non-nuclear or peaceful nuclear uses.

Nuclear-related issues in the countries of eastern Europe and the former USSR continued to be of international concern.

The issues that were addressed included: the application of safeguards to the large nuclear programmes in some of these States; the safety of nuclear installations; the need to establish adequate infrastructures for nuclear safety and radiation protection and the problems of radioactive contamination. IAEA helped to make significant advances towards resolving such issues. Missions were carried out to all major nuclear facilities in Armenia, Belarus, Kazakstan, Kyrgyzstan, Ukraine and Uzbekistan in connection with the development of safeguards approaches, the future implementation of safeguards and the assessment of national infrastructure requirements. In the safety area, IAEA concentrated on establishing priorities for safety upgradings of the various reactor types and on providing expert assistance and guidance.

An expanded safety programme was adopted covering the areas of safety of nuclear installations, radiation protection, health, radioactive waste management, nuclear power and the nuclear fuel cycle.

IAEA advises and assists Governments, at their request, on atomic energy programmes. The main objective of its technical assistance programme is to promote the transfer of skills and knowledge so that recipient countries can carry out their atomic energy programmes more efficiently and safely. It provides advisers, equipment and training to member States, the majority of which are developing countries.

Total new resources available for technical cooperation in 1994 amounted to $52.8 million.

IAEA formulates basic safety standards for radiation protection and issues regulations and codes of practice on specific types of operations, including the safe transport of radioactive materials. It also facilitates emergency assistance to member States in the event of a radiation accident. The capability of the Agency to perform its functions under the Convention on Assistance in the Case of a Nuclear Accident or Radiological Emergency and under the Convention on Early Notification of a Nuclear Accident was strengthened through arrangements for use of WMO's Global Telecommunication System to transmit measured radiological data.

Information on virtually every aspect of nuclear science and technology is collected and disseminated by IAEA through its International Nuclear Information System in Vienna. With UNESCO, it operates the International Centre for Theoretical Physics in Trieste, Italy, and maintains three laboratories for studies in basic uses. IAEA works with FAO in research on atomic energy in food and agriculture, and with WHO on radiation in medicine and biology. IAEA's Marine Environment Laboratory in Monaco carries out worldwide marine pollution studies with UNEP and UNESCO.

Administration

IAEA's policies and programmes are directed by the General Conference, composed of all IAEA's member States, which meets annually, and by a 35-member Board of Governors.

Director-General: Hans Blix.

Headquarters: Vienna International Centre, Wagramerstrasse 5, P.O. Box 100, A-1400 Vienna, Austria.
Tel: (43) (1) 2060; Cable: INATOM VIENNA;
Telex: 112645 ATOM A; Fax: (43) (1) 20607.

WORLD TRADE ORGANIZATION

The World Trade Organization (WTO) was established on 1 January 1995, replacing the General Agreement on Tariffs and Trade (GATT) as the major entity overseeing international trade.

Aims and activities

The WTO administers, through various councils and committees, the 28 agreements on international trading relations contained in the final act of the Uruguay Round of trade negotiations, which was approved at a meeting in Marrakesh, Morocco, in 1994. In addition, WTO administers a number of plurilateral agreements, notably on government procurement and civil aircraft.

The WTO goes further than GATT in that it provides the sole legal and institutional foundation for the multilateral trading system. Whereas GATT was applied on a provisional basis, the WTO will be legally binding. It will also provide the principal contractual obligations determining how Governments frame and implement domestic trade legislation and regulations.

The WTO has five essential functions:
♦ to administer and implement the multilateral and plurilateral trade agreements which make up the WTO Agreements;
♦ to act as a forum for multilateral trade negotiations among its members;
♦ to seek to resolve trade disputes among WTO members;
♦ to oversee national trade policies of its members;
♦ to cooperate with other international institutions involved in global economic policy-making.

The WTO is a watchdog on international trade, regularly examining the trade regimes of individual members. In its various bodies, members flag proposed or draft measures by others that can cause trade conflicts. Members are also required to notify in detail various trade measures and statistics, which are maintained by WTO on a large data base. Trade disputes between members that cannot be solved through bilateral talks are adjudicated under the WTO Dispute Settlement Body.

The WTO continues, in a strengthened form, the code of conduct for international trade established by GATT, which came into force in 1948. This includes the principle of non-discrimination between trading partners the "most-favoured nation" clause—and equal treatment for imports and domestic goods in internal markets.

WTO rules also cover trade in services, intellectual property and investment. Under the WTO Agreements, protectionistic policies in important areas such as textile and clothing and agriculture will be phased out or reduced.

The WTO secretariat assists developing countries in the implementation of the Round through a newly established Development Division and a strengthened Technical Cooperation and Training Division.

Eight major negotiating "rounds" in GATT brought about far-reaching reductions in tariffs and other trade barriers. The most significant were the first (Geneva, 1947), the Kennedy (1964-67), the Tokyo (1973-79) and the Uruguay (1986-1994) Rounds.

The International Trade Centre, established by GATT in 1964, is a joint subsidiary organ of WTO and the United Nations, the latter acting through the United Nations Conference on Trade and Development (see Trade and Development in Chapter 3). The Centre assists developing countries in export promotion. It provides information and advice on export markets and marketing techniques and helps in establishing export services and training personnel.

Administration

All 128 member countries of GATT automatically become WTO members upon acceptance of the Uruguay Round Agreements and submission of commitments on trade in goods and services. The highest body of WTO is the Ministerial Conference, which meets at least once every two years and can take decisions on all matters under any of the multilateral trade agreements. The General Council is responsible for WTO's day-to-day activities. Its mandate includes supervising bodies relating to dispute settlement and trade policy reviews of WTO members. It also delegates responsibility to other committees and bodies, namely the Council for Trade in Goods, the Council for Trade in Services and the Council on Trade-Related Aspects of Intellectual Property Rights.

Director-General: Renato Ruggiero.

Headquarters: Centre William Rappard, 154 rue de Lausanne, 1211 Geneva 21, Switzerland.
Tel: (41) (22) 739 51 11; Cable: GATT GENEVA;
Telex: 412324 GATT CH; Fax: (41) (22) 731 42 06.

APPENDICES

GROWTH OF UNITED NATIONS
MEMBERSHIP, 1945-1994

Year	Number	Member States
1945	Original 51	Argentina, Australia, Belgium, Bolivia, Brazil, Byelorussian Soviet Socialist Republic, Canada, Chile, China, Colombia, Costa Rica, Cuba, Czechoslovakia, Denmark, Dominican Republic, Ecuador, Egypt, El Salvador, Ethiopia, France, Greece, Guatemala, Haiti, Honduras, India, Iran, Iraq, Lebanon, Liberia, Luxembourg, Mexico, Netherlands, New Zealand, Nicaragua, Norway, Panama, Paraguay, Peru, Philippines, Poland, Saudi Arabia, South Africa, Syrian Arab Republic, Turkey, Ukrainian Soviet Socialist Republic, Union of Soviet Socialist Republics, United Kingdom of Great Britain and Northern Ireland, United States of America, Uruguay, Venezuela, Yugoslavia
1946	55	Afghanistan, Iceland, Sweden, Thailand
1947	57	Pakistan, Yemen[1]
1948	58	Myanmar
1949	59	Israel
1950	60	Indonesia
1955	76	Albania, Austria, Bulgaria, Cambodia, Finland, Hungary, Ireland, Italy, Jordan, Lao People's Democratic Republic, Libyan Arab Jamahiriya, Nepal, Portugal, Romania, Spain, Sri Lanka
1956	80	Japan, Morocco, Sudan, Tunisia
1957	82	Ghana, Malaysia
1958	83	Guinea
1960	100	Benin, Burkina Faso, Cameroon, Central African Republic, Chad, Congo, Côte d'Ivoire, Cyprus, Gabon, Madagascar, Mali, Niger, Nigeria, Senegal, Somalia, Togo, Zaire
1961	104	Mauritania, Mongolia, Sierra Leone, United Republic of Tanzania
1962	110	Algeria, Burundi, Jamaica, Rwanda, Trinidad and Tobago, Uganda
1963	112	Kenya, Kuwait
1964	115	Malawi, Malta, Zambia
1965	118	Gambia, Maldives, Singapore
1966	122	Barbados, Botswana, Guyana, Lesotho
1967	123	Democratic Yemen[1]

[1] Yemen was admitted to membership in the United Nations on 30 September 1947 and Democratic Yemen on 14 December 1967. On 22 May 1990, the two countries merged and have since been represented as one Member with the name "Yemen".

Year	Number	Member States
1968	126	Equatorial Guinea, Mauritius, Swaziland
1970	127	Fiji
1971	132	Bahrain, Bhutan, Oman, Qatar, United Arab Emirates
1973	134	Bahamas, Germany[2]
1974	137	Bangladesh, Grenada, Guinea-Bissau
1975	143	Cape Verde, Comoros, Mozambique, Papua New Guinea, Sao Tome and Principe, Suriname
1976	146	Angola, Samoa, Seychelles
1977	148	Djibouti, Viet Nam
1978	150	Dominica, Solomon Islands
1979	151	Saint Lucia
1980	153	Saint Vincent and the Grenadines, Zimbabwe
1981	156	Antigua and Barbuda, Belize, Vanuatu
1983	157	Saint Kitts and Nevis
1984	158	Brunei Darussalam
1990	160	Liechtenstein, Namibia
1991	167	Democratic People's Republic of Korea, Estonia, Federated States of Micronesia, Latvia, Lithuania, Marshall Islands, Republic of Korea
1992	179	Armenia, Azerbaijan, Bosnia and Herzegovina, Croatia, Georgia, Kazakstan, Kyrgyzstan, Moldova, San Marino, Slovenia, Tajikistan, Turkmenistan, Uzbekistan
1993	184	Andorra, Czech Republic[3], Eritrea, Monaco, Slovak Republic[3], The former Yugoslav Republic of Macedonia
1994	185	Palau

---

[2] The Federal Republic of Germany and the German Democratic Republic were admitted to membership in the United Nations on 18 September 1973. Through the accession of the German Democratic Republic to the Federal Republic of Germany, effective from 3 October 1990, the two German States have united to form one sovereign State.

[3] Czechoslovakia was an original Member of the United Nations from 24 October 1945. In a letter dated 10 December 1992, its Permanent Representative informed the Secretary-General that the Czech and Slovak Federal Republic would cease to exist on 31 December 1992 and that the Czech Republic and the Slovak Republic, as successor States, would apply for membership in the United Nations. Following the receipt of such applications, the Security Council, on 8 January, recommended to the General Assembly that the Czech Republic and the Slovak Republic be admitted to United Nations membership. They were thus admitted on 19 January as Member States.

UNITED NATIONS MEMBER STATES
(at 31 December 1994)

Member State	Date of admission	Scale of assessments (per cent)	Population (est.)
Afghanistan	19 November 1946	0.01	17,690,000
Albania	14 December 1955	0.01	3,389,000
Algeria	8 October 1962	0.16	26,722,000
Andorra	28 July 1993	0.01	61,000
Angola	1 December 1976	0.01	10,276,000
Antigua and Barbuda	11 November 1981	0.01	65,000
Argentina	24 October 1945	0.57	34,180,000
Armenia	2 March 1992	0.13	3,732,000
Australia	1 November 1945	1.51	17,627,000
Austria	14 December 1955	0.75	8,015,000
Azerbaijan	2 March 1992	0.22	7,391,000
Bahamas	18 September 1973	0.02	269,000
Bahrain	21 September 1971	0.03	539,000
Bangladesh	17 September 1974	0.01	115,203,143
Barbados	9 December 1966	0.01	260,000
Belarus[a]	2 March 1992	0.48	10,188,000
Belgium	27 December 1945	1.06	10,046,000
Belize	25 September 1981	0.01	205,000
Benin	20 September 1960	0.01	5,215,000
Bhutan	21 September 1971	0.01	1,596,000
Bolivia	14 November 1945	0.01	7,237,000
Bosnia and Herzegovina	22 May 1992	0.04	3,707,000
Botswana	17 October 1966	0.01	1,443,000
Brazil	24 October 1945	1.59	153,792,000
Brunei Darussalam	21 September 1984	0.03	274,000
Bulgaria	14 December 1955	0.13	8,452,000
Burkina Faso	20 September 1960	0.01	9,682,000
Burundi	18 September 1962	0.01	5,958,000
Cambodia	14 December 1955	0.01	9,308,000
Cameroon	20 September 1960	0.01	12,522,000
Canada	9 November 1945	3.11	28,973,000
Cape Verde	16 September 1975	0.01	370,000
Central African Republic	20 September 1960	0.01	3,156,000
Chad	20 September 1960	0.01	6,098,000
Chile	24 October 1945	0.08	14,026,000
China	24 October 1945	0.77	1,196,360,000
Colombia	5 November 1945	0.13	34,520,000
Comoros	12 November 1975	0.01	607,000
Congo	20 September 1960	0.01	2,443,000
Costa Rica	2 November 1945	0.01	3,199,000

Member State	Date of admission	Scale of assessments (per cent)	Population (est.)
Côte d'Ivoire	20 September 1960	0.02	13,316,000
Croatia	22 May 1992	0.13	4,511,000
Cuba	24 October 1945	0.09	10,941,000
Cyprus	20 September 1960	0.02	726,000
Czech Republic	19 January 1993	0.42	10,331,000
Democratic People's Republic of Korea	17 September 1991	0.05	23,048,000
Denmark	24 October 1945	0.60	5,205,000
Djibouti	20 September 1977	0.01	557,000
Dominica	18 December 1978	0.01	71,000
Dominican Republic	24 October 1945	0.02	7,608,000
Ecuador	21 December 1945	0.03	11,221,000
Egypt[b]	24 October 1945	0.07	56,488,000
El Salvador	24 October 1945	0.01	5,517,000
Equatorial Guinea	12 November 1968	0.01	379,000
Eritrea	28 May 1993	0.01	3,345,000
Estonia	17 September 1991	0.07	1,507,000
Ethiopia	13 November 1945	0.01	56,900,000
Federated States of Micronesia	17 September 1991	0.01	105,000
Fiji	13 October 1970	0.01	762,000
Finland	14 December 1955	0.57	5,082,000
France	24 October 1945	6.00	57,804,000
Gabon	20 September 1960	0.02	1,012,000
Gambia	21 September 1965	0.01	1,026,000
Georgia	31 July 1992	0.21	5,471,000
Germany	18 September 1973	8.93	81,255,000
Ghana	8 March 1957	0.01	16,446,000
Greece	25 October 1945	0.35	10,350,000
Grenada	17 September 1974	0.01	92,000
Guatemala	21 November 1945	0.02	10,322,000
Guinea	12 December 1958	0.01	6,306,000
Guinea-Bissau	17 September 1974	0.01	1,028,000
Guyana	20 September 1966	0.01	816,000
Haiti	24 October 1945	0.01	7,041,000
Honduras	17 December 1945	0.01	5,770,000
Hungary	14 December 1955	0.18	10,275,000
Iceland	19 November 1946	0.03	263,000
India	30 October 1945	0.36	901,459,000
Indonesia[c]	28 September 1950	0.16	189,136,000
Iran (Islamic Republic of)	24 October 1945	0.77	59,359,000
Iraq	21 December 1945	0.13	19,454,000
Ireland	14 December 1955	0.18	3,503,000

Member State	Date of admission	Scale of assessments (per cent)	Population (est.)
Israel	11 May 1949	0.23	5,383,000
Italy	14 December 1955	4.29	57,057,000
Jamaica	18 September 1962	0.01	2,411,000
Japan	18 December 1956	12.45	124,536,000
Jordan	14 December 1955	0.01	4,936,000
Kazakstan	2 March 1992	0.35	16,925,000
Kenya	16 December 1963	0.01	28,113,000
Kuwait	14 May 1963	0.25	1,433,000
Kyrgyzstan	2 March 1992	0.06	4,474,000
Lao People's Democratic Republic . . .	14 December 1955	0.01	4,605,000
Latvia	17 September 1991	0.13	2,544,000
Lebanon	24 October 1945	0.01	2,806,000
Lesotho	17 October 1966	0.01	1,943,000
Liberia	2 November 1945	0.01	2,640,000
Libyan Arab Jamahiriya . .	14 December 1955	0.24	4,700,000
Liechtenstein	18 September 1990	0.01	30,000
Lithuania	17 September 1991	0.15	3,735,000
Luxembourg	24 October 1945	0.06	395,000
Madagascar	20 September 1960	0.01	12,092,000
Malawi	1 December 1964	0.01	9,135,000
Malaysia[d]	17 September 1957	0.12	19,247,000
Maldives	21 September 1965	0.01	238,000
Mali	28 September 1960	0.01	10,135,000
Malta	1 December 1964	0.01	366,000
Marshall Islands	17 September 1991	0.01	52,000
Mauritania	27 October 1961	0.01	2,161,000
Mauritius	24 April 1968	0.01	1,098,000
Mexico	7 November 1945	0.88	93,008,000
Monaco	28 May 1993	0.01	31,000
Mongolia	27 October 1961	0.01	2,318,000
Morocco	12 November 1956	0.03	26,069,000
Mozambique	16 September 1975	0.01	15,583,000
Myanmar	19 April 1948	0.01	44,596,000
Namibia	23 April 1990	0.01	1,461,000
Nepal	14 December 1955	0.01	20,812,000
Netherlands	10 December 1945	1.50	15,352,000
New Zealand	24 October 1945	0.24	3,493,000
Nicaragua	24 October 1945	0.01	4,401,000
Niger	20 September 1960	0.01	8,361,000
Nigeria	7 October 1960	0.20	105,264,000
Norway	27 November 1945	0.55	4,331,000

Member State	Date of Admission	Scale of Assessments (per cent)	Population (est.)
Oman	7 October 1971	0.03	2,018,000
Pakistan	30 September 1947	0.06	122,802,000
Palau	15 December 1994	*	16,000
Panama	13 November 1945	0.02	2,583,000
Papua New Guinea	10 October 1975	0.01	3,922,000
Paraguay	24 October 1945	0.02	4,643,000
Peru	31 October 1945	0.06	22,454,000
Philippines	24 October 1945	0.07	65,649,000
Poland	24 October 1945	0.47	38,513,000
Portugal	14 December 1955	0.20	9,868,000
Qatar	21 September 1971	0.05	486,000
Republic of Korea	17 September 1991	0.69	43,500,000
Republic of Moldova	2 March 1992	0.15	4,356,000
Romania	14 December 1955	0.17	22,755,000
Russian Federation[e]	24 October 1945	6.71	148,366,000
Rwanda	18 September 1962	0.01	7,554,000
Saint Kitts and Nevis . . .	23 September 1983	0.01	42,000
Saint Lucia	18 September 1979	0.01	139,000
Saint Vincent and the Grenadines	16 September 1980	0.01	110,000
Samoa	15 December 1976	0.01	163,000
San Marino	2 March 1992	0.01	24,000
Sao Tome and Principe . .	16 September 1975	0.01	122,000
Saudi Arabia	24 October 1945	0.96	17,119,000
Senegal	28 September 1960	0.01	7,902,000
Seychelles	21 September 1976	0.01	72,000
Sierra Leone	27 September 1961	0.01	4,297,000
Singapore	21 September 1965	0.12	2,874,000
Slovak Republic	19 January 1993	0.13	5,333,000
Slovenia	22 May 1992	0.09	1,989,000
Solomon Islands	19 September 1978	0.01	355,000
Somalia	20 September 1960	0.01	8,954,000
South Africa	7 November 1945	0.41	40,436,000
Spain	14 December 1955	1.98	39,150,000
Sri Lanka	14 December 1955	0.01	17,619,000
Sudan	12 November 1956	0.01	28,129,000
Suriname	4 December 1975	0.01	414,000
Swaziland	24 September 1968	0.01	809,000
Sweden	19 November 1946	1.11	8,765,000
Syrian Arab Republic[f]	24 October 1945	0.04	13,393,000
Tajikistan	2 March 1992	0.05	5,767,000
Thailand	16 December 1946	0.11	58,584,000

Member State	Date of Admission	Scale of Assessments (per cent)	Population (est.)
The former Yugoslav Republic of Macedonia[g]	8 April 1993	0.02	2,083,000
Togo	20 September 1960	0.01	3,885,000
Trinidad and Tobago	18 September 1962	0.05	1,260,000
Tunisia	12 November 1956	0.03	8,570,000
Turkey	24 October 1945	0.27	60,227,000
Turkmenistan	2 March 1992	0.06	3,921,000
Uganda	25 October 1962	0.01	19,940,000
Ukraine	24 October 1945	1.87	52,114,000
United Arab Emirates	9 December 1971	0.21	1,206,000
United Kingdom	24 October 1945	5.02	58,191,000
United Republic of Tanzania[h]	14 December 1961	0.01	28,019,000
United States of America	24 October 1945	25.00	258,233,000
Uruguay	18 December 1945	0.04	3,149,000
Uzbekistan	2 March 1992	0.26	21,860,000
Vanuatu	15 September 1981	0.01	156,000
Venezuela	15 November 1945	0.49	20,712,000
Viet Nam	20 September 1977	0.01	71,324,000
Yemen	30 September 1947	0.01	12,302,000
Yugoslavia	24 October 1945	0.14	10,507,000
Zaire	20 September 1960	0.01	41,231,000
Zambia	1 December 1964	0.01	8,936,000
Zimbabwe	25 August 1980	0.01	10,739,000

States which are not Members of the United Nations but which participate in certain of its activities, have been called upon to contribute on the basis of the following rates:

Holy See	0.01
Nauru	0.01
Switzerland	1.16
Tonga	0.01

* Rate of assessment to be determined.

[a] On 19 September 1991, Byelorussia informed the United Nations that it had changed its name to Belarus.

[b] Egypt and Syria were original Members of the United Nations from 24 October 1945. Following a plebiscite on 21 February 1958, the United Arab Republic was established by a union of Egypt and Syria and continued as a single Member. On 13 October 1961, Syria, having resumed its status as an independent State, resumed its separate membership in the United Nations. On 2 September 1971, the United Arab Republic changed its name to the Arab Republic of Egypt.

[c] By letter of 20 January 1965, Indonesia announced its decision to withdraw from the United Nations "at this stage and under the present circumstances". By

telegram of 19 September 1966, it announced its decision "to resume full cooperation with the United Nations and to resume participation in its activities". On 28 September 1966, the General Assembly took note of this decision and the President invited representatives of Indonesia to take seats in the Assembly.

d The Federation of Malaya joined the United Nations on 17 September 1957. On 16 September 1963, its name was changed to Malaysia, following the admission to the new federation of Singapore, Sabah (North Borneo) and Sarawak. Singapore became an independent State on 9 August 1965 and a United Nations Member on 21 September 1965.

e The Union of Soviet Socialist Republics was an original Member of the United Nations from 24 October 1945. In a letter dated 24 December 1991, Boris Yeltsin, the President of the Russian Federation, informed the Secretary-General that the membership of the Soviet Union in the Security Council and all other United Nations organs was being continued by the Russian Federation with the support of the 11 member countries of the Commonwealth of Independent States.

f Egypt and Syria were original Members of the United Nations from 24 October 1945. Following a plebiscite on 21 January 1958, the United Arab Republic was established by a union of Egypt and Syria and continued as a single Member. On 13 October 1961, Syria, having resumed its status as an independent State, resumed its separate membership in the United Nations.

g The General Assembly decided on 8 April 1993 to admit to United Nations membership the States being provisionally referred to for all purposes within the United Nations as "The former Yugoslav Republic of Macedonia" pending settlement of the difference that had arisen over its name.

h Tanganyika was a United Nations Member from 14 December 1961 and Zanzibar was a Member from 16 December 1963. Following the ratification on 26 April 1964 of Articles of Union between Tanganyika and Zanzibar, the United Republic of Tanganyika and Zanzibar continued as a single Member, changing its name to the United Republic of Tanzania on 1 November 1964.

UNITED NATIONS INFORMATION CENTRES AND SERVICES
(at 31 May 1995)

CENTRES AND SERVICES IN AFRICA

ACCRA ◆ United Nations Information Centre, Gamel Abdul Nassar/Liberia Roads (Post Office Box 2339), Accra, Ghana
Services to: Ghana, Sierra Leone

ADDIS ABABA ◆ United Nations Information Service, Economic Commission for Africa, Africa Hall (Post Office Box 3001), Addis Ababa, Ethiopia
Services to: Ethiopia, Economic Commission for Africa

ALGIERS ◆ United Nations Information Centre, 19, avenue Chahid El Ouali, Mustapha Sayed (Boîte postale 823), Algiers, Algeria
Services to: Algeria

ANTANANARIVO ◆ United Nations Information Centre, 22, rue Rainitovo, Antsahavola (Boîte Postale 1348), Antananarivo, Madagascar
Services to: Madagascar

BRAZZAVILLE ◆ United Nations Information Centre, Avenue Foch, Case Ortf 15 (Boîte postale 13210 or 1018), Brazzaville, Congo
Services to: Congo

BUJUMBURA ◆ United Nations Information Centre, 117 Avenue de la Révolution (Boîte postale 2160), Bujumbura, Burundi
Services to: Burundi

CAIRO ◆ United Nations Information Centre, 1191 Corniche El Nile, World Trade Centre (Boîte postale 262), Cairo, Egypt
Services to: Egypt, Saudi Arabia

DAKAR ◆ United Nations Information Centre, 12 Avenue Roume, Immeuble UNESCO (Boîte postale 154), Dakar, Senegal
Services to: Cape Verde, Côte d'Ivoire, Gambia, Guinea, Guinea-Bissau, Mauritania, Senegal

DAR ES SALAAM ◆ United Nations Information Centre, Old Boma Building, Ground Floor, Marogoro Road/Sokoine Drive (Post Office Box 9224), Dar es Salaam, United Republic of Tanzania
Services to: United Republic of Tanzania

HARARE ◆ United Nations Information Centre, Dolphin House, Ground Floor, 123 L. Takawira Street/Union Avenue (Post Office Box 4408), Harare, Zimbabwe
Services to: Zimbabwe

KHARTOUM ◆ United Nations Information Centre, United Nations Compound, University Avenue (Post Office Box 1992), Khartoum, Sudan
Services to: Somalia, Sudan

KINSHASA ◆ United Nations Information Centre, Bâtiment Deuxième République, Boulevard du 30 Juin (Boîte postale 7248), Kinshasa, Zaire
Services to: Zaire

LAGOS ♦ United Nations Information Centre, 17 Kingsway Road, Ikoyi (Post Office Box 1068), Lagos, Nigeria
Services to: Nigeria

LOME ♦ United Nations Information Centre, 107 Boulevard du 13 Janvier (Boîte Postale 911), Lomé, Togo
Services to: Benin, Togo

LUSAKA ♦ United Nations Information Centre, Post Office Box 32905, Lusaka, Zambia
Services to: Botswana, Malawi, Swaziland, Zambia

MASERU ♦ United Nations Information Centre, Letsie Road, Food Aid Compound Road, Behind Hotel Victoria (Post Office Box 301), Maseru 100, Lesotho
Services to: Lesotho

NAIROBI ♦ United Nations Information Centre, United Nations Office, Gigiri (Post Office Box 30552), Nairobi, Kenya
Services to: Kenya, Seychelles, Uganda

OUAGADOUGOU ♦ United Nations Information Centre, Avenue Georges Konseiga, Secteur No. 4 (Boîte Postale 135), Ouagadougou 01, Burkina Faso
Services to: Burkina Faso, Chad, Mali, Niger

RABAT ♦ United Nations Information Centre, Angle Charia Ibnouzaid, Et Zankat Roundanat, No. 6 (Boîte postale 601), Rabat, Morocco
Services to: Morocco

TRIPOLI ♦ United Nations Information Centre, Muzzafar Al Aftas Street, Hay El-Andalous (2) (Post Office Box 286), Tripoli, Libyan Arab Jamahiriya
Services to: Libyan Arab Jamahiriya

TUNIS ♦ United Nations Information Centre, 61 boulevard Bab-Benat (Boîte Postale 863), Tunis, Tunisia
Services to: Tunisia

WINDHOEK ♦ United Nations Information Centre, 372 Paratus Building, Independence Avenue (Private Bag 13351), Windhoek, Namibia
Services to: Namibia

YAOUNDE ♦ United Nations Information Centre, Immeuble Kamden, rue Joseph Clère (Boîte Postale 836), Yaoundé, Republic of Cameroon
Services to: Cameroon, Central African Republic, Gabon

CENTRES AND SERVICES IN THE AMERICAS

ASUNCION ♦ United Nations Information Centre, Estrella 345, Edificio City, 3er Piso (Casilla de Correo 1107), Asunción, Paraguay
Services to: Paraguay

BUENOS AIRES ♦ United Nations Information Centre, Junín 1940, 1er piso, 1113 Buenos Aires, Argentina
Services to: Argentina, Uruguay

LA PAZ ◆ United Nations Information Centre, Avenida Mariscal Santa Cruz No. 1350 (Apartado Postal 9072), La Paz, Bolivia
Services to: Bolivia

LIMA ◆ United Nations Information Centre, 320/326 General Jacinto Lara, San Isidro (Apartado Postal 14-0199), Lima, Peru
Services to: Peru

MANAGUA ◆ United Nations Information Centre, Reparto Bolonia, Porton Hospital Militar 1c al Lago, 1c abajo, 3260 Managua, Nicaragua
Services to: Nicaragua

MEXICO CITY ◆ United Nations Information Centre, Presidente Masaryk 29-6º piso, 11570 México, D.F., México
Services to: Cuba, Dominican Republic, Mexico

PANAMA CITY ◆ United Nations Information Centre, Street 53 and Via Ricardo Arango, Mitsui Bank Building, First Floor (Apartado Postal 6-9083, El Dorado), Panama City, Panama
Services to: Panama

PORT OF SPAIN ◆ United Nations Information Centre, 2nd Floor, Bretton Hall, 16 Victoria Avenue (Post Office Box 130), Port of Spain, Trinidad
Services to: Antigua and Barbuda, Bahamas, Barbados, Belize, Dominica, Grenada, Guyana, Jamaica, Netherlands Antilles, Saint Kitts and Nevis, Saint Lucia, Saint Vincent and the Grenadines, Suriname, Trinidad and Tobago

RIO DE JANEIRO ◆ United Nations Information Centre, Palácio Itamaraty, Avenida Marechal Floriano 196, 20080 Rio de Janeiro, RJ Brazil
Services to: Brazil

SAN SALVADOR ◆ United Nations Information Centre, Edificio Escalón, 2º piso, Paseo General Escalón y 87 Avenida Norte, Colonia Escalón (Apartado Postal 2157), San Salvador, El Salvador
Services to: El Salvador

SANTA FE DE BOGOTA ◆ United Nations Information Centre, Calle 100, No. 8A-55, Oficina 815 (Apartado Aéreo 058964), Santa Fé de Bogotá 2, Colombia
Services to: Colombia, Ecuador, Venezuela

SANTIAGO ◆ United Nations Information Service, Economic Commission for Latin America and the Caribbean, Edificio Naciones Unidas, Avenida Dag Hammarskjöld (Casilla 179-D), Santiago, Chile
Services to: Chile, Economic Commission for Latin America and the Caribbean

WASHINGTON D.C. ◆ United Nations Information Centre, 1775 K Street, N.W., Suite 400, Washington, D.C. 20006, United States
Services to: United States

CENTRES AND SERVICES IN ASIA AND THE PACIFIC

AMMAN ♦ United Nations Information Service, Economic and Social Commission for Western Asia, 28 Abdul Hameed Sharaf Street (Post Office Box 927115), Amman, Jordan
Services to: Iraq, Economic and Social Commission for Western Asia

BANGKOK ♦ United Nations Information Service, Economic and Social Commission for Asia and the Pacific, United Nations Building, Rajdamnern Avenue, Bangkok 10200, Thailand
Services to: Cambodia, Hong Kong, Lao People's Democratic Republic, Malaysia, Singapore, Thailand, Viet Nam, Economic and Social Commission for Asia and the Pacific

BEIRUT ♦ United Nations Information Centre, Apartment No. 1, Fakhoury Building, Montée Bain Militaire, Ardati Street (Post Office Box 4656), Beirut, Lebanon
Services to: Jordan, Kuwait, Lebanon, Syrian Arab Republic

COLOMBO ♦ United Nations Information Centre, 202-204 Bauddhaloka Mawatha (Post Office Box 1505), Colombo 7, Sri Lanka
Services to: Sri Lanka

DHAKA ♦ United Nations Information Centre, House 60, Road 11A (General Post Office Box 3658, Dhaka 1000), Dhanmandi, Dhaka 1209, Bangladesh
Services to: Bangladesh

ISLAMABAD ♦ United Nations Information Centre, House No. 26, 88th Street, G-6/3 (Post Office Box 1107), Islamabad, Pakistan
Services to: Pakistan

JAKARTA ♦ United Nations Information Centre, Gedung Dewan Pers, 5th Floor, 32-34 Jalan Kebon Sirih, Jakarta, Indonesia
Services to: Indonesia

KABUL ♦ United Nations Information Centre, Shah Mahmoud Ghazi Watt (Post Office Box 5), Kabul, Afghanistan
Services to: Afghanistan

KATHMANDU ♦ United Nations Information Centre, Pulchowk, Patan (Post Office Box 107, Pulchowk), Kathmandu, Nepal
Services to: Nepal

MANAMA ♦ United Nations Information Centre, Villa 131, Road 2803, Segaya, (Post Office Box 26004), Manama 238, Bahrain
Services to: Bahrain, Qatar, United Arab Emirates

MANILA ♦ United Nations Information Centre, Ground Floor, NEDA Building, 106 Amorsolo Street, Legaspi Village, Makati (Post Office Box 7285 (DAPO), 1300 Domestic Road, Pasay City), Metro Manila, Philippines
Services to: Papua New Guinea, Philippines, Solomon Islands

NEW DELHI ♦ United Nations Information Centre, 55 Lodi Estate, New Delhi–110 003, India
Services to: Bhutan, India

SANA'A ♦ United Nations Information Centre, 4 Handhal Street, Al-Boniya Area (Post Office Box 237), Sana'a, Republic of Yemen
Services to: Yemen

SYDNEY ♦ United Nations Information Centre, Suite 1, 2nd Floor, 125 York Street, Sydney NSW 2000 (Post Office Box 4045, Sydney, N.S.W. 2001), Australia
Services to: Australia, Fiji, Kiribati, Nauru, New Zealand, Samoa, Tonga, Tuvalu, Vanuatu

TEHERAN ♦ United Nations Information Centre, 185 Ghaem Magham Farahani Avenue (Post Office Box 15875-4557), Teheran 15868, Iran
Services to: Iran

TOKYO ♦ United Nations Information Centre, United Nations University Building, 8th Floor, 53-70, Jingumae 5-chome, Shibuya-ku, Tokyo 150, Japan
Services to: Japan, Palau

YANGON ♦ United Nations Information Centre, 6 Natmauk Road (Post Office Box 230), Yangon, Myanmar
Services to: Myanmar

CENTRES AND SERVICES IN EUROPE

ANKARA ♦ United Nations Information Centre, 197 Atatürk Bulvari (P.K. 407), Ankara, Turkey
Services to: Turkey

ATHENS ♦ United Nations Information Centre, 36 Amalia Avenue, GR-10558, Athens, Greece
Services to: Cyprus, Greece, Israel

BRUSSELS ♦ United Nations Information Centre and Liaison Office with European Community, Avenue de Broqueville 40, 1200 Brussels, Belgium
Services to: Belgium, Luxembourg, Netherlands

BUCHAREST ♦ United Nations Information Centre, 16 Aurel Vlaic Street (Post Office Box 1-701), Bucharest, Romania
Services to: Romania

COPENHAGEN ♦ United Nations Information Centre, 37 H. C. Andersens Boulevard, DK-1553 Copenhagen V, Denmark
Services to: Denmark, Finland, Iceland, Norway, Sweden

GENEVA ♦ United Nations Information Service, United Nations Office at Geneva, Palais des Nations, 1211 Geneva 10, Switzerland
Services to: Bulgaria, Poland, Switzerland

LISBON ♦ United Nations Information Centre, Rua Latino Coelho No. 1, Edificio Aviz, Bloco A-1, 10°, 1000 Lisbon, Portugal
Services to: Portugal

LONDON ♦ United Nations Information Centre, 18 Buckingham Gate, London SW1E 6LB, United Kingdom
Services to: Ireland, United Kingdom

MADRID ♦ United Nations Information Centre, Avenida General Perón, 32-1 (Post Office Box 3400, 28080 Madrid), 28020 Madrid, Spain
Services to: Spain

MOSCOW ♦ United Nations Information Centre, 4/16 Ulitsa Lunacharskogo, Moscow 121002, Russian Federation
Services to: Russian Federation

PARIS ♦ United Nations Information Centre, 1 rue Miollis, 75732, Paris Cedex 15, France
Services to: France

PRAGUE ♦ United Nations Information Centre, Panska 5, 11000 Prague 1, Czech Republic
Services to: Czech Republic, Slovak Republic

ROME ♦ United Nations Information Centre, Palazzetto Venezia, Piazza San Marco 50, 00186 Rome, Italy
Services to: Holy See, Italy, Malta

VIENNA ♦ United Nations Information Service, United Nations Office at Vienna, Vienna International Centre, Wagramer Strasse 5 (Post Office Box 500, A-1400 Vienna) A-1220 Vienna, Austria
Services to: Austria, Germany, Hungary

OFFICES IN THE COMMONWEALTH OF INDEPENDENT STATES AND ERITREA

ALMATY ♦ United Nations Office, Room 1312, Hotel Kazakstan, Lenin Avenue, Almaty, Kazakstan
Services to: Kazakstan

ASMARA ♦ United Nations Office, Andinet Street, Zone 4 Admin. 07, Airport Road (Post Office Box 5366) Asmara, Eritrea
Services to: Eritrea

BAKU ♦ United Nations Office, 3 Isteglaliyat Street, Baku 1, Azerbaijan
Services to: Azerbaijan

KIEV ♦ United Nations Office, 6 Klovsky Uzviz 1, Kiev 252020, Ukraine
Services to: Ukraine

MINSK ♦ United Nations Office, Ulitsa Kirova 17, 6th Floor (G.P.O. Box 103), 220050 Minsk, Belarus
Services to: Belarus

TASHKENT ♦ United Nations Office, 4 Taras Shevchenko Street, Tashkent 700029, Uzbekistan
Services to: Uzbekistan

TBILISI ♦ United Nations Office, Kazbegi Avenue 2a (Former Pavlova), Tbilisi 380060, Republic of Georgia
Services to: Georgia

YEREVAN ♦ United Nations Office, Hrazdan Hotel, 2nd Floor, 2 Pionerskaya Street, Yerevan, Armenia
Services to: Armenia

UNITED NATIONS SPECIAL OBSERVANCES

International Decades and Years

1985-1996	Transport and Communications Decade for Asia and the Pacific
1988-1997	World Decade for Cultural Development
1990s	Third Disarmament Decade
1990s	International Decade for Natural Disaster Reduction
1990-2000	International Decade for the Eradication of Colonialism
1990-1999	United Nations Decade of International Law
1991-2000	Fourth United Nations Development Decade
1991-2000	Second Transport and Communications Decade in Africa
1991-2000	United Nations Decade against Drug Abuse
1993-2002	Second Industrial Development Decade for Africa
1993-2002	Asian and Pacific Decade of Disabled Persons
1993-2003	Third Decade to Combat Racism and Racial Discrimination
1994-2004	International Decade of the World's Indigenous People
1995-2005	United Nations Decade for Human Rights Education
1994	International Year of the Family
1994	International Year of Sport and the Olympic Ideal
1995	United Nations Year for Tolerance
1995	World Year of Peoples' Commemoration of the Victims of the Second World War
1996	International Year for the Eradication of Poverty
1998	International Year of the Ocean
1999	International Year of Older Persons

Annual Days and Weeks

21 March	International Day for the Elimination of Racial Discrimination
Beginning 21 March	Week of Solidarity with the Peoples Struggling against Racism and Racial Discrimination
22 March	World Day for Water
3 May	World Press Freedom Day
15 May	International Day of Families
5 June	World Environment Day
17 June	World Day to Combat Desertification and Drought
26 June	International Day against Drug Abuse and Illicit Trafficking
First Saturday of July	International Day of Cooperatives
11 July	World Population Day
9 August	International Day of the World's Indigenous People

16 September	International Day for the Preservation of the Ozone Layer
Third Tuesday of September	International Day of Peace
1 October	International Day for the Elderly
First Monday of October	World Habitat Day
Second Wednesday of October	International Day for Natural Disaster Reduction
16 October	World Food Day
17 October	International Day for the Eradication of Poverty
24 October	United Nations Day
24-30 October	Disarmament Week
Week of 11 November	International Week of Science and Peace
20 November	Africa Industrialization Day
29 November	International Day of Solidarity with the Palestinian People
3 December	International Day of Disabled Persons
10 December	Human Rights Day
29 December	International Day for Biological Diversity

Other International Days

Other international days observed throughout the United Nations system include:

8 March	International Women's Day
23 March	World Meteorological Day
7 April	World Health Day
17 May	World Telecommunication Day
31 May	World No-Tobacco Day
8 September	International Literacy Day
Last week in September	World Maritime Day
9 October	World Post Day
24 October	World Development Information Day
20 November, varies	Universal Children's Day
1 December	World AIDS Day
5 December	International Volunteer Day for Economic and Social Development
7 December	International Civil Aviation Day

UNITED NATIONS PUBLICATIONS
OF RELATED INTEREST

The following UN publications may be obtained from the addresses indicated below, or at your local distributor:

About the United Nations. Video and teaching guide sets for classroom use. (Video length, 15-20 minutes; teaching guides average 35 pages). Subjects covered in the series include: Peace-keeping (Sales No. E.91.I.27); Human Rights (Sales No. E.91.I.40); Palestine (Sales No. E.91.I.30); Africa Recovery (Sales No. E.91.I.33); Environment and Development (Sales No. 92.I.9); Decolonization (Sales No. E.92.I.11); Literacy (Sales No. E.91.I.36). (Each video and teaching guide set, $29.95; each video alone, $24.00; each book alone, $9.95)

Africa Recovery (quarterly newsletter) (annual subscription for institutions, $35.00; for individuals, $20.00)

An Agenda for Peace (Second edition, 1995) by Boutros Boutros-Ghali, Secretary-General of the United Nations (155 pages) (Sales No. E.95.I.15; $7.50)

An Agenda for Development, 1995 by Boutros Boutros-Ghali, Secretary-General of the United Nations (133 pages) (Sales No. E.95.I.16; $7.50)

The Blue Helmets, a review of United Nations peace-keeping (571 pages) (DPI/1065; Sales No. E.90.I,18, soft; $8.95)

Building Peace and Development, 1994. Annual Report on the Work of the Organization by Boutros Boutros-Ghali, Secretary-General of the United Nations (299 pages) (Sales No. E.95.I.3; $9.95)

Charter of the United Nations and Statute of the International Court of Justice (87 pages) (DPI/511; $1.00)

Demographic Yearbook (Vol. 44, 1994) (823 pages) (Sales No. B.94.XIII.I; $125.00)

Disarmament—New Realities: Disarmament, Peace-Building and Global Security (397 pages) (Sales No. E.93.IX.14; $35.00)

United Nations Disarmament Yearbook (Vol. 18, 1994) (419 pages) (Sales No. 94.IX.I; $50.00)

Image & Reality, questions and answers about United Nations management, finance and people (104 pages) (DPI/1288; $1.25)

The International Bill of Human Rights (42 pages) (DPI/925; $2.00)

The Model United Nations. Video and Book set (Video length, 20 minutes; book, 32 pages(Video Sales No. E.92.I.24; Book Sales No. E.92.I.23. Video and book set, $20.00. Book alone, $5.00)

New Dimensions of Arms Regulations and Disarmament in the Post–Cold War Era, by Boutros Boutros-Ghali, Secretary-General of the United Nations (53 pages) (Sales No. E.93.IX.8; $9.95)

Statistical Yearbook (39th edition) (1,174 pages) (Sales No. B.94.XVII.I H; $110)

UN Chronicle. Quarterly journal (Annual subscription, $20.00)

The United Nations and Drug Abuse Control (100 pages) (DPI/1015/Rev. 1; Sales No. E.92.I.31; $5.00)

The Universal Declaration of Human Rights (15 pages) (DPI/876, 35 cents)

Women: Challenges to the Year 2000 (96 pages) (Sales No. E.91.I.21, $12.95)

World Economic and Social Survey, 1995 (308 pages) (Sales No. E.94.II.C.1, $12.95)

World Investment Report 1994—Transnational Corporations, Employment and the Work Place (446 pages) (Sales No. E.94.II.A.14, $45.00)

Yearbook of the United Nations. Vol. 47, 1993 (1,428 pages) (Sales No. E.94.I.1, $150)

* * *

THE UNITED NATIONS BLUE BOOKS SERIES

The United Nations and Apartheid, 1948-1994 (565 pages) (Sales No. E.95.I.7, $29.95)

The United Nations and Cambodia, 1991-1995 (360 pages) (Sales No. E.95.I.9, $29.95)

The United Nations and El Salvador, 1990-1995 (612 pages) (Sales No. E.95.I.12, $29.95)

The United Nations and Nuclear Non-Proliferation (199 pages) (Sales No. E.95.I.17, $29.95)

The United Nations and Mozambique, 1992-1995 (321 pages) (Sales No. E.95.I.20, $29.95)

FORTHCOMING:

The United Nations and the Advancement of Women, 1945-1995

The United Nations and Human Rights, 1945-1995

The United Nations and Population

The United Nations and Somalia

For a complete list of United Nations publications in print, write to:

United Nations Publications
Sales Section
Room DC2-0853
New York, N.Y. 10017
United States of America
Tel. (212) 963-8302; 1 (800) 253-9646
Fax (212) 963-3489

United Nations Publications
Sales Office and Bookshop
CH-1211 Geneva 10
Switzerland
Tel. 41 (22) 917-2613
    41 (22) 917-2614
Fax 41 (22) 917-0027

INDEX

A

Acronyms, xi

Administrative Committee on Coordination, 274

Advisory Committee on Administrative and Budgetary Questions, 19

Afghanistan, 64; Coordinator of UN Humanitarian and Economic Assistance Programmes relating to (UNOCA), 65, 66, 67, 68; Geneva Accords (1988), 65; Personal Representative, 66; UN Good Offices Mission in and Pakistan (UNGOMAP), 65

Africa: a United Nations priority, 138; Convention Governing the Specific Aspects of Refugee Problems in (1969), 225; Green Revolution in, 162; Industrialization Day, 324; New Agenda for the Development of in the 1990s, 138, 145; Second Industrial Development Decade for (1993-2002), 323; Second Transport and Communications Decade in (1991-2000), 323

African Economic Recovery and Development, UN Programme of Action for (1986-1990), 138

African National Congress of South Africa (ANC), 210

Ageing and older persons, 173; Banyan Fund (1991), 174; international conference (1992)/Proclamation, 174; International Day, 324; International Institute, 174; International Year (1999), 174, 323/conceptual framework, 174; targets for the year 2001, 174; UN Principles (1991), 174; UN Trust Fund, 173-174; World Assembly (Vienna, 1982), 173/International Plan of Action, 174

Agricultural development: see International Fund for Agricultural Development

Aircraft: Convention for the Suppression of Unlawful Seizure of (The Hague, 1970), 267; Convention on Offences and Certain Other Acts Committed on Board (Tokyo, 1963), 267

Angola, 33; Verification Mission, UN (UNAVEM/UNAVEM II/UNAVEM III), 21, 33-35, 37

Antarctic Treaty (1959), 123

Apartheid, 207; Declaration on and its Destructive Consequences in Southern Africa, 212; dismantling, 211; International Anti-Apartheid Year (1978), 211; International Convention on the Suppression and Punishment of the Crime of (1973), 210; international efforts for eliminating, 208; Programme of Action against (1976), 211; UN Special Committee against, 209, 213

Arbitration: UNCITRAL Model Law on International Commercial (1985), 260; UNCITRAL Rules (1976), 261

Artificial earth satellites, Principles governing the use by States of (1982), 127

Asia and the Pacific: Decade of Disabled Persons, 323; Transport and Communications Decade for (1985-1996), 323

Assessments of Member States, 20, 21, 31, 311-315

Astronauts, Agreement on the Rescue of, the Return of, and the Return of Objects Launched into Outer Space (1967), 127

B

Bacteriological (Biological) and Toxin Weapons, Convention on the Prohibition of the Development, Production and Stockpiling of and on

Their Destruction (BW Convention, 1972), 123; Ad Hoc Group, 125

Biological Diversity, International Day for, 324

Budget of the UN, 19, 22

C

Cambodia, 69; Agreements on (Paris, 1991), 70, 71, 72; elections (1993), 71-72; International Committee on the Reconstruction of, 72; Paris Conference (1989), 69; Representative to, 72; Special Representative, 70; UN Advance Mission in (UNAMIC), 70; UN Border Relief Operations (UNBRO), 69; UN Transitional Authority in (UNTAC), 70

Capital Development Fund (UN), 141

Carriage of Goods by Sea, Convention on ("Hamburg Rules", 1978), 145, 260

Central America, 56; Esquipulas II agreement, 56; United Nations Observer Group in (ONUCA), 57; see also El Salvador; Guatemala; Nicaragua

Charter of the UN, 3, 203; amendments to the, 268; Preamble, 3-4; Special Committee on the and on the Strengthening of the Role of the Organization, 268

Chemical Weapons Convention (1993), 121, 124

Child, Rights of the, 205; Committee on 205; Convention on (1989), 170, 205; Declaration of (1959), 205

Children: assistance to, 169; Universal Day, 324; World Summit for (New York, 1990)/ Declaration and Plan of Action, 170

Children's Fund, UN (UNICEF), 22, 169; "baby-friendly hospital initiative" (1992), 171; Emergency Programme Fund, 222; Nobel Peace Prize (1965), 172; see also Humani-

tarian Assistance; Rights of the Child; World Health Organization

Civil Aviation, Convention for the Suppression of Unlawful Acts against the Safety of (Montreal, 1971), 257; Protocol for the Suppression of Unlawful Acts of Violence at Airports Serving International Civil Aviation (Montreal, 1988), 267; see also International Civil Aviation Organization

Civil and Political Rights, International Covenant on, 191, 192/First and Second Optional Protocols, 191, 193

Civilian Persons in Time of War, Fourth Geneva Convention relating to the Protection of (1949), 97, 101

Colonial Countries and Peoples, Declaration on the Granting of Independence to (1960), 231, 234, 236, 237; Special Committee on the Situation with regard to the Implementation of the Declaration (Special Committee of 24), 236; Territories to which the Declaration continues to apply (as at 31 December 1994), 235; Trust and Non-Self-Governing Territories that have achieved independence since the adoption of the Declaration, 238

Colonialism, International Decade for the Eradication of (1990-2000), 237, 323

Committee for Programme and Coordination, 19

Committee on Contributions, 20

Commodities: Common Fund for (1989), 144; international agreements, 144

Commonwealth of Independent States, 9

Conciliation Rules, UNCITRAL (1980), 261

Congo, 37; UN Operation in the (ONUC), 37

Consular Relations, Vienna Convention on (1963), 258

Continental Shelf, Convention on the (1958), 258; Commission on the Limits of the, 263; Protocol for the Suppression of Unlawful Acts against the Safety of Fixed Platforms located on (Rome, 1988), 267

Conventional Armed Forces in Europe, CFE Treaty (1990), 124

Conventional Arms, Register of (1992), 125

Conventional Weapons, Convention on Prohibitions or Restrictions on the Use of Certain (Inhumane weapons Convention, 1981), 124, 125; review conference (Vienna, 1995), 125

Conventions: see under subjects

Cooperatives, International Day of, 323

Credentials Committee, 8

Credit Transfers, UNCITRAL Model Law on International (1992), 260

Crime: International Conference on Preventing and Controlling Money Laundering and the Use of the Proceeds of (Italy, 1994), 178; World Ministerial Conference on Organized Transnational (Naples, 1994)/Political Declaration and Global Action Plan, 178

Crime and Abuse of Power, Declaration on Basic Principles of Justice for Victims of (1985), 177

Crime and Justice Research Institute, United Nations Interregional (UNICRI), 178

Crime Prevention and Criminal Justice, 176; Commission on (1992), 178; Guiding Principles for in the Context of Development and a New International Economic Order (1985), 177; Milan Plan of Action for strengthening international cooperation in (1985), 177

Crime, prevention of and treatment of offenders/UN Congresses on (1955-1995), 176-178

Crimes, Code of against the Peace and Security of Mankind, 259

Croatia, United Nations Confidence Restoration Operation in (UN-CRO), 119

Cultural Development, World Decade for (1988-1997), 323

Cyprus, 72; confidence-building measures, 75, 76; Coordinator of UN Humanitarian Assistance for, 73; overall framework agreement, 74, 75; proximity talks, 74, 75, 76, 77, 78; Special Representative, 73, 75; territorial adjustments and displaced persons, 75; UN Peace-keeping Force in (UNFICYP), 21, 72, 73, 74, 78

D

Death Penalty, Second Optional Protocol of the International Covenant on Civil and Political Rights Aiming at Abolition of the (1989), 193

Debt: guidelines for international action in the area of debt rescheduling (1980), 145; resolution on retroactive adjustment of terms of the Official Development Assistance debt of low-income developing countries (1978), 145

Declarations: see under subjects

Decolonization, 231

Desertification, 154; UN Conference on (Nairobi, 1977)/Plan of Action, 155; Convention to combat (1994), 154, 155; UNDP/UNEP Joint Venture, 155; World Day to Combat, 323; see also Environment and development; Sahel; Sudano-Sahelian activities

Detention arbitrary: preventing, 201; Working Group, 198, 201

El Salvador: elections (1994), 59; Peace Accords (1992), 58; UN Observer Mission in (ONUSAL), 21, 58, 59

Emergency Force, UN (UNEF), 93; UNEF II, 94

Energy, New and Renewable Sources of: Committee, 157; UN Conference on (Nairobi, 1981)/Programme of Action, 157

Environment and Development, Conference on (Rio de Janeiro, 1992), 142, 152, 154; Agenda 21, 150, 152, 153, 154; finance and technology, 153; Rio Declaration (1992), 153; World Commission, 150

Environment Programme (UNEP), 142, 150, 218; Basel Convention (1989), 152; Biological Diversity Convention (1992), 152, 153; Climate Change Framework Convention (1992), 152, 153; Environment Fund, 150; Global Environment Facility, 142, 154; Global Environment Monitoring System (GEMS), 151; Global Resource Information Database (GRID), 151; Governing Council, 150; Industry and Environment Office, 151; INFOTERRA, 151; International Register of Potentially Toxic Chemicals (IRPTC), 151; International Trade in Endangered Species, Convention (1973), 152; Mediterranean Action Plan, 151; Montreal Protocol (1987), 152/London (1990) and Copenhagen (1992) Amendments, 152; regional seas programme, 151; secretariat, 150; Vienna Convention (1983), 152

Environment, UN Conference (Stockholm, 1972), 150; World Day, 152, 323

Environmental Modification Techniques, Convention on the Prohibition of Military or Any Other Hostile Use of (ENMOD Convention, 1977), 123

Environmental protection: ICJ case, 255

Eritrea, 38; United Nations Observer Mission to Verify the Referendum in (UNOVER), 39

Executions and disappearances, preventing extrajudicial, 200; Special Rapporteur, 200; Working Group, 198, 200

F

Fact-finding, Declaration on by the UN in the Field of Maintenance of International Peace and Security, (1991) 269

Family/Families, 175; International Conference (1994), 176; International Day, 323; International Year (1994), 175, 323

Financial situation of the United Nations, 20

Fish Stocks, United Nations Conference on straddling and highly migratory, (New York, 1993), 154; legal agreement, 154

Food and agriculture, 160; World Day, 324; World Food Conference (Rome, 1974), 160; see also FAO; Food Security, IFAD; WFC; WFP

Food and Agriculture Organization of the United Nations (FAO), 160, 275; Food Security Assistance Scheme, 277; Global Information and Early Warning System, 163, 221, 276; Office for Special Relief Operations, 221; People's Participation Programme, 276; see also Humanitarian Assistance

Food Council, World (WFC), 160, 162

Food Programme, World (WFP), 22, 133, 160, International Emergency Food Reserve, 223; see also Humanitarian Assistance

Food Security, Committee on World, 160, 163

Frontier delimitation, ICJ cases, 254-255

G

General Assembly, 6; emergency special sessions, 8; functions and powers, 6; general debate, 8; Main Committees, 8; President/Vice-Presidents, 8; sessions, 7; special sessions, 8; voting, 8

General Committee, 8

Genocide, Convention on the Prevention and Punishment of the Crime of, 257

Georgia-Abkhazia, 110; cease-fire agreement (1994), 112; Special Envoy, 111, 112, 113; Memorandum of Understanding (1993), 112; return of refugees and displaced persons, 113; UN appeal for emergency humanitarian assistance, 111; United Nations Observer Mission in (UNOMIG), 21, 111

Guatemala, 59; agreements on human rights, resettlement, and indigenous people, 59-60; Framework Agreement, 59; United Nations Human Rights Verification Mission in (MINUGUA), 60

H

Haiti, 60; Friends of the Secretary-General for, 62; Governors Island Agreement, 62; Pact of New York, 62; Special Envoy for, 61; United Nations Mission in (UNMIH), 21, 62; United Nations Observer Group for the Verification of the Elections in (ONUVEH), 60

High seas: Convention on the (1958), 258; Convention on Fishing and Conservation of the Living Resources of the (1958), 258

Hostages, Convention against the Taking of (1979), 267

Humanitarian assistance, 217; Central Emergency Revolving Fund, 220; Central Register of Disaster Management Capacities, 221; Department of Humanitarian Affairs (DHA), 217; Disaster Management Training Programme, 221; Emergency Relief Coordinator, 219; Humanitarian Coordinator, 220; Inter-Agency Standing Committee (IASC), 219; Operational Agencies (FAO, 219, 221; UNICEF 219, 222; UNDP, 219, 222; WFP, 219, 223; WHO, 219, 223); Resident Coordinator, 220; UN Disaster Assessment and Coordination Team, 221; UN Disaster Management Teams, 220; see also Refugees

Human rights, 189; advisory services and technical assistance, 202; and development, 206; Day, 189, 324; International Conference on (Teheran, 1968), 194; International Year for (1968), 194; specialized treaties, 193

Human Rights: Centre for, 197; Commission, 193, 197; Committee, 192, 193; High Commissioner for, 195, 196; Special Rapporteurs, 198; UN bodies, 193; Working Group, 198

Human Rights Education, Decade for (1995-2005), 323

Human Rights, International Covenants on, 190

Human Rights, Universal Declaration of, 189, 191, 203

Human rights violations: complaints of under 1503 procedure/specialized treaties, 199; putting an end to, 197

Human Rights, World Conference on (Vienna, June 1993)/Vienna Declaration and Programme of Action, 194, 195, 196

Human settlements, 158; Commission on, 158, 160; Global Strategy for

Shelter to the Year 2000, 159, 160; Sustainable Cities Programme, 159; Urban Environmental Management, 159; UN Centre for (Habitat), 158-159; Urban Management Programme, 159; World Habitat Day, 160, 324
UN Conference on (Habitat II) (Turkey, 1996), 160

I

India-Pakistan, 105; Bangladesh, 105, 108; Declaration at Tashkent, 107; Simla agreement, 108; Special Representative, 107; UN Commission for, 106, 107; UN Military Observer Group in (UNMOGIP), 107, 108; UN Observation Mission (UNIPOM), 107
Indigenous people/populations: International Day, 323; International Decade (1994-2004), 207, 323; International Year (1993), 207; protecting, 206; Universal Declaration on the Rights of, 206; UN Voluntary Fund for, 207; Working Group on, 206
Industrial development; *see* United Nations Industrial Development Organization
Industrial Works, UNCITRAL Legal Guide on Drawing Up International Contracts for the Construction of (1987), 261
Intergovernmental agencies related to the United Nations, 273; *see also* names of organizations
International Atomic Energy Agency (IAEA), 273, 299; International Centre for Theoretical Physics, 302; International Nuclear Information System, 302; Marine Environment Laboratory, 302; safeguards agreements, 299-300
International Bills of Exchange and International Promissory Notes, UN Convention on (1988), 260

International Civil Aviation Organization (ICAO), 286; International Day, 323
International Committee of the Red Cross (ICRC), 219
International Countertrade Transactions, UNCITRAL Legal Guide (1992), 261
International Court of Justice, 15, 29, 253; advisory opinions, 16, 253, 256; contentious cases, 253-255, 256-257; Chamber for Environmental Matters, 17; Chamber of Summary Procedures, 17; jurisdiction, 16; membership, 16; Statute, 15; *see also* International Law
International Economic Cooperation: Declaration on, in particular, the Revitalization of Economic Growth and Development of the Developing Countries (1990), 134; special session of General Assembly (1990), 134
International Federation of Red Cross and Red Crescent Societies, 219
International Fund for Agricultural Development (IFAD), 160, 296
International Labour Organization (ILO), 274; International Institute for Labour Studies (Geneva), 275; International Training Centre (Turin), 275; Nobel Peace Prize (1969), 275
International Law, 253; development and codification of, 257; UN Decade of (1990-1999), 323
International Law Commission, 257; Conventions, 258
International Maritime Organization (IMO), 293; World Maritime Day, 324; World Maritime University, 294
International Monetary Fund (IMF), 284
International Peace and security, 25; draft Declaration on the Enhance-

Law Enforcement Officials, Code of Conduct for (1979), 177

Law of the Sea, 261; Agreement (1994), 265; Convention (1982), 262-264/Impact of, 265-266; deep seabed mining, 264; ICJ cases, 254; International Tribunal for, 264; UN Conferences (1958, 1960, 1973, 1982), 261, 262

Law of treaties: *see* Treaties

Least developed countries: Substantial New Programme of Action for the (1981), 145; Programme of Action for the 1990s (1990), 145

Lebanon, 99; Observer Group Beirut, 100; release of hostages and prisoners in, 103; Taif agreement, 103; UN Interim Force in (UNIFIL), 21, 100, 101, 102, 103, 104

Legal Affairs, Office of, 269

Liberia, 39; Economic Community of West African States (ECOWAS), 40, 41, 42; United Nations Observer Mission in (UNOMIL), 21, 41, 42

Liner Conferences, Code of Conduct for (1974), 145

Literacy Day, International, 324

M

Macedonia, United Nations Preventive Deployment Force in the former Yugoslav Republic of (UNPREDEP), 119

Maritime Liens and Mortgages, Convention on (1993), 145

Maritime Navigation, Convention for the Suppression of Unlawful Acts against the Safety of (Rome, 1988), 267

Marriage, Convention on Consent to, Minimum Age for and Registration of (1962), 204-205

Medical Ethics, Principles of (1982), 201

Mentally Retarded Persons, Declaration on the Rights of (1971), 174

Mercenaries, International Convention against the Recruitment, Use, Financing and Training of (1989), 268

Middle East, 92; Agreement on the Gaza Strip and the Jericho Area, 99; Camp David accords, 96; Declaration of Principles on Interim Self-Government Arrangements (1993), 98; Military Working Group, 95; Peace Conferences: (Geneva, 1973), 94, (Madrid, 1991), 97; Presidential Statement (1990), 97; resolution 242 (1967), 94, 96, 97; resolution 338 (1973), 94, 96, 97; Special Coordinator in the Occupied Territories, 99; Special Representatives (1967), 94, (1991), 97; UN Mediator, 93; Washington Declaration (1994), 99; *see also* Palestine; Disengagement Observer Force, UN; Emergency Force, UN; Truce Supervision Organization, UN

Migrant workers: Convention (1990), 207/proposed Committee, 207; protecting, 207

Migration, International Organization for, 219

Minorities: Declaration on the Rights of Persons Belonging to National, Ethnic, Religious and Linguistic (1992), 206; protecting, 206; Sub-commission on Prevention of Discrimination and Protection of, 194, 197-198

Moon and Other Celestial Bodies, Agreement Governing Activities of States on (1979), 123, 127; Treaty (1966), 126, 127

Mozambique, 42; United Nations Operation in (ONUMOZ), 21, 43, 44, 45, 46

Multimodal transport of goods, International, Convention on (1980), 145

N

Namibia, 240; Decree for the Protection of the Natural Resources of (1974), 241; elections in (1989), 241, 243, 244; ICJ opinions (1950), 240, 255; (1971), 241, 255; independence, 243, 244; Institute for, 241; membership in UN, 244; President of the Republic, 244; resolution 435 (1978), 242; Special Representative for, 242, 243; special session on (1978), 242; tripartite agreement (1988), 243; UN Council for, 240; UN plan for independence of, 242; UN Transition Assistance Group (UNTAG), 242, 243

Narcotic Drugs and Psychotropic Substances, UN Convention against Illicit Traffic in (1988), 179; see also Drug abuse; Psychotropic Substances

Narcotic drugs, Commission on, 180

Narcotic drugs, Single Convention on (1961), 179, Protocol amending (1972), 172

Narcotics Control Board, International, 180

Natural Disaster Reduction: International Decade for (1990s), 218, 323; World Conference (Yokohama, 1994), 218

Natural resources and energy, 156; Committee, 156, 157

New international economic order, 134; Declaration and Programme of Action on the Establishment of a (1974), 134

Nicaragua, UN Observer Mission for the Verification of the Elections in (ONUVEN), 57; see also Central America

Non-custodial Measures, UN Standard Minimum Rules for (Tokyo Rules, 1990), 178

Non-Self-Governing Territories, 234, 237; Charter Declaration regarding, 234; see also Decolonization

North Atlantic Treaty Organization (NATO), 121

Nuclear Accident: IAEA Convention on Assistance in the Case of or Radiological Emergency (1987), 301; IAEA Convention on Early Notification of (1986), 301

Nuclear Energy, UN Conference for the Promotion of International Cooperation in the Peaceful Uses of (Geneva, 1987), 157

Nuclear Material, Convention on the Physical Protection of (Vienna, 1980), 267

Nuclear Weapons, Treaty on the Non-Proliferation of (1968), 123; Conference of parties to the Treaty (1995), 124

Nuclear weapons tests, Treaty Banning in the Atmosphere, in Outer Space and Under Water (partial test-ban Treaty, 1963), 122-123

O

Ocean, International Year of the (1998), 323

Operators of Transport Terminals in International Trade, UN Convention on the Liability of (1991), 260

Organization of African Unity (OAU), 210

Organization of American States (OAS), 57

Outer space, 126; Committee on the Peaceful Uses of, 126, 127-128; Convention on Registration of Objects Launched into (1974), 127; Legal Subcommittee, 126; International Space Year (1992), 129; Scientific and Technical Subcommittee, 126; Treaty (1967), 123; UN Conferences on the Exploration and Peaceful Uses of (1968, 1982),

128-129; UN Programme on Space Applications, 128
Ozone Layer, International Day for the Preservation of the, 324

P

Pacific Islands, Trust Territory of the, 232
Palestine: Geneva Declaration on (1983), 96; International Conference on the Question of (Geneva, 1983), 96; National Council (PNC), 97; UN Special Committee on, 92
Palestine Liberation Organization (PLO), 95, 98, 99
Palestine Refugees in the Near East, UN Relief and Works Agency for (UNRWA), 22, 104
Palestinian Authority in the Gaza Strip and the Jericho Area, 105
Palestinian People: Committee on the Exercise of the Inalienable Rights of the, 96; International Day of Solidarity with the, 96, 324; Special Committee to Investigate Israeli Practices Affecting the Human Rights of the and Other Arabs of the Occupied Territories, 95
Pan Africanist Congress of Azania, 210
Peace: An Agenda for 19, 28-30; United Nations action for, 33
Peace: International Day, 26, 324; International Week of Science and, 324; International Year (1986), 26; resolution on Uniting for (1950), 7; University for (San José, Costa Rica), 26
Peace-building, 30
Peace-keeping operations, 21, 27, 28, 30; assessed contributions by Member States for, 21, 31; current and past operations (list), 32-33
Peacemaking, 29; and peace-keeping, 26

Plastic Explosives, Convention on the Marking of for the Purpose of Detection (Montreal, 1991), 267
Policy Coordination and Sustainable Development, Department for, 139, 149, 153, 163
Population and Development, 163; Commission, 163, 164; Division, 163; International Conference (Mexico City, 1984), 165; World Day, 323; World Conference (Bucharest, 1974)/World Plan of Action, 165
Population and Development, International Conference on (Cairo, 1994)/Programme of Action, 165, 166
Population Fund (UNFPA), 22, 164
Poverty, Eradication of: International Day, 324; International Year (1996), 323
Preferences, Generalized System of (1971) 144
Preventive diplomacy, 29
Prisoners: Basic Principles for the Treatment of (1990), 178; Model Agreement on the Transfer of Foreign (1985), 177; Standard Minimum Rules for the Treatment of (1955), 176
Procurement of Goods, Construction and Services, UNCITRAL Model Law on (1994), 261
Promoting peaceful relations, 25
Psychotropic Substances, Convention on (1971), 179

R

Racial discrimination: Committee on the Elimination of, 203; Decades for Action to Combat Racism and (1973, 1983, 1993), 203, 323; eliminating, 202; International Convention on the Elimination of All Forms of (1965), 202, 203; International Day for the Elimination of,

209, 323; UN Declaration on the Elimination of All Forms of (1963), 202; Week of Solidarity with the Peoples Struggling against Racism and, 323; *see also* Apartheid

Refugees: assistance to, 224; Convention relating to the Status of (1951), and Protocol (1967), 225; General/ Special Programmes, 226; non-refoulement, 224; refugees worldwide, 226; *see also* United Nations Relief and Works Agency for Palestine Refugees in the Near East

Refugees, Office of the UN High Commissioner for (UNHCR), 22, 224; Nobel Peace Prize (1954 and 1981), 226

Regional organizations, 30

Remote sensing, Principles relating to (1986), 127

Representation of States in Their Relations with Organizations of a Universal Character, Vienna Convention on the (1975), 258

Restrictive business practices, set of principles and rules for the control of (1980), 144

Rwanda, 46; Arusha Peace Agreement, 47; Commission of Experts, 49; humanitarian appeal (1994), 50; Special Rapporteur to investigate human rights situation in, 49; International Tribunal for, 50, 266; United Nations Assistance Mission for (UNAMIR), 21, 47, 48, 49; United Nations Observer Mission in Uganda-Rwanda (UNOMUR), 47, 49

S

Sahel, Permanent Inter-State Committee for Drought Control in the (CILSS), 155

Sahelian Relief Operations, Office for, 155

Science and technology for development, 148; capacity building and resource mobilization, 149; Commission on (ECOSOC), 146, 149; Division for (UNCTAD), 149; Division for Science, Technology and the Private Sector (UNDP), 149; investment and technology, 149; technology assessment and information services, 149; UN Conference on (Vienna, 1979)/Programme of Action, 148, 149; UN Conference on the Application of Science and Technology for the Development of the Less Developed Areas (Geneva, 1963), 148; UN Fund for (UNDP), 149; *see also* Trade and Development

Seabed and the Ocean Floor beyond the Limits of National Jurisdiction, Committee on the Peaceful Uses of, 261; Declaration of Principles, 261

Sea-bed and the Ocean Floor, Treaty Banning Nuclear Weapons on (Seabed Treaty, 1971), 123

Sea-Bed Authority, International, 264

Second World War, World Year of Peoples' Commemoration of the Victims of the, 323

Secretariat (UN), 17

Secretary-General, 18

Security Council, 9; first Summit Meeting of (New York, 1992), 10; functions and powers, 10; members, 9; veto, right of, 9; voting, 9

Ships, Convention on Conditions for Registration of (1986), 145

Small Islands, Global Conference on the Sustainable Development of (Barbados, 1994), 154

Social development, Commission on, 139

Social Development, United Nations Research Institute for (UNRISD), 184

Social Development, World Summit for (Copenhagen, 1995), 137; Declaration and Programme of Action, 137-138

Somalia, 50; Special Representative for, 52; Unified Task Force (UNITAF), 53; United Nations Operation in (UNOSOM), 21, 51; UNOSOM II, 53-56

South Africa: arms embargo, 209, 214; bantustans, 208; elections (1994), 213-214; Group Areas Act (1950), 208; International Day of Solidarity with the Struggle of Women in, 211; International Day of Solidarity with the Struggling People of, 211; International Year of Mobilization for Sanctions against (1982), 211; National Peace Accord/Goldstone Commission, 211, 212; oil embargo against, 209; Population Registration Act (1950), 208; racial policies of, 208; Special Representative for, 213; see also Apartheid

South Africa, United Nations Observer Mission in (UNOMSA), 212

South African Political Prisoners, Day of Solidarity with, 210

South Asia subcontinent: see India-Pakistan

South Pacific Nuclear-Free Zone Treaty (Treaty of Rarotonga, 1985), 123

South West Africa People's Organization (SWAPO), 242

Space Objects, Convention on International Liability for Damage Caused by (1971), 127; see also Outer Space

Special Missions, Convention on (1969), 258

Sport and the Olympic Ideal, International Year (1994), 323

Sports, apartheid in: International Convention against (1985), 210; International Declaration against (1977), 210

Staff assessment (UN), 20

Statelessness, Convention on the Reduction of (1961), 258

State Property, Archives and Debts, Vienna Convention on Succession of States in Respect of (1983), 259

Strategic offensive arms reduction treaties, START I (1991) and START II (1993), 124

Sudano-Sahelian activities, UN Trust for 155; Sudano-Sahelian Office (UNSO), 155; see also Desertification

Sustainable development, 149; Commission on, 153, 157; see also Environment and development

T

Tajikistan, 108; Special Envoy for, 109; United Nations Mission of Observers in (UNMOT), 21, 110; UN humanitarian and emergency appeals (1994), 109, 110; WFP emergency relief operation (1993), 109

Territorial rights: ICJ cases, 253-254

Terrorism, International, 266; Declaration on Measures to Eliminate (1994), 266; international conventions on, 267; see also aircraft; civil aviation; continental shelf; hostage-taking; internationally protected persons; maritime navigation; nuclear material; plastic explosives

Tolerance, United Nations Year for (1995), 323

Torture: Committee Against, 201; Convention against (1984), 201; Declaration on the Protection of All Persons from Being Subjected to (1975), 177, 201; the fight against, 201; Special Rapporteur, 202; UN Voluntary Fund for Victims of, 202

Trade and development, UN Conference on (UNCTAD), 143; Ad Hoc Working Groups, 146; Board (UNCTAD), 145; Cartagena Commitment, 144, 146; sessions, 143; Standing Committees, 145-146; *see also* Investment and transnational corporations; Science and technology for development

Trade Preferences, Global System of (1989), 144

Training and research, 182; UN Institute for (UNITAR), 182

Treaties: Convention on the Law of (1969), 258; Vienna Convention on Succession of States in Respect of (1978), 258; Vienna Convention on the Law of between States and International Organizations or between International Organizations (1986), 259; *see also under* subjects

Truce Supervision Organization, UN (UNTSO), 93, 99

Trusteeship Council, 14, 232; functions and powers, 15

Trusteeship System, International, 14, 15, 231; Trust Territories which have exercised the right to self-determination, 233

U

United Nations: Day, 3, 324; Declaration by (1942), 3; growth of membership, 1945-1994, 309; Information Centres and Services (at 31 May 1995), 317; membership, 5; Member States (at 31 December 1994), 311; official languages, 6; origin, 3; purposes and principles, 4; rules of procedure, 269; special observances, 323; structure, 6

United Nations Educational, Scientific and Cultural Organization (UNESCO), 277; International Literacy Day, 324; International Programme for the Development of Communication, 279; World Heritage List, 278

United Nations Industrial Development Organization (UNIDO), 297

United Nations peace-keeping forces, 21; Nobel Peace Prize (1988), 28

United Nations and Associated Personnel, Convention on the Safety of (1994), 267

United Nations Protection Force (UN-PROFOR), 21, 114, 115, 117, 118, 119; *see also* Yugoslavia, former

United Nations University (UNU), 183

Universal Postal Union (UPU), 287; World Post Day, 324

V

Volunteers, UN, 142; International Day, 143, 324; TOKTEN and UNISTAR programmes, 142

W

Warsaw Treaty Organization, 121

Water: International Conference on and the Environment (Dublin, 1992), 156; UN Conference (Mar del Plata, 1977)/Action Plan, 156; World Day for, 323

Western Sahara, 244; ICJ advisory opinion (1975), 245; Identification Commission, 248, 249; OAU summit (1981), 246; peace agreement (1979), 245; United Nations Mission for the Referendum in (MINURSO), 21, 246, 247, 249

Women: International Day, 324; International Year (1975), 167; Nairobi Forward-looking Strategies for the Advancement of to the year 2000, 167; promoting the rights of, 203; role of in development, 167; UN Decade for (1976-1985), 167; World Conference of International Women's Year (Mexico City, 1975), 167; World Conference on the UN Decade for (Copenhagen, 1980), 167; World Conference to Review and Appraise the Achieve-